STARTING POINT

THE AVA GUIDE
TO
900+ UNIQUE TRAILS IN AMERICA

American Volkssport Association
1001 Pat Booker Road, Suite 101
Universal City, Texas 78148-4147

Dedication

STARTING POINT *The AVA Guide to 900+ Unique Trails in America* is dedicated to the clubs and individuals who have made Volkssporting possible in the United States. Welcome to volkssporting!

DISCLAIMER: The AVA and its officers, members, and agents shall not be liable or responsible for, and shall be held harmless for and against any and all claims and damages to or loss of property arising out of or attributed to the operations of events conducted by the AVA.

ISBN 0-9644794-0-0
LCCCN 94-074164

Thank you for your purchase of the American Volkssport Association's (AVA) **STARTING POINT** *The AVA Guide to 900+ Unique Trails in America*. **STARTING POINT** contains more than 900 listings of sporting events that are available on a daily basis for your personal physical fitness programs. Listings of events are provided by state in alphabetical order in this easy-to-read, compact booklet.

The following general information is provided to help get you acquainted with the AVA and our year-round walking events.

Who is the AVA? Founded in 1979, the AVA is a non-profit, tax-exempt, national organization dedicated to promoting the benefits of health and physical fitness for people of all ages. The AVA promotes physical fitness by sponsoring, through its affiliate clubs, non-competitive sports events in safe, stress-free environments.

What is volkssporting? A volkssporting event is an organized walk, bike, swim, or cross-country ski designed to appeal to everyone. Events are non-competitive, and participants exercise at their own pace.

Types of events: Most volkssport events are walks (referred to as volksmarches) that are 10 kilometers (6.2 miles) in length, however, the distance varies depending on the event. Bicycle events are 25 kilometers or more; swimming events are 300 meters or more; cross-country ski events are 10 kilometers or more. Other events may include rollerblading, ice skating or snowshoeing.

Weekend events: Sometimes referred to as "regular events," these events occur on weekends, usually both Saturday and Sunday, with published start and finish times. Participants may start an event individually or in a group at any time during a specified 3-5 hour time period and are allowed more than adequate time to finish. Many 5 kilometer walks are available for the beginner. Special provisions also allow for the physically challenged to participate in most events. Participation is open to the general public and free of charge. A nominal fee is charged if a participant wishes to earn credit or to purchase an award. Weekend events are published in the AVA's bimonthly newspaper, *The American Wanderer*. For subscription information see page 121.

Year-Round and Seasonal events: STARTING POINT features Year-Round events (YRE), which are events that are available any day of the year. There are some restrictions, most notably, closures during holidays at some locations. Seasonal events, as the name suggests, are open during a limited time frame (eleven months or less) due to weather conditions.

Trail Ratings:

1. Easy walk on pavement or a well-maintained trail. Usually suitable for wheelchairs and strollers.
2. A moderately easy walk on some pavement or some woodland or open field trails. No significant difficulty with hills. Possibly not suitable for wheelchairs and strollers.
3. A moderate walk in any setting with some difficult terrain, substantial hills and/or steps.
4. A more difficult walk. Most likely settings with natural paths and steep or hilly inclines.
5. A very difficult walk on rough terrain. Steep hills and high altitude trails. Unsuitable for persons not in good health.

Clubs: You are welcome to join one or more of our 550 + volkssporting clubs. Membership in these clubs is usually less than $10 per year. Of course, you may remain unaffiliated as AVA sporting events are open to everyone regardless of membership.

International Achievement Awards Program: A great incentive for participating in volkssporting is collecting "credits" for each event and distance accomplished. The AVA offers a voluntary International Achievement Awards program for those who wish to track their progress and credit. International Record Books are available for purchase at every regular event (and at some YRE events) for $4 each. An Event book is a record for the number of events in which you participate and a Distance book is a record of actual number of kilometers walked.

When you register at an AVA sanctioned event, you indicate that you are walking "For Credit" and pay a small registration fee (not more than $2.00) and a nominal fee if you want to purchase an award, which is a memento of the event. At the finish, your record books are stamped. When your books are completed, you send them to the AVA Headquarters to receive your certificate, patch and pin. You earn your first Achievement Award after 10 events and/or 500 kilometers. You may order Event and Distance books at any time through the AVA National Headquarters.

Volkssports Associate: Included in **STARTING POINT** on page 121 is information on joining **Volkssports Associate**. When you become an associate, you receive the AVA's bi-monthly newspaper, *The American Wanderer*, travel discounts at **Choice** Hotels, **Alamo Rent-A-Car** and special offers on AVA specialties. Your membership helps support the local clubs and the association overall as we can use associate fees for headquarters operations and development of volkssporting in the United States. To receive a free general information packet about volkssporting and the AVA call 1-800-830-WALK(9255).

Events in this book are sanctioned by the AVA in the IVV. Information was furnished by the sponsoring club. Updates to **STARTING POINT** are published in *The American Wanderer*. To subscribe, see page 121.

All participants must complete a Start Card & carry it with them throughout the event & must surrender the card upon completion of the event. Events are open to all persons free of charge.

You may walk an event for credit twice in the same day on the same start card for one fee. A new start card must be purchased each time you do a bike event for credit.

Anyone doing an event **other than a walk** must sign a waiver.

Participate during daylight hours only. Observe local laws regarding your pets.

If the club has more than one route available, check to make sure they have sanctions (look for the YR# in this book) on all trails. If not, you can only receive one event credit, even if doing all of the trails.
Remember to bring your books. Some YREs may not have them available for sale. You may order books from the AVA National Headquarters for $4.00 each including shipping & handling.

Hint: Use address labels to register. Sometimes even printing is hard to read.

Start/Finish personnel are our hosts. Let them attend to their customers first.

Top Ten Year Round Events for 1994

These events were voted as the best by volkssporters from all 50 states. Visit them in 1995 and see if you agree. They will be designated by a ☆ in the event listing.

1st Place: YR037, West Point, NY	6th Place: YR019, Monterey, CA
2nd Place: YR055, San Antonio, TX	7th Place: YR445, Point Lobos, CA
3rd Place: YR522, Devils Tower, WY	8th Place: YR231, Washington, DC
4th Place: YR214, Niagara Falls, NY	9th Place: YR061, Alexandria, VA
5th Place: YR388, Guernsey, WY	10th Place: YR105, Virginia City, MT

An order blank for additional copies of *STARTING POINT* and a form for Volkssports Associate Membership are located on pages 123 and 121, respectively.

ALABAMA

Mobile - 10km Walk (YR338) **Jan 1-Dec 31**
Sponsoring Club: AVA-310, Magnolia State Volkssport Club
POC: Al Sager, 205-653-1400. PO Box 636, Pascagoula, MS 39568

Start Point: Mobile Visitors Center (Ft Conde), 205-434-7304. Located just off the Water St exit of I-10.

Event Info: Daily, 8-5. Rated 1. Suitable for strollers & wheelchairs. Pets must be leashed.

Montgomery - 10km Walk (YR398) & 25km Bike (YR217) **Jan 1-Dec 31**
Sponsoring Club: AVA-261, Capital City Wanderers
POC: Elwood Hintz, 205-272-5986. 3914 Meredith Dr, Montgomery AL 36109

Start Point: Riverfront Inn Hotel, 200 Coosa St. I-65 North. Exit Herron St. right. I-65 South, turn left on Herron, go downtown to Cousa St. For bike: 7.7 mile drive from Riverfront Inn to Wares Ferry Elementary School where you can park your car.

Event Info: Daily, dawn to dusk. Walk rated 2. Bike rated 1.

Tallassee - 10km Walk (YR129) **Jan 2-Dec 31**
Sponsoring Club: AVA-261, Capital City Wanderers
POC: John Kosick, 205-285-9029. 6810 Buttercup Drive, Elmore, AL 36025

Start Point: Talisi Hotel, 205-283-2769. Sistrunk St. I-85. Exit #26 Tallassee. Turn right on Hwy 14. Turn right on Sistrunk St. before the bridge.

Event Info: Daily, dawn to dusk. Closed major holidays. Rated 3. Not for strollers or wheelchairs. Pets must be leashed and you must carry your own water for them.

Wetumpka - 10km Walk (YR574) **Jan 1-Dec 31**
Sponsoring Club: AVA-261, Capital City Wanderers
POC: John Kosick, 205-285-9029. 6810 Buttercup Dr, Elmore AL 36025

Start Point: Wetumpka Police Station, corner of Main & Ready. I-65 North of Montgomery. Exit Hwy 14. Follow to downtown Wetumpka.

Event Info: Daily, dawn to dusk. Rated 2. Suitable for strollers, no wheelchairs. Pets must be leashed.

ALASKA

Anchorage - 10km Walk (YR902) **Jun 1-Oct 1**
Sponsoring Club: AVA-754, The Over-The-Hill-Gang Volkssport Club
POC: Ron Crenshaw, 907-277-8735. 1553-H St, Anchorage, AK 99501 or Alicia Maxcy, 206-927-4580. PO Box 23057, Federal Way, WA 98093

Start Point: Public Lands Information Office, 605 West 4th Ave (the old Federal Bldg located on the corner of 4th & F Street across from the Log Cabin Visitors Center). From the airport, take Airport Road to Minnesota St. Turn left drive to 4th Ave, turn right to start.

Event Info: Jun 1-Aug 31: daily, 9-5:30. Sept 1-Oct 1: Mon-Fri only, 11-5:30. Rated 1. Restrooms & water available at start/finish only.

Juneau - 10km Walk (YR863) **May 1-Oct 1**
Sponsoring Club: AVA-754, The Over-The-Hill-Gang Volkssport Club
POC: Barbara Coate, 907-789-9230. PO Box 211206, Auke Bay, AK 98821 or Alicia Maxcy, 206-927-4580. PO Box 23057, Federal Way, WA 98093.

Start Point: Galligaskin's Gift Shop, 207 S. Franklin St. From Cruise Ship Terminal: Exit on S Franklin. Turn left and go to start. From Airport: Drive south (towards town) on Egan Dr to Marine Dr. Take Marine Dr staying to the right to S Franklin St. Turn right and go to start.

Event Info: Daily, 9 A.M.-10 P.M. No restrooms at start but available elsewhere. Rated 3.

ARKANSAS

Garfield - 10km Walk, (YR145) **Jan 2-Dec 31**
Sponsoring Club: AVA-619, Ozark Hill Hikers
POC: Radine Trees Nehring, 501-787-5930. Rt 1, Box 55, Gravette AR 72736-9611

Register: The Buss Stop-Phillips 66 Gas Station & Convenience Store, 501-359-3430. US Hwy 62 in Garfield (three miles east of Pea Ridge National Military Park).

Start Point: Pea Ridge National Military Park Visitors Center.

Event Info: $2.00 park entrance fee. Daily, 8-5. Closed Thanksgiving, Christmas & New Years. Rated 1+. Suitable for strollers with a strong pusher. Not recommended for wheelchairs. Pets must be leashed.

ARIZONA

Bisbee - 10km Walk (YR669) **Jan 2-Dec 31**
Sponsoring Club: AVA-746, Thunder Mountain Trekkers
POC: Dave & Wendy Breen, 602-378-1763. 3288 Sky Hawk Dr, Sierra Vista, AZ 85635-6623

Start Point: School House Inn, 602-432-2996. 818 Tombstone Canyon.

Event Info: Trail is rated 3+. Not suitable for strollers or wheelchairs because of hills & stairs. Pets allowed but there are numerous loose dogs in town.

Mesa - 11km Walk (YR025) **Jan 1-Dec 31** Credit Only Event
Sponsoring Club: AVA-332, Valley Volkssporters Association
POC: John Shoemaker, 602-345-1852. 948 W. Osage, Mesa AZ 85210

Start Point: Mezona Best Western, 602-834-9233. 800-528-8299. 250 W. Main. I-10 to US 60 East. North on Country Club to Main. Start at NE corner.

Event Info: Special rate for volkssporters. Daily, dawn to dusk. Rated 1. Strollers & wheelchairs may have difficulty along canal bank. Carry water in hot weather. Leashed pets.

Naco - 10km Walk (YR670) **Jan 2-Dec 31**
Sponsoring Club: AVA-746, Thunder Mountain Trekkers
POC: Dave & Wendy Breen, 602-378-1763. 3288 Sky Hawk Dr., Sierra Vista, AZ 85635-6623

Start Point: Turquoise Valley Country Club, 602-432-3091. W Newell St.

Event Info: Walk goes into Mexico. All participants **must** sign the waiver. Identification needed to cross the border. Naturalized citizens & all aliens must have proof of citizenship, resident alien card or passport with visa. Trail is rated 1. **No** pets. Carry your own water.

Phoenix - 10km Walk (YR139) 13km Walk (YR230) & 25/50km Bike (YR452) **Jan 1-Dec 31**
Sponsoring Club: AVA-332, Valley Volkssporters Association
POC: Hal Witter, 602-990-1515. 3606 North Kachina Lane, Scottsdale AZ 85251-5156.

Start Point: MON THRU FRI: Norton House, 602-262-6412. 2700 N 15th Ave.
WEEKENDS/HOLIDAYS: Encanto Park Sports Complex, 602-261-8443. By the tennis courts at 15th Ave & Encanto Blvd. I-10 exit 7th Ave N. West on McDowell to 15th Ave. North to start.

Event Info: Mon-Fri, 9-5; Weekends & Holidays, 10-sunset. Trails are rated 1. Suitable for strollers. Wheelchairs may experience some difficulty. Pets must be leashed.

Phoenix - 10km Walk (YR849-Mall) & 11km Walk (YR851) **Jan 1-Dec 31**
Sponsoring Club: AVA-332, Valley Volkssporters Association
POC: Bob Gary, 602-841-0252. 3829 W. Keim Drive, Phoenix, AZ 85019-1723

Start Point: Phoenix Baptist Hospital Wellness Connection (inside Chris-Town Mall), 602-995-9355. 1703 West Bethany Home Road. I-17, exit Bethany Home Rd. Go east 3/4 mile to Mall at 17th Ave. Start is near food court in Southeast section.

Event Info: Mon-Fri, 10-9; Sat, 10-7; Sun, noon-5. Early start forms at Info Desk at main entrance. Trails are rated 1. Suitable for strollers & wheelchairs. Pets must be leashed.

Phoenix - 10km Walk (YR848) **Jan 1-Dec 31**
Sponsoring Club: AVA-332, Valley Volkssporters Association
POC: Bob Gary, 602-841-0252. 3829 W Keim Dr, Phoenix, AZ 85019-1723

Start Point: SAS Shoes (in Metro Market Place), 602-678-1668. 9201 N 29th Ave. I-17 exit Dunlap Ave. Go west 1/4 mile to 29th Ave. Go north 1 block to start.

Event Info: Mon-Sat, 10-6; Sun, Closed. (Early/late start box locate outside). Rated 1. Suitable for strollers. Wheelchairs may have some difficulty. Pets must be leashed.

Scottsdale - Three 10km Walks(YR563, YR564 & YR850) & 29km Bike (YR565) **Jan 1-Dec 31**
Sponsoring Club: AVA-332, Valley Volkssporters Association
POC: Hal Witter, 602-990-1515. 3606 N. Kachina Lane, Scottsdale AZ 85251-5156.

Start: SAS Shoes in the Pavilions, 602-443-8091. 9180 E Indian Bend. In Scottsdale, East to Pima & Indian Bend Roads.

Event Info: Mon-Sat, 10-6. Closed Sunday. (Early/Late Start mailbox located outside.) Bicycle rental available at Tempe Bicycle Shop (two doors down). Trails are rated 1. Suitable for strollers & wheelchairs. Pets must be leashed.

Sierra Vista - 11km Walk (YR447-Coronado Nat'l Monument), 11/13km Walk (YR372-San Pedro Riparian Nat'l Conservation Area) & 12km Walk (YR499-Fort Hauchuca) **Jan 1-Dec 31**
Sponsoring Club: AVA-746, Thunder Mountain Trekkers
POC: Dave & Wendy Breen, 602-378-1763. 3288 Sky Hawk Dr., Sierra Vista, AZ 85635-6623

Register: Registration for all events is at the Thunder Mountain Inn, 602-458-7900. 1631 S Hwy 92. You then drive to start locations shown below.

Start YR447-Coronado: From the Thunder Mountain Inn, turn left onto SR 92 as you leave the parking lot. Follow SR 92 south approximately 12 miles. Shortly after the highway makes a 90 degree turn to the left, you should see a brown & white highway sign which shows the road to the Memorial is on your right. Turn right on this road & follow it until you reach the visitor center/museum bldg (about 5 miles).

Start YR372-San Pedro: From the Inn parking lot, turn right onto SR 92 and proceed north to 2nd traffic light (intersection of SR 90, SR 92 & Fry Blvd). Right onto SR 90 and proceed east for 6.7 miles. The San Pedro House parking area is on the right, just past milepost 328 and just before you cross the river.

Start YR499-Ft Huachuca: Leave the Thunder Mountain Inn and turn right on Hwy 92. Turn left at the 2nd traffic light (Fry Blvd). Follow Fry to the main gate of Ft Huachuca. If you do not have a DOD sticker on your auto, you must stop and get a visitor's pass. You will need your driver's license, vehicle registration & proof of insurance (or car rental agreement). After getting pass, proceed to the NCO club (Club La Hacienda) to start.

Event Info: **YR447** is rated 5. Elevation starts at 5400' with a 1600' gain. Bring your own water. **No** pets allowed. **YR372** is rated 2+. Not suitable for strollers or wheelchairs. **Do not** wear shorts. you **must** bring your own water. Pets must be leashed. **YR499** is rated 1+. Pets must be leashed.

Tempe - 12km Walk (YR524) **Jan 1-Dec 31** Credit Only Event
Sponsoring Club: AVA-332, Valley Volkssporters Association
POC: Steve Bartley, 602-491-6017. 18 W Louis Way, Tempe AZ 85284

Start Point: Tyke's World Toys and Playcenter, 602-491-6017. 3136 S McClintock. I-10 to US 60 East. North at McClintock to start.

Event Info: Mon-Sat, 9-6; Sun, 12-5. Closed January 1-2, Easter, Thanksgiving, & December 25 & 26. May also be closed on other major holidays. Call if in doubt. Rated 1. Suitable for strollers & wheelchairs. Pets must be leashed.

Tucson - 10km Walk (YR321) & 31km Bike (YR459) **Jan 1-Dec 31**
Sponsoring Club: AVA-374, Tucson Volkssport Klub
POC: Fred E. Barton, 602-298-4340. 270 South Candlestick Dr, Tucson AZ 85748-6743

Start Point: Park Inn, 602-622-4000. 88 East Broadway Blvd.

Event Info: Daily, dawn to dusk. Pets must be leashed. Trails are rated 1. Suitable for strollers & wheelchairs.

CALIFORNIA

Alameda - 10km Walk (YR620) & 11km Walk (YR619) **Jan 2-Dec 31** Credit Only Events
Sponsoring Club: AVA-196, Golden Bear Paw Prints, Inc.
POC: Ben/Berta Wilkes, 707-994-4135. Box 2461, Clearlake CA 95422 or Diane Eatherly, 510-482-0817.

Start Point: Encinal Market, 3211 Encinal Ave at High St. Into Oakland take I-580 or I-880. Then SE on High Street to Encinal.

Event Info: Mon-Sat, 9:15-9; Sun, 9:15-7. Closed on holidays. Trails are rated 1. Suitable for strollers & wheelchairs. Pets must be leashed.

Campbell - 10/13km Walk (YR853) **Jan 1-Dec 31**
Sponsoring Club: AVA-338, South Bay Striders
POC: Jacquie Christensen, 408-356-3954. 16389 E. LaChiquita, Los Gatos, CA 95032

Start Point: Campbell Inn, 408-374-4300. 675 East Campbell Ave. From Hwy 17/880, take the Hamilton Avenue exit and go east to Bascom Avenue. Turn right and continue to Campbell Ave (Pruneyard Shopping Center on your right) and turn right again. Cross under the 17/880 Hwy and the Inn will be on your right.

Event Info: Daily, 8-dusk. Rated 1. Suitable for strollers & wheelchairs. Pets must be leashed. Only one event credit even if completing both trails.

Carlsbad - 10km Walk (YR200) 14km Walk (YR271) **Jan 1-Dec 31**
Sponsoring Club: AVA-392, San Diego County Rockhoppers
POC: Irja Graham, 619-758-5667. 1391 Broken Hitch Road, Oceanside, CA 92056 or
L. M. Rursch, 619-728-5931. 716 Hillcrest Lane, Fallbrook, CA 92028

Start Point: Carlsbad-by-the-Sea, A California Lutheran Retirement Community, 619-729-2377, 2855 Carlsbad Blvd. Located 30 miles North of San Diego.

Event Info: Daily, dawn to dusk. Trails are rated 1+. Not suitable for strollers or wheelchairs. Pets must be leashed & are not allowed on the seawall or beach areas.

☆Carmel/Point Lobos - Two 10km Walks (YR443 & YR445) **Jan 1-Dec 31** Credit Only Events
Sponsoring Club: AVA-005, Monterey Walking Club
POC: Art Plummer, 408-384-0218. 484 Reindollar, Marina CA 93933

Start Point: Power Juice Co., behind Chevy's Restaurant in Crossroads Shopping Ctr. 408-384-0218. Take Hwy 1 South to Rio Rd in Carmel. Turn left at Rio Rd and right at Crossroads Shopping Center.

Event Info: Mon-Sat, 9-5; Sun, 10-5. Carmel is rated 1+ and Point Lobos is rated 3. Neither trail is suitable for strollers or wheelchairs. Pets are not allowed in the park.

Cherry Valley - 10km Walk (YR543) **Jan 1-Dec 31** Credit Only Event
Sponsoring Club: AVA-285, Green Valley Gaiters
POC: Lois Wilson, 909-845-5872. 10315 Frontier Trail, Cherry Valley, CA 92223

Start Point: Vienna Liquor & Delicatessen, 38761 Cherry Valley Blvd. From I-10 exit onto Cherry Valley off-ramp. Proceed East (left for east bound; right for west bound) on Cherry Valley Blvd approximately 2 1/2 miles. Start is on the right.

Event Info: Daily, 9-5. Rated 2+. Not advisable for strollers or wheelchairs.

Chico - 11km Walk (YR579) & 33km Bike (YR700) **Jan 2-Dec 30**
Sponsoring Club: AVA-575, Ye Olde Chico Walking Club
POC: Linda Detling, 916-343-7887. 1304 Arbutus Ave, Chico CA 95926

Start Point: Fleet Feet Sports, 916-345-1000. 222 W 3rd St. From Hwy 99, take East First Ave exit and go west. Turn left at The Esplanade to West 3rd St. The Esplanade curves and becomes Broadway. From Broadway go right on West Third St.

Event Info: Mon-Fri, 10-6; Sat, 10-5; Sun, 12-4. Open Sundays Apr & May & Sept-Dec only. Pets must be leashed. Trails are rated 1. Suitable for strollers. Wheelchairs may have some difficulty with curbs.

Chico - 11km Walk (YR698) **Jan 1-Dec 31** Credit Only Event
Sponsoring Club: AVA-575, Ye Olde Chico Walking Club
POC: Linda Detling, 916-343-7887. 1304 Arbutus Ave, Chico CA 95926

Start Point: Johnson's Comfort Shoes-Chico Mall, 916-342-2310. 1950 E 20th. From Hwy 99, take the East 20th St. exit and go east. Go left at the traffic light into the Mall parking lot. Park close to Gottschalk's and enter mall to start.

Event Info: Mon-Fri, 10-9; Sat, 10-6; Sun, 11-6. Closed major holidays. Rated 1. Strollers & wheelchairs may have difficulty. Pets must be leashed.

Chico - 14km Walk (YR699) **Jan 1-Dec 31** Credit Only Event
Sponsoring Club: AVA-575, Ye Olde Chico Walking Club
POC: Linda Detling, 916-343-7887. 1304 Arbutus Ave, Chico, CA 95926

Start Point: Johnson's Shoes, #7 North Valley. (Plaza Mall, 916-343-8923). From the south on Hwy 99, take Cohasset Hwy exit. Turn left immediately on Pillsbury Rd to the Mall parking lot on the right. Start is near the center of the Mall. From the North on Hwy 99, take East Ave exit and go left on East Ave. Turn right on Pillsbury Rd and then left into Mall parking lot. Start is near the center of the Mall.

Event Info: Mon-Fri, 10-9; Sat, 10-6; Sun, 11-6. Closed major holidays. Rated 1+. Strollers & wheelchairs may have difficulty. Pets must be leashed.

Chula Vista - Two 10km Walks (YR747) & (YR748-Mexico) **Jan 1-Dec 31**
Sponsoring Club: AVA-535, Avocado Country Pathfinders (YR747) & AVA-CA, California Volkssport Assn. (YR748)
POC: Arthur Sederholm, 619-728-1827. 2592 Daily Dr, Fallbrook, CA 92028

Start Point: Best Western Motel, 619-728-1827. 710 "E" St.

Event Info: YR748 goes into Mexico. ALL PARTICIPANTS MUST SIGN WAIVER. No pets.

Citrus Heights - Three 10km Walks (YR224, YR289 & YR290) **Jan 2-Dec 31** Credit Only Events
Sponsoring Club: AVA-196, Golden Bear Paw Prints, Inc.
POC: Berta/Ben Wilkes, 707-994-4135. Box 2461, Clearlake CA 95422 or Jean Davis, 916-944-1087.

Start Point: SAS Store, 7175 Greenback Ln. From Sacramento take I-80 N then East on Greenback; or US 56 East then Sunrise North to Greenback Lane. Store is located behind the Red Tomato Restaurant.

Event Info: Mon-Thurs & Sat, 10-6; Fri, 10-8; Sun, 12-5. Trails are rated 1+. Suitable for strollers & wheelchairs. Pets must be leashed.

Corona - 10km Walk (YR913) **Jan 1-Dec 31**
Sponsoring Club: AVA-157, Low Desert Roadrunners
POC: Joe Obradovitz, 909-735-0457. 4410 Crestview Dr, Norco, CA 91760 or Jean Vik, 909-737-8341. 19310 Ontario Ave, Corona, CA 91720

Start Point: Corona Regional Medical Center, 909-737-4343. 800 S Main St.From I-15, exit Corona or Beach Cities to 91 west. Then exit at Main Street and turn left. Travel south on Main to 8th. Turn right on 8th. Medical Center covers entire block. Please park on streets rather than in the lot.

Event Info: Daily, 8-5. Rated 1. Suitable for strollers & wheelchairs. Pets must be leashed.

Fair Oaks - 11km Walk (YR559) **Jan 1-Dec 31**
Sponsoring Club: AVA-218, Sutter Strutters Volkssport Club
POC: David M. Lynch, 916-784-8284. 403 Tanner Ct, Roseville CA 95678.

Start Point: Fleet Feet Sports, 8128 Madison Ave; 916-965-8326.

Event Info: Mon-Fri, 10-8; Sat, 10-6; Sun, 12-5. Pets must be leashed. Rated 1+. Suitable for strollers & wheelchairs.

Fairfield - 10km Walk (YR696) **Jan 1-Dec 31**
Sponsoring Club: AVA-376, Vaca Valley Volks
POC: Ruth A. Redd, 707-429-1899. 2000 Claybank Rd #E1, Fairfield, CA 94533

Start Point: North Bay Medical Center, 1800 Pennsylvania Ave (main lobby, old bldg.)

Fresno - 10km Walk (YR456) **Jan 1-Dec 30** Credit Only Event
Sponsoring Club: AVA-371, Big Valley Vagabonds
POC: Mary L. Mott, 209-297-7685. 3212 E Tenaya Ave, Fresno CA 93710

Start Point: IHOP Restaurant, 3020 Tulare St. From US99 go East on 41. Take Tulare Exit, turn left and go to IHOP on left.

Event Info: Daily, dawn to dusk. Rated 1. Suitable for strollers and wheelchairs. Pets must be leashed.

Fresno - 10km Walk (YR457) **Jan 1-Dec 31** Credit Only Event
Sponsoring Club: AVA-371, Big Valley Vagabonds
POC: Mary L. Mott, 209-297-7685. 3212 E Tenaya Ave, Fresno CA 93710-5925

Start Point: San Joaquin Hotel, 1309 W Shaw. North on US 99 take 41 East to Shaw Exit. Turn left to 1300 block. South on US 99, exit Shaw. Left across freeway to 1300 block.

Event Info: Daily, dawn to dusk. Rated 1. Suitable for strollers if determined. No wheelchairs. Pets must be leashed.

Homewood - 32/47km Bike (YR389) & 11/15km Walk (YR235) **May 15-Oct 15**
Sponsoring Club: AVA-683, Sierra Nevada Striders
POC: David Sampson, 702-746-1740. 5215 Mountcrest Ln, Reno NV 89523

Start Point: Tahoe Gear, 5095 W Lake Blvd (Hwy 89); 916-525-5233.

Event Info: Daily 9-5. Bike rentals available at start. Trails are rated 1+. Suitable for strollers & wheelchairs. Pets must be leashed. SNOW and/or ICE CANCELS EVENTS.

Huntington Beach - 10km Walk (YR899) **Jan 1-Dec 31** Credit Only Event
Sponsoring Club: AVA-427, Hollywood Star Trekkers
POC: Kathy & John Shirtz, 310-374-3189. 346 27th St, Hermosa Beach, CA 90254

Start Point: Grinder Restaurant, 714-536-1664. 21002 Pacific Coast Hwy (just south of pier).

Event Info: Daily, dawn to dusk. Please call for holiday hours. Rated 1+. Suitable for strollers but difficult for wheelchairs. Pets must be leashed.

Ione/Jackson - 10km Walk (YR606), 12km Walk (YR255) & 10/15km Walk (YR378) **Jan 1-Dec 31** Credit Only Events
Sponsoring Club: AVA-196, Golden Bear Paw Prints, Inc.
POC: Berta/Ben Wilkes, 707-994-4135. PO Box 2461, Clearlake CA 95422 or Dorothy Williamson, 209-274-4339.

Start Point: Best Western-Amador Inn, 200 S Hwy 49. The start point is on Main Street which is also SH 49 & 88. It is on the SE corner where SH 88 turns NE and SH 49 continues SE. This is the registration for YR606. After registering, drive 10 miles south of Jackson on Route 88 then right on Route 104. Park in back of police station at Iron Ivan RR Engine, on Church St off W Main to start the event.

Event Info: If staying at the Inn, be sure to ask for the Volkssporter Discount. Daily, dawn to dusk. Pets must be leashed. Jackson events, YR255 & YR378 are rated 2+. Strollers may have difficulty. Not suitable for wheelchairs. YR606 is rated 1+. Strollers ok but not recommended for wheelchairs.

Los Gatos - 25km Bike (YR241) **Jan 1-Dec 31** Credit Only Event
Sponsoring Club: AVA-338, South Bay Striders
POC: Ernest Christiansen, 408-370-2668. 123 Carlton Ave NR3, Los Gatos CA 95032-2749

Start Point: Los Gatos Cyclery, 15954 Los Gatos Blvd. From Hwy 280 or 101 take 880 south towards Santa Cruz. Take the Lark Ave exit and at the light turn left (Lark Ave). Continue to Los Gatos Blvd, turn right. Continue to Blossom Hill Ave. Los Gatos Cyclery will be in the shopping center on your left before the stop light.

Event Info: Mon-Thu, 9-6; Fri, 9-8; Sat, 9-5 & Sun, 11-5. Rated 1+. Participants must sign waiver. No bike rentals available.

Los Gatos - 10km Walk (YR074) **Jan 1-Dec 31**
Sponsoring Club: AVA-338, South Bay Striders
POC: Mary Florsheim, 408-867-3966. 14638 Placida Ct, Saratoga, CA 95070

Start Point: Village Inn, 235 W Main St. From Hwy 280 or 101 take 880 south towards Santa Cruz. Take the Los Gatos-Saratoga exit (not east Los Gatos). At the signal, University Ave, turn left and proceed to the end. You will be at Main St. Turn right and go past the signal (Santa Cruz Ave) and the Inn is on the left.

Event Info: Daily, 8-dusk. Rated 1+. Suitable for strollers. Pets must be leashed.

Merced - 10km Walk (YR750) **Jan 2-Dec 30** Credit Only Event
Sponsoring Club: AVA-371, Big Valley Vagabonds
POC: Mary L. Mott, 209-297-7685. 3212 E. Tenaya Ave, Fresno CA 93710

Start Point: Mercy Hospital, 2740 "M" St. From US 99 take M.L. King exit. Go W to 13th St. Right on 13th to "M" St. Right on "M" to hospital. Use main entrance lot beyond 27th St.

Event Info: Daily, 8-8. Closed Easter, Thanksgiving & Christmas. Rated 1. Suitable for strollers & wheelchairs. Pets must be leashed.

Mill Valley - 10km Walk (YR391) **Jan 1-Dec 31** Credit Only Event
Sponsoring Club: AVA-204, Bay Bandits Volksmarch Club
POC: Robert P. Glasson, 415-457-1073. 59 Convent Ct, San Rafael CA 94901

Start Point: Mill Valley Parks & Recreation Dept, 415-383-1370. 180 Camino Alto.

Event Info: Mon-Fri, 9-5; Closed Sat, Sun & Holidays. Rated 2. Not suitable for strollers or wheelchairs. Pets must be leashed.

Mokelumne Hill - 10km Walk (YR225) **Jan 1-Dec 31** Credit Only Event
Sponsoring Club: AVA-196, Golden Bear Paw Prints, Inc.
POC: Berta/Ben Wilkes, 707-994-4135. Box 2461, Clearlake CA 95422 or Dorothy Williamson, 209-274-4339.

Register: Best Western-Amador Inn, 200 S. Highway 49, in Jackson.

Start Point: Drive 7 miles to Mokelumne Hill for start of walk.

Event Info: If staying at the Best Western, be sure to ask for the Volkssporter Discount. Daily, dawn to dusk. Rated 2+. Pets must be leashed. Strollers OK with some difficulty. Not suitable for wheelchairs.

☆ **Monterey** - 10km Walk (YR019) & 25km Bike (YR020) **Jan 1-Dec 31**
Sponsoring Club: AVA-005, Monterey Walking Club
POC: Art Plummer, 408-384-0218. 484 Reindollar, Marina CA 93933

Start Point: La Casa Bodega Deli & General Store, 500 Del Monte Ave. Take Hwy 1 South to Del Monte exit. La Casa Bodega is on left across from Fisherman's Wharf parking.

Event Info: Daily, 9-5. Trails are rated 1. Suitable for strollers & wheelchairs. Leashed pets.

Morgan Hill - 10km Walk (YR328) & 27km Bike (YR749) **Jan 1-Dec 31** Credit Only Events
Sponsoring Club: AVA-338, South Bay Striders
POC: Diane LeGore, 408-779-5013. 16755 Ranger Court, Morgan Hill, CA 95037

Start Point: Get Fit, 850 Tennant Ave. From Hwy 101 take the Tennant Ave exit West. After the Vineyard Blvd stoplight, turn left into the shopping center. Get Fit is located on the left between the cinemas & Radio Shack. Drive from Get Fit to start for bike event.

Event Info: Mon-Fri, 5-10; Sat, 7-10; Sun, 8-6. Walk dawn to dusk only. Trails are rated 1+. No strollers or wheelchairs. Carry water in summer. No water or restrooms are located on the bike trail. Bike rentals are not available. Pets must be leashed.

Oakland - Two 10km Walks (YR401 & YR509)) **Jan 1-Dec 31**
Sponsoring Club: AVA-CA, California Volkssport Association
POC: Rosanna Poret, 510-420-0778. 3922 Cerrito, Oakland, CA 94611

Start Point: WalkAbout Footware, 510-655-2265. 6012 College Ave.

Pleasant Hill - 10km Walk (YR537) **Jan 1-Dec 31**
Sponsoring Club: AVA-764, Walnut Creek Walk-A-Nuts
POC: Lorri Dane, 310-932-8965. 130 Sharene Lane #25, Walnut Creek, CA 94596

Start Point: The Shoe Walk, 510-676-2918. 1924 Contra Costa Blvd.

Redding - 10km Walk (YR238) 11km Walk (YR133) & 25km Bike (YR621) **Jan 1-Dec 31**
Sponsoring Club: AVA-645, Redding Road Ramblers
POC: Beverly Severance, 916-275-2793. 18251 Ranchera Rd, Redding, CA 96003

Start Point: Mercy Medical Center Laboratory, Rosaline Ave & Airpark Dr. From I-5 take 299 West; left on Court St; right on Rosaline Ave; left on Airpark Dr.

Event Info: Daily, dawn to dusk. Walks are rated 1+. Bike is rated 2+. Bikers must sign waiver. Helmets are required.

Redlands - 10km Walk (YR584) **Jan 1-Dec 31** Credit Only Event
Sponsoring Club: AVA-285, Green Valley Gaiters
POC: Gerry & JoAnne Myers, 909-794-1534. 20 Maria Ct, Redlands, CA 92374

Start Point: Family Fitness Center, 700 E Redlands Blvd, #AA. Behind Thrifty Drugs.

Event Info: Daily, 7-5. Pets must be leashed. Rated 1+. Strollers & wheelchairs will have difficulty with curbs. Do not park in green curbed areas.

Redondo Beach - Two 10km Walks (YR490-Redondo Beach & YR491-Manhattan Beach) **Jan 1-Dec 31**
Credit Only Events
Sponsoring Club: AVA-427, Hollywood Star Trekkers
POC: John & Kathy Shirtz, 310-374-3189. 346 27th St, Hermosa Beach, CA 90254

Start Point: Best Western Sunrise Hotel, 310-376-0746. King Harbor Marina, 400 N Harbor.

Event Info: Daily, dawn to dusk. Pets must be leashed. Trails are rated 2. Manhattan Beach may be difficult for strollers & wheelchairs.

Roseville - 10km Walk (YR560) **Jan 1-Dec 31**
Sponsoring Club: AVA-218, Sutter Strutters Volkssport Club
POC: David M. Lynch 916-784-8284. 403 Tanner Ct, Roseville CA 95678.

Start Point: Fleet Feet Sports, 1730-3 Santa Clara Drive; 916-783-4558.

Event Info: Mon-Fri, 10-8; Sat, 10-6; Sun, 12-5. Pets must be leashed. Rated 1+. Suitable for strollers & wheelchairs.

Sacramento - 11km Walk (YR003) & 30/52km Bike (YR006) **Jan 1-Dec 31** Bike is a Credit Only Event
Sponsoring Club: AVA-CA, California Volkssport Association
POC: Don Ratliff, 916-645-8280. 1515 Quail Rd, New Castle, CA 95658

Start Point: Sandman Motel, 236 Jibboom St. Near I-5 & Richards Blvd.

Event Info: Daily, dawn to dusk. Trails are rated 1. Walk is suitable for strollers & wheelchairs. Pets must be leashed and are not allowed in the Capitol Bldg. Bikers must sign waiver. Carry water in hot weather.

Sacramento - 10km Walk (YR558) 27km Bike (YR607) **Jan 1-Dec 31** Credit Only Events
Sponsoring Club: AVA-265, Sacramento Walking Sticks
POC: Myrna Jackson, 916-41-6714. 1501 Castec Drive, Sacramento, CA 9564

Start Point: Earth Alive, 4329 Arden Way (Arden Plaza).

Event Info: Mon-Fri, 9:30-7; Sat, 9-6; Sun, Closed. Trails are rated 1. Suitable for strollers but wheelchairs may experience difficulty with curbs. Pets must be leashed.

Sacramento - 10km Walk (YR583) **Jan 1-Dec 31** Credit Only Event
Sponsoring Club: AVA-265, Sacramento Walking Sticks
POC: Jean Rosenberg, 916-457-1269. 5777 11th Ave, Sacramento CA 94820

Start Point: Mercy General Hospital, Greenhouse Cafeteria, 4001 J St.

Event Info: Daily, 6am-8 P.M. Pets must be leashed. Rated 1. Suitable for strollers but curbs may cause trouble for wheelchairs.

San Jose - 11km Walk (YR240) **Jan 1-Dec 31** Credit Only Event
Sponsoring Club: AVA-338, South Bay Striders
POC: Clark & Cheryl Hanson, 408-432-9807. 116 El Basque Dr, San Jose, CA 95134

Start Point: Best Western Inn, 455 South 2nd St. From Hwy 280, take the 7th St exit and go north on 7th. Turn left onto San Salvador and left again at 2nd St.

Event Info: Daily, 8-dusk. Pets are discouraged. Rated 1. Suitable for strollers and wheelchairs.

San Luis Obispo - 10km Walk (YR458) **Jan 1-Dec 31** Credit Only Event
Sponsoring Club: AVA-371, Big Valley Vagabonds
POC: Ed Ritchie, 805-937-4719. 1650 Clarke Ave Sp 285, Santa Maria Ca 93455

Start Point: Holiday Inn Express, 805-544-8600. 1800 Monterey St. N on US101, Grand exit. Right to Monterey St. S on US101, Monterey St exit. Motel is on right.

Event Info: Daily, dawn to dusk. Leashed pets. Rated 2. Suitable for strollers & wheelchairs with some difficulty.

Sausalito - 12km Walk (YR392) **Jan 1-Dec 31** Credit Only Event
Sponsoring Club: AVA-204, Bay Bandits Volksmarch Club
POC: Robert P. Glasson, 415-457-1073. 59 Convent Ct, San Rafael CA 94901

Start Point: Mill Valley Parks & Rec Dept, 415-383-1370. 180 Camino Alto.

Event Info: Mon-Fri, 9-5; closed Sat, Sun & Holidays. Rated 1. Suitable for strollers & wheelchairs. Pets must be leashed.

Stockton - 10km Walk (YR170) **Jan 2-Dec 31** Credit Only Event
Sponsoring Club: AVA-416, Delta Tule Trekkers
POC: Willard Kolb, 209-368-2451. 1237 S. Avena Ave, Lodi, CA 95240

Start Point: Archie's Giant Burgers & Breakfast, 1304 East Hammer Ln.

Event Info: Daily, 7-dusk. Closed New Year's, Thanksgiving & Christmas Eve and Day. Rated 1. Suitable for strollers & wheelchairs. Pets must be leashed. Ask for the Volkssporters Discount when purchasing from Archie's.

Sun City - 12km Walk (YR701) **Jan 1-Dec 31** Credit Only Event
Sponsoring Club: AVA-157, Low Desert Roadrunners
POC: Rick Bundy, 909-678-3337. 21671 Darby St, Wildomar CA 92395

Start Point: Sun City Motel (main lobby), 909-672-1861. 27680 Encanto Dr. From I-215 take the McCall Blvd exit and then drive east to the traffic light (Encanto Dr). Turn left and proceed to start point on the right.

Event Info: Daily, dawn to dusk. Rated 1. Suitable for strollers, no wheelchairs. Pets must be leashed.

Sutter Creek - 10km Walk (YR103) **Jan 1-Dec 31** Credit Only Event
Sponsoring Club: AVA-196, Golden Bear Paw Prints, Inc.
POC: Berta/Ben Wilkes, 707-994-4135. Box 2461, Clearlake CA 95422 or Dorothy Williamson, 209-274-4339.

Register: Gold Quartz Inn, 15 Bryson Dr. Located on the south end of Sutter Creek. Turn east off SH 49 on Bryson Dr. Inn is 1/2 block down on the left. Drive to start point in town.

Event Info: Inn offers a 10% discount to volkssporters. Daily, 8-5. Rated 2+. Not recommended for strollers or wheelchairs. Pets must be leashed.

Truckee - 10km Walk (YR695) **May 1-Nov 30**
Sponsoring Club: AVA-489, Tahoe Trail Trekkers
POC: Gisela Steiner, 916-546-3452. Box 499, Tahoe Vista, CA 96148

Start Point: Sierra Mountaineer, 916-546-3452. Bridge & Jibbom St.

Vacaville - 10km Walk (YR331) **Jan 1-Dec 31**
Sponsoring Club: AVA-376, Vaca Valley Volks
POC: Ruth A. Redd, 707-429-1899. 2000 Claybank Rd #E1, Fairfield, CA 94535

Start Point: Vaca Valley Hospital, 1000 Nut Tree Rd

Ventura - 10km Walk (YR860) **Jan 1-Dec 31** Credit Only Event
Sponsoring Club: AVA-371, Big Valley Vagabonds
POC: Marsha Polk, 805-986-1485. 918 Lighthouse Way, Port Hueneme, CA 93041-3259 or Mary Mott, 209-297-7685.

Start Point: Vagabond Motel, 805-648-5371. 756 E. Thompson Blvd. Northbound on US 101 take California St exit to East Thompson Blvd, then right 2 1/2 blocks to Motel. From southbound on US 101, take Ventura Ave exit to East Thompson Blvd. Turn right and go 7 blocks to Motel.

Event Info: Daily, dawn to dusk. Rated 1+. Suitable for strollers. Pets must be leashed.

Visalia - 10km Walk (YR861) **Jan 1-Dec 31** Credit Only Event
Sponsoring Club: AVA-371, Big Valley Vagabonds
POC: Bob Golden, 209-732-9435. 3521 Cutter Ave, Visalia, CA 93277 or Jim Scofield, 209-734-5464.

Start Point: Carrows Restaurant, 209-732-0934. 900 S Mooney Blvd. From Hwy 99 take Hwy 198 East to Mooney Blvd, turn right. Start is on the left across from College of the Sequoias. (Sequoia National park can be reached via Hwy 198.)

Event Info: Daily, dawn to dusk. Rated 1. Suitable for strollers & wheelchairs. Pets must be leashed.

Walnut Creek - 10km Walk (YR852) **Jan 1-Dec 31** Credit Only Event
Sponsoring Club: AVA-764, Walnut Creek Walk-A-Nuts
POC: Lorri Dane, 510-932-8965. 130 Shareen Lane #25, Walnut Creek, CA 94596

Start Point: The Walking Company, 510-210-1900. 1155 Broadway Plaza

Event Info: Mon-Fri, 10-9; Sat, 10-8; Sun, 11-7. Rated 1+. Suitable for strollers & wheelchairs. Pets must be leashed.

Weimar - 10km Walk (YR854) **Jan 1-Dec 31**
Sponsoring Club: AVA-686, Placer Pacers
POC: Dave Davidson, 916-878-8470/Herb Webber, 916-878-7023. PO Box 142, Auburn, CA 95604-0142

Start Point: Weimar Institute, 916-637-4111. 20601 W. Paoli Lane. From Auburn drive east on I-80 approximately 9 miles to West Paoli Lane exit. Turn left over the highway and right into the campus.

Event Info: Daily, dawn to dusk (not earlier than 6:30). Rated 3. Elevation 2200 ft. Not suitable for strollers or wheelchairs. Pets must be leashed. NO SMOKING. Occasional snow or ice may close trails in winter. Call ahead.

Yuba City - 11km Walk (YR111) & 10km Walk (YR397) **Jan 1-Dec 31**
Sponsoring Club: AVA-266, California Camel Clompers
POC: Audrey Stricker, 916-673-5058. 1160 Cecily Ct, Yuba City CA 95991

Start Point: The Bonanza Inn, (Best Western), 916-674-8824. 1001 Clark Ave.

Event Info: Daily, dawn to dusk. Trails are rated 1. Suitable for strollers & wheelchairs. Pets must be leashed.

COLORADO

Aurora - 10km Walk (YR317) **Jan 2-Dec 31**
Sponsoring Club: AVA-024, Rocky Mountain Wanderers
POC: Mary Humphrey, 303-690-9601. 17330 E. Greenwood Circle, Aurora, CO 80013-2246

Start Point: Helga's German Delicatessen, 728 Peoria St. Just west of I-225 at 6th & Peoria.

Event Info: Mon, 8-8; Tue-Sat, 9-9; Sun, 11-8. Closed major holidays. Rated 1+. Elevation is 5,500 ft. Suitable for strollers & wheelchairs. Pets must be leashed.

Boulder - 10km Walk (YR826) **Jan 1-Dec 31**
Sponsoring Club: AVA-024, Rocky Mountain Wanderers
POC: Kathryn Miller, 303-443-8898. 235 Linden Drive, Boulder, CO 80304-0472

Start Point: University Inn, 1632 Broadway.

Event Info: Daily, dawn to dusk. Rated 1+. Suitable for strollers & wheelchairs with some difficulty due to curbs. Elev xation is 5,344 ft. Pets must be leashed.

Cañon City - 11km Walk (YR277) **Jan 1-Dec 31**
Sponsoring Club: AVA-072, Falcon Wanderers
POC: Falcon Wanderers, 719-275-6669. PO Box 17162, Colorado Springs, CO 80935

Start Point: Best Western Royal Gorge Motel, 1925 Fremont Dr; 800-231-7317.

Event Info: Daily, dawn to dusk. Rated 3. Not recommended for strollers or wheelchairs. Pets must be leashed. Water not available on trail. Carrying water strongly recommended.

Colorado Springs - 11km Walk (YR095) **Mar 1-Dec 31**
Sponsoring Club: AVA-072, Falcon Wanderers
POC: Falcon Wanderers, 719-684-9462. PO Box 17162, Colorado Springs CO 80935

Start Point: Bear Creek Park, 7-11 Store, 1011 S. 21st St; 719-635-0183. I-25 exit 141.

Event Info: Daily, dawn to dusk. Rated 3+. Strollers or wheelchairs cannot complete trail. Pets are not allowed. Carrying water is highly recommended.

Colorado Springs - 25km Bike (YR467) **Jan 3-Dec 30**
Sponsoring Club: AVA-072, Falcon Wanderers
POC: Falcon Wanderers, 719-684-9462. PO Box 17162, Colorado Springs CO 80935-7162

Start Point: Ted's Bicycle, 3016 N Hancock Ave; 719-473-6915.

Event Info: Mon-Sat, 9-6. Closed Sundays and all holidays. Rated 2+.

Colorado Springs - 11km Walk (YR464) **Jan 8-Dec 31**
Sponsoring Club: AVA-072, Falcon Wanderers
POC: Falcon Wanderers, 719-475-1671. PO Box 17162, Colorado Springs CO 80935

Start Point: Garden of the Gods Trading Post, 324 Beckers Ln; 719-685-9045.

Event Info: Summer: daily, 8-8. Winter: daily, 9-4:30. Rated 3. Strollers and wheelchairs will not be able to complete the trail. Pets must be leashed.

Colorado Springs - 10km Walk (YR465) **Jan 2-Dec 31**
Sponsoring Club: AVA-072, Falcon Wanderers
POC: Falcon Wanderers, 719-633-8971. PO Box 17162, Colorado Springs CO 80935-7162

Start Point: Mountain Chalet, 226 N Tejon; 719-633-0732.

Event Info: Mon, Tues & Sat, 9:30-6; Wed-Fri, 9:30-8. Contact event coordinator for special summer & holiday hours. Rated 1+. Suitable for strollers but not wheelchairs. Leashed pets.

Colorado Springs - 10km Walk (YR777) **Jan 1-Dec 31**
Sponsoring Club: AVA-072, Falcon Wanderers
POC: Falcon Wanderers, 719-684-9462. PO Box 17162, Colorado Springs, CO 80935

Start Point: 7-11 Store (Prospect Lake), 719-633-8889. 331 S Hancock Ave

Event Info: Daily, dawn to dusk. Rated 1+. Suitable for strollers & wheelchairs with assistance. Pets must be leashed.

Creede - Four 10km Walks (YR128-Phoenix Park, YR209-Miners Creek, YR355-Shallow Creek & YR396-Willow Canyon) **Jun 17-Oct 1**
Sponsoring Club: AVA-597, Upper Rio Grande Mountain Walkers
POC: BJ Myers, 719-658-2736. PO Box 272, Creede CO 81130

Start Point: Abbey Lane Gallery, 719-658-2736. 131 North Main St.

Event Info: YR128 is rated 4+. Altitude goes from 9,960 ft to 10,760 ft. Not suitable for wheelchairs or strollers. YR209 is rated 4. Altitude goes from 8,850 ft to 9,300 ft. It is not suitable for strollers or wheelchairs. YR355 is rated 3+. Altitude goes from 8,850 ft to 9,000 ft. It is not suitable for strollers or wheelchairs. YR396 is rated 3+. Altitude goes from 8,740 ft to 9,960 ft. It is suitable for strollers and wheelchairs. People considering attempting these events with strollers or wheelchairs should be in excellent physical condition.

Denver - 10km Walk (YR048) **Jan 2-Dec 31**
Sponsoring Club: AVA-024, Rocky Mountain Wanderers
POC: Nancy Reisdorff, 303-343-3806. 303 S. Troy, Aurora, CO 80012

Start Point: Larry's Shoes, 175 Fillmore St. Just north of the Cherry Creek Mall.

Event Info: Mon-Fri, 10-9; Sat, 10-7; & Sun 12-6. Rated 1+. Elevation is 5,280 ft. Suitable for strollers & wheelchairs. Pets must be leashed.

Evergreen - Two 10km Walks (YR195) & (YR375) **Jan 2-Dec 31**
Sponsoring Club: AVA-671, Lakewood On Parade Walkers
POC: Kathleen Finley, 303-233-7338. 70 Cody Ct, Lakewood CO 80226

Register: Paragon Sports, 303-670-0092. 2962 Hwy 74. I-70 to Evergreen Exit.

Start Point (YR195): Alderfer/Three Sisters Park.

Start Point (YR375): Elk Meadow Park.

Event Info: Daily, 10-6. Call to verify hours. Rated 3 due to altitude. No strollers or wheelchairs. Pets must be leashed.

Fountain - 10km Walk (YR153) **Jan 1-Dec 31**
Sponsoring Club: AVA-072, Falcon Wanderers
POC: Falcon Wanderers, 719-540-8755. PO Box 17162, Colorado Springs CO 80935

Start Point: Loaf 'N Jug Store, 719-390-7675. 7055 Alegre Circle.

Event Info: Daily, dawn to dusk. Rated 2. No wheelchairs. Strollers can complete with difficulty. Pets must be leashed.

Franktown - 11km Walk (YR827) **Jan 1-Dec 31**
Sponsoring Club: AVA-024, Rocky Mountain Wanderers
POC: Patty Gibson, 303-660-2807. 8630 Sun Country Dr, Elizabeth, CO 80107

Start Point: Castlewood Canyon State Park Visitor's Center, 303-688-5242.

Event Info: Park gates open at 9. Must finish by 4. Daily park pass is required. Carry your own water. Rated 4. Not suitable for strollers or wheelchairs. Elevation ranges from 6,200 ft to 6,500 ft. Pets must be leashed.

Georgetown - 10km Walk (YR541) **May 27-Sept 30**
Sponsoring Club: AVA-024, Rocky Mountain Wanderers
POC: Dottie Baars, 303-237-9788. 2010 Kendall, Edgewater, CO 80214

Start Point: Hamill House. 3rd & Argentine Sts. 45 miles west of Denver on I-70, exit 228.

Event Info: Daily, 10-5. Rated 3+. Elevation is 8,600 ft. Not suitable for strollers or wheelchairs.

Grand Lake - 12km Walk (YR283) **May 27-Sept 30**
Sponsoring Club: AVA-024, Rocky Mountain Wanderers
POC: John Burdan, 303-972-9296. 10118 W. Roxbury Ave, Littleton, CO 80127

Start Point: Grand Lake Chamber of Commerce, 303-627-3372. Located at the intersection of Hwy 34 & Grand Ave.

Event Info: Daily, 10-5. Rated 3+. Elevation is 8,400 ft. Not suitable for strollers or wheelchairs. Pets must be leashed.

Manitou Springs - 10km Walk (YR353) **Jan 1-Dec 31**
Sponsoring Club: AVA-072, Falcon Wanderers
POC: Falcon Wanderers, 719-597-5469. PO Box 17162, Colorado Springs CO 80935

Start Point: Loaf 'N Jug, 137 Manitou Ave; 719-685-1740.

Event Info: Daily, dawn to dusk. Rated 3 due to hills and altitude. Not recommended for wheelchairs. Strollers with difficulty. Pets must be leashed.

Monument - 11km Walk (YR466) & 25km Bike (YR337) **Jan 7-Dec 31**
Sponsoring Club: AVA-072, Falcon Wanderers
POC: Falcon Wanderers, 719-495-0404. PO Box 17162, Colorado Springs CO 80935

Start Point: High Country Feed Store, 243 Washington St; 719-481-3477.

Event Info: Mon-Fri, 8-6; Sat, 8-5; Sun, 9-5 in May & Jun. Trails are rated 3. Not suitable for wheelchairs. Strollers with difficulty. Pets must be leashed. Water not available at Start/Finish. Carrying water on trail is recommended.

Pueblo - 11km Walk (YR480) **Jan 1-Dec 31**
Sponsoring Club: AVA-072, Falcon Wanderers
POC: Falcon Wanderers, 719-948-3156. PO Box 17162, Colorado Springs CO 80935-7162

Start Point: Loaf 'N Jug, 120 South Sante Fe.

Event Info: Daily, dawn to dusk. Rated 2. Suitable for strollers but wheelchairs are not recommended. Pets must be leashed.

Pueblo - 10km Walk (YR842) **Jan 3-Dec 31**
Sponsoring Club: AVA-072, Falcon Wanderers
POC: Falcon Wanderers, 719-948-3156. PO Box 17162, Colorado Springs, CO 80935

Start Point: Pueblo Greenway & Nature Center, 719-545-9114. 5200 Nature Center Rd

Event Info: Tue-Sun, 9-5. Call for hours Dec 25-31. Rated 1+. Suitable for strollers & wheelchairs. Pets must be leashed.

USAF Academy - 10km Walk (YR197) **May 1-Oct 31**
Sponsoring Club: AVA-072, Falcon Wanderers
POC: Falcon Wanderers, 719-591-8193. PO Box 17162, Colorado Springs, CO 80935S

Start Point: Loaf 'N Jug, 719-488-9373. 13854 Glen Eagle Drive.

Event Info: Daily, dawn to dusk. Rated 3+. Strollers & wheelchairs cannot complete this trail. Walking sticks & hiking boots are recommended.

CONNECTICUT

Farmington - 10km Walk (YR923) **Jan 1-Dec 31**
Sponsoring Club: AVA-784, Connecticut Valley Volkssport Club
POC: Vern Tompkins, 203-621-8089. 91 Lowery Dr, Southington, CT 06479

Start Point: Farmington Inn, 203-677-2821. 827 Farmington Avenue. Follow I-84 exit 39, to Rt 4 West to Farmington Center. Farmington Inn is on the left after junction with Rt 10.

Event Info: Rated 1+.

Glastonbury - 10km Walk (YR925) **Jan 1-Dec 31**
Sponsoring Club: AVA-784, Connecticut Valley Volkssport Club
POC: Bob McDougall, 203-342-3062. PO Box 251, Glastonbury, CT 06033-0251

Start Point: Wawa Food Market, 203-659-3902. 103 New London Turnpike. Take I-91 to exit 25. Rt 3 East to Rt 2 South, Hebron Ave exit. Turn left to light at New London Turnpike, turn right at light, Wawa is 1/2 block down on right.

Event Info: Daily, dawn to dusk. Rated 1+.

Hartford - 12km Walk (YR567) **Jan 1-Dec 31**
Sponsoring Club: AVA-784, Connecticut Valley Volkssport Club
POC: Bob McDougall, 203-342-3062. PO Box 251, Glastonbury CT 06033-0251

Start Point: Ramada Inn, 203-246-6591. 440 Asylum Ave. From I-84 take exit 18. At end of ramp: westbound turn left, eastbound turn right. Ramada Inn is one block past railroad overpass on the left.

Event Info: Daily, dawn to dusk. Rated 1+.

Plantsville - 10km Walk (YR924) **Jan 1-Dec 31**
Sponsoring Club: AVA-784, Connecticut Valley Volkssport Club
POC: Vern Tompkins, 203-621-8089. 91 Lowery Dr, Southington, CT 06479

Start Point: Taylors Market, 203-628-6418. 44 W Main St. I-84 to exit 30. At end of ramp: from westbound turn left; from eastbound turn right. Taylor's Market will be on the right after the railroad crossing. Park in municipal parking.

Event Info: Rated 1+.

Portland - 10km Walk (YR254) **Jan 1-Dec 31**
Sponsoring Club: AVA-784, Connecticut Valley Volkssport Club
POC: Bob McDougall, 203-342-3062. PO Box 251, Glastonbury CT 06033-0251

Start Point: Dunkin' Donuts, 203-342-1490. 152 Main St. Follow I-91 to exit 22, Rt 9 South. Follow signs for Rt 17 North to Portland, turning right at the light under the bridge. After crossing the bridge, DUNKIN' DONUTS will be on the left.

Event Info: Daily, dawn to dusk. Rated 1+.

Wethersfield - 11km Walk (YR717) **Jan 1-Dec 31**
Sponsoring Club: AVA-784, Connecticut Valley Volkssport Club
POC: William Webb, 203-529-5577. 7 Fernwood St, Wethersfield, CT 06109

Start Point: Ramada Inn, 203-563-2311. 1330 Silas Dean Highway. Follow I-91 to exit 24. At end of ramp follow Rt 99 North. Ramada Inn is on the right one block north on Rt 99.

Event Info: Daily, dawn to dusk. Rated 1+.

Windsor - 10km Walk (YR706) **Jan 1-Dec 31**
Sponsoring Club: AVA-784, Connecticut Valley Volkssport Club
POC: William Webb, 203-529-5577. 7 Fernwood St, Wethersfield, CT 06109

Start Point: Bart's Restaurant & Deli, 203-688-9035. 55 Palisado Ave. Follow I-91 to exit 37 to Rt 305 East. Follow signs to Rt 159 North (Palisado Ave). Bart's will be on the left after the railroad overpass.

Event Info: Mon-Fri, 7 A.M.-8 P.M., Sat, 7 A.M.-4 P.M. Closed most Sundays. Rated 1+.

WASHINGTON DC

DC - 11km Walk (YR157) **Jan 1-Dec 31**
Sponsoring Club: AVA-246, Walter Reed Wandervogel
POC: Klaus J. Waibel, 301-681-9084. PO Box 59652, Washington DC 20012

Start Point: National Museum of Health & Medicine, Bldg 54, Walter Reed Army Medical Ctr.

Event Info: Daily, 10-2. Finish by 5. Closed Christmas. Rated 1+. Not suitable for strollers or wheelchairs. Pets must be leashed. Weekday parking extremely limited.

☆ **DC** - 10/13km Walk (YR231) **Jan 2-Dec 31**
Sponsoring Club: AVA-021, Washington DC Volksmarching Club
POC: Nancy Stenger, 703-631-8512. 14402 William Carr Lane, Centreville, VA 22020-2813

Start Point: Columbia Plaza Gourmet, 202-887-8240. 538 - 23rd St, NW. Mon-Fri, 7:30-8 P.M.; Sat, 10-6; closed on Sunday; Holidays, limited hours.

Alternate Start Point: Columbia Plaza Pharmacy, 202-331-5800. 516 - 23rd St, NW. Mon-Fri, 5:30am-7 P.M.; Sat, 7:30-6; Sun, 7:30-3; & Holidays, 7-4. Weekend hours may change during the summer. Call to verify.

Event Info: Rated 1+. Both Start Points are closed Thanksgiving, Christmas & New Years. Pets must be leashed.

DC - Two 10km Walks (YR552 & YR553) **Jan 1-Dec 31**
Sponsoring Club: AVA-419, Seneca Valley Sugarloafers Volksmarch Club
POC: Ed Branges, 301-340-9418. 1830 Greenplace Terr, Rockville, MD 20850-2942

Start Point: Washington Park Gourmet Deli, 2331 Calvert St, N.W. Take Metro Red Line to Woodley Park/Zoo Station. Walk one block to corner of 24th & Calvert Sts.

Event Info: Daily, 9-5. Closed Thanksgiving & Christmas. Trails are rated 2. Suitable for strollers & wheelchairs. No pets allowed.

DELAWARE

Dover - 11km Walk (YR150) & 37km Bike (YR207) **Jan 2-Dec 30**
Sponsoring Club: AVA-636, Diamond State Trekkers
POC: Ingrid Rockett, 302-697-3008. 11-B North Railroad Ave, Wyoming DE 19934

Start Point: The Pancake House, 950 North State St; 302-674-8310.

Event Info: Mon-Sat, 7-6; Sun, 7-2. Closed Memorial Day, July 4th, Labor Day, Thanksgiving, Christmas, & New Year's. Rated 1. Suitable for strollers but some sidewalks lack cuts. Pets must be leashed.

New Castle - 10km Walk (YR912) **Jan 2-Dec 30**
Sponsoring Club: AVA-636, Diamond State Trekkers
POC: Ingrid Rockett, 302-697-3008. 11-B North Railroad Ave, Wyoming, DE 19934-1043

Start Point: The Cellar Gourmet Restaurant, 302-323-0999. 208 Delaware St.

Event Info: Jun-Aug, daily, 8-6 (finish by 5:30). Sept-May, daily, 8-3 (finish by 2:30). Closed Easter, Thanksgiving, Christmas, New Year's. During extreme bad weather event is closed. Rated 1+. Not suitable for wheelchairs but okay for strollers. Pets must be leashed. Restrooms available only at start/finish.

Rehoboth Beach - 10km Walk (YR741) **Jan 14-Dec 15**
Sponsoring Club: AVA-065, First State Webfooters
POC: Paul Hewett, 302-945-2020. 1189 Alls Well Alley, F-6PNN, Long Neck, DE 10066

Start Point: Atlantic Sands Hotel front desk, on the boardwalk at Baltimore Ave.

Event Info: Daily, 8-5. Be off the trail by dark or 5 P.M., whichever comes first. Rated 1. Modified trail available for handicapped, wheelchairs & strollers. Dogs are not permitted on the beach or boardwalk from Apr 1- Oct 31. Pets must be leashed at all other times.

FLORIDA

Apopka - 10km Walk (YR267) **Jan 1-Dec 31**
Sponsoring Club: AVA-FL, Florida Volkssport Association
POC: Bill Woolgar, 407-696-4367. 1260 Park Dr, Casselberry, FL 32707

Start Point: Wekiwa Springs State Park Entrance, 407-884-2009. 1800 Wekiwa Cir.

Event Info: Daily, 8-dusk. Rated 1+. One brochure lists all 12 State Parks. When you complete the walks in all 12 parks, you will receive a beautifully colored certificate.

Bristol - 10km Walk (YR708) **Jan 1-Dec 31**
Sponsoring Club: AVA-773, Miccosukee Milers
POC: Joe Sexton, 904-488-8631/904-576-9492. 1330 Burgess Dr, Tallahassee FL 32304

Start Point: Apalachee Diner, 904-643-2264. Hwy 20.

Event Info: Daily, 6:30-dusk. Closed Thanksgiving & Christmas. Rated 1+. Not suitable for strollers. Pets must be leashed.

Brooksville - 10km Walk (YR520) **Jan 1-Dec 31**
Sponsoring Club: AVA-FL, Florida Volkssport Association
POC: Bob Lazzell, 904-597-3912. 14979 Rialto Ave, Brooksville, FL 34613

Register: Lake Lindsey Grocery Store, 904-796-0109. 14351 Snow Memorial Hwy.

Start Point: Withlacoochee State Forest.

Event Info: Daily, 8-dusk. One brochure lists all 12 state parks. Special certificate when completing all 12.

Bushnell - 10km Walk (YR548) **Jan 1-Dec 31**
Sponsoring Club: AVA-FL, Florida Volkssport Association
POC: Joan Jarrett, 904-521-0615. PO Box 802, Dade City, FL 33526

Start Point: Dade Battlefield State Historic Site Visitor Center, 904-793-4781. 7200 S. Battlefield Dr

Event Info: Park open 8-dusk. Center open 9-5. Rated 1. One brochure lists all 12 state parks. Special certificate when completing all 12.

Cocoa Village - 10km Walk (YR070) **Jan 1-Dec 31**
Sponsoring Club: AVA-140, Patrick Pacers Volkssport Club
POC: Ron Barnett, 407-452-9448. 101 Tequesta Harbor Dr, Merritt Island FL 32952

Start Point: Dixie Restaurant, 300 N Cocoa Blvd (US 1). I-95 exit 75 on SR 520 to N Cocoa Blvd (US 1). Turn left (north) on No Cocoa Blvd (US 1). Start is on your right.

Event Info: Mon-Fri, 7-10; Sat-Sun, 7-11. Rated 1.

Dade City - 10km Walk (YR576) **Jan 1-Dec 31**
Sponsoring Club: AVA-219, Suncoast Sandpipers Volkssport Club
POC: Kay Tanno, 904-567-7211. 511 W Meridan, Dade City FL 33525

Register: Mr. C's Warehouse Foods, 7th St. From I-75 exit at SR52. Travel East 9 miles to Dade City. Left on US 301 for 1/2 mile to Mr. C's in shopping center on left.

Start Point: Withlacoochee River Park. 4.7 miles from Mr. C's.

Event Info: Daily, 7:30-3. Rated 1+. Not suitable for strollers or wheelchairs.

Daytona Beach/Ponce Inlet - 10km Walk (YR725) **Jan 1-Dec 31**
Sponsoring Club: AVA-717, Happy Wanderers
POC: Alan or Elaine Brayton, 904-760-1410. 1212 Ryan St, Port Orange, FL 32119

Start Point: Ponce de Leon Inlet Lighthouse Gift Shop, 4931 S. Peninsula Dr. I-95 exit 85. Proceed East (SR427) Dunlawton Ave. Cross intra-coastal bridge. Right at S Atlantic Ave (2nd intersection CR 4075) 5.2 miles to Beach St. Right to S Peninsula Dr, left to Lighthouse.

Event Info: Daily, fall/winter, 10-5; summer, 10-8. Rated 1+. Not suitable for wheelchairs or strollers. No pets allowed.

DeLand - 10km Walk (YR440) **Jan 1-Dec 31**
Sponsoring Club: AVA-717, Happy Wanderers
POC: Alan & Elaine Brayton, 904-760-1410. 1212 Ryan St, Port Orange, FL 32119

Start Point: Volusia County Public Library, 130 E. Howry Ave. I-4 exit 54. Follow signs to DeLand (approx 4 miles) on 17/92. Turn right on Howry Ave (SR44E). Start is on right.

Event Info: Mon,Wed, Fri & Sat, 10-5; Tue & Thurs, 10-8. Closed Sunday and Holidays. Rated 1+. Strollers & wheelchairs will have slight difficulties. Pets must be leashed.

DeLand - 10km Walk (YR549) **Jan 1-Dec 31**
Sponsoring Club: AVA-FL, Florida Volkssport Association
POC: Hank Rossi, 904-228-2740. 1205 Emmel Rd, Cassadaga, FL 32709

Start Point: Hontoon Island State Park, Hontoon Landing Ship's Store, 800-248-2474. 2317 River Ridge Rd.

Event Info: Park is open daily, 8-dusk. Ship's Store is open 6am-7 P.M. One brochure lists all 12 state parks. Special certificate when walking all 12.

Dunedin - 10km Walk (YR573) **Jan 1-Dec 31**
Sponsoring Club: AVA-FL, Florida Volkssport Association
POC: Al Barbieri, 813-584-7975. 131 Bluff View Dr, #409, Belleair Bluffs, FL 34640

Start Point: Honeymoon Island State Rec Area, Park entrance, 813-469-5942. #1 Causeway Blvd.

Event Info: Daily, 8-dusk. Rated 1+. One brochure lists all 12 State Parks. Complete the walk in each one and receive a beautifully colored certificate.

Ft Myers - 11km Walk (YR446) **Jan 1-Dec 31**
Sponsoring Club: AVA-755, Fort Myers Meandering Manatees
POC: Maxine Johnson, 813-997-6384. 666 Brigantine Blvd, N. Ft Myers, FL 33917

Start Point: Sheraton Harbor Place, 2500 Edwards Dr. Located opposite the Yacht Basin on the Caloosahatchee River between US 41 & Business US 41.

Event Info: Rated 1. Suitable for strollers & wheelchairs.

Ft Myers - 25km Bike (YR818) **Jan 1-Dec 31**
Sponsoring Club: AVA-755, Fort Myers Meandering Manatees
POC: Maxine Johnson, 813-997-6384. 666 Brigantine Blvd, N. Ft Myers, FL 33917

Start Point: Hess Mart, Daniels Parkway. 4/10 of a mile west of exit 21 from I-75.

Event Info: Rated 1. Participants must sign waiver. Use of helmets is encouraged.

Ft Myers - 10km Walk (YR817) **Jan 1-Dec 31**
Sponsoring Club: AVA-755, Fort Myers Meandering Manatees
POC: Maxine Johnson, 813-997-6384. 666 Brigantine Blvd, N. Ft Myers, FL 33917

Start Point: Lakes Park, 813-481-7946. 7330 Gladiolus Dr. From I-75 take Daniels Rd/SW Regional Airport Exit #21 and go west. In about three miles, turn left on Six Mile Cypress Pkwy. After crossing US 41, this becomes Gladiolus.

Event Info: Park entrance fee is $3.00 per car. Rated 1+. Most of trail is suitable for strollers & wheelchairs. No pets allowed.

Hobe Sound - 10km Walk (YR643) **Jan 1-Dec 31**
Sponsoring Club: AVA-FL, Florida Volkssport Association
POC: Lynne Rourke, 407-474-3339. 92 Turtle Creek Dr, Tequesta, FL 33469

Start Point: Jonathan Dickinson State Park, 407-546-2771. 16450 SE Federal Hwy.

Event Info: Daily, 8-dusk. Rated 1+. One brochure lists all 12 State Parks. Walk in all 12 parks and receive a beautifully colored certificate.

Indialantic - 11km Walk (YR617) **Jan 1-Dec 31**
Sponsoring Club: AVA-140, Patrick Pacers Volkssport Club
POC: Ron Barnett, 407-452-9448. 101 Tequesta Harbor Dr, Merritt Island FL 32952

Start Point: Blueberry Muffin Restaurant, 1130 N. Hwy A1A. I-95 exit 71 east on US 192 to N Hwy A1A. Turn left on N Hwy A1A. Start is on the left.

Event Info: Mon-Sat, 6:30-3; Sun, 7-3. Rated 1+.

Inverness - 10km Walk (YR582) **Jan 1-Dec 31**
Sponsoring Club: AVA-FL, Florida Volkssport Association
POC: Jack Thiele, 904-523-1485. 32651 Trilby Rd, Dade City, FL 33525

Register: Lil' Champ Store, 904-344-3967. 745 S Hwy US41.

Start Point: Fort Cooper State Park.

Event Info: Daily, 8-dusk. Rated 1+. One brochure lists all 12 state parks. Receive a beautifully colored certificate when completing events in all 12 parks.

Jupiter - 10km Walk (YR650) **Jan 1-Dec 31**
Sponsoring Club: AVA-758, Barefoot Pelicans
POC: Lynn Rourke, 407-747-3339. 92 Turtle Creek Dr, Tequesta FL 33469-1508

Start Point: The Log Cabin Restaurant, 631 North Hwy A1A. I-95/Turnpike to SR706 East to A1A. Left (North) to Log Cabin Restaurant.

Event Info: Daily, 7-dusk. Rated 2. Pets not allowed.

Lake Buena Vista (Disney Village) - 10km Walk (YR841) **Jan 1-Dec 31**
Sponsoring Club: AVA-629 Mid-Florida Milers
POC: Jim Davern, 407-295-7146. 2077 Oneta Ct, Orlando, FL 32818

Start Point: Pirates Cove Adventure Golf, Crossroads Shopping Center. I-4 to exit 27, Lake Buena Vista (SR 535) north to Crossroads (1st light). Turn right and go straight to Start.

Event Info: Daily, 9am-11:30 P.M. Rated 1.

Lake Wales - 10km Walk (YR572) **Jan 1-Dec 31**
Sponsoring Club: AVA-FL, Florida Volkssport Association
POC: Rosie & Chuck Trimpey, 813-646-8165. 5804 Yarborough Lane, Lakeland, FL 33813

Start Point: Lake Kissimmee State Park, 813-696-1112. 14248 Camp Mack Rd.

Event Info: Daily, 7-dusk. Rated 1+. One brochure lists all 12 State Parks. Walk in all 12 and receive a special certificate.

Melbourne - 10km Walk (YR498) **Jan 1-Dec 31**
Sponsoring Club: AVA-140, Patrick Pacers Volkssport Club
POC: Ron Barnett, 407-452-9448. 101 Tequesta Harbor Dr, Merritt Island, FL 32952

Start Point: Burger King, 1514 S Harbor City Blvd (US1). I-95 exit 71 east on US 192 to S Harbor City Blvd (US 1). Turn left on S Harbor City Blvd (US 1). Start is on the left.

Event Info: Mon-Fri, 6am-10 P.M.; Sat & Sun, 6-12. Rated 1.

Melbourne Beach - 10km Walk (YR751) **Jan 1-Dec 31**
Sponsoring Club: AVA-FL, Florida Volkssport Association
POC: Chuck Woodward, 407-722-0463. 1177 N Hwy A1A #402, Indialantic, FL 32903

Start Point: Sebastian Inlet State Recreation Area Concession Store, 407-725-6828. 9700 South A1A

Event Info: Daily, 8-dusk. Closed Thanksgiving & Christmas. Rated 1+. One brochure lists all 12 state parks. Special Certificate when all 12 are completed.

Mt. Dora - 10km Walk (YR726) **Jan 1-Dec 31**
Sponsoring Club: AVA-717, Happy Wanderers
POC: Alan & Elaine Brayton, 904-760-1410. 1212 Ryan St, Port Orange, FL 32119 or Bob Rausch, 904-357-1420. 2818 Pineapple Lane, Eustis, FL 32726

Start Point: Chamber of Commerce, 341 Alexander St. I-4 to exit 51 (SR 46 to Old US 441 to downtown). Turn (S) Alexander St, 3 blocks to Chamber in old train depot.

Event Info: Mon-Fri, 9-5; Sat, 1-4; Sun, 12-4. Rated 1+. Not suitable for wheelchairs or strollers. No pets allowed.

Orlando - 10km Walk (YR152) **Jan 1-Dec 31**
Sponsoring Club: AVA-629, Mid-Florida Milers
POC: Jim Davern, 407-295-7146. 2077 Oneta Court, Orlando, FL 32818

Start Point: Orlando Regional Medical Center, Information Desk, 1414 Kuhl. From I-4 take Exit 38, Anderson St east to 2nd light. Turn right on Orange Ave. At the 5th light, turn right on Copeland Dr. One block and left on Kuhl Ave. 1/2 block and right on Copeland again. Left into 2nd entrance of parking bldg.

Event Info: Daily, dawn to dusk. Rated 1. Suitable for strollers & wheelchairs. Pets must be leashed.

Orange City - 10km Walk (YR581) **Jan 1-Dec 31**
Sponsoring Club: AVA-FL, Florida Volkssport Association
POC: Rena & John McMahon, 407-275-5748. 1112 Spring Lite Way, Orlando, FL 32825

Start Point: Blue Spring State Park Entrance, 904-775-3663. 2100 W. French Ave.

Event Info: Daily, 8-dusk. Rated 1+. One brochure lists all 12 State Parks. Receive a special certificate when completing all 12.

Osprey - 10km Walk (YR642) **Jan 1-Dec 31**
Sponsoring Club: AVA-FL, Florida Volkssport Association
POC: Bill Murphy, 813-966-6225. 634 Leger Dr, Nokomis, FL 43275

Start Point: Oscar Scherer State Park Entrance, 813-966-3154. 1843 S. Tamiami Trail.

Event Info: Daily, 8-dusk. Rated 1+. One brochure lists all 12 State Parks. Receive a certificate when you complete all 12.

Pensacola - 11km Walk (YR345) **Jan 2-Dec 31**
Sponsoring Club: AVA-240, Pensacola Volksmarch Club
POC: Strictly Walking & More, 904-479-1612. 4771 Bayou Blvd #7, Pensacola, FL 32503

Start Point: National Museum Naval Aviation

Event Info: Daily, 9-5. Closed Thanksgiving & Christmas. Trail is rated 1+. Portions not suitable for strollers or wheelchairs. No pets allowed.

Pensacola - 10km Walk (YR274) **Jan 1-Dec 31**
Sponsoring Club: AVA-240, Pensacola Volksmarch Club
POC: Lillian Baines, 904-477-3174. 3721 Swan Ln, Pensacola FL 32504

Start Point: Pensacola Police Dept, 711 N Haynes St. 904-435-1900.

Event Info: Daily, dawn to dusk. Rated 1+. Suitable for strollers. Wheelchairs may have difficulty with busy intersections. Pets must be leashed.

Pensacola - 11km Walk (YR342) & 26km Bike (YR343) **Jan 1-Dec 31** Credit Only Events
Sponsoring Club: AVA-240, Pensacola Volksmarch Club
POC: Bob Howerton, 904-477-5528. 4510 Treeline Dr, Pensacola, FL 32504

Start Point: Circle K Convenience Store, 2825 Langley Ave. (Near the airport)

Event Info: Daily, dawn to dusk. Walk is rated 1. Suitable for strollers and wheelchairs. Bikers are required to wear helmets and sign waiver. Pets must be leashed.

Ponte Vedra Beach - 10km Walk (YR644) **Jan 1-Dec 31**
Sponsoring Club: AVA-FL, Florida Volkssport Association
POC: Nita & Chuck Stalfort, 904-264-3069. 517 Lakefield Lane, Orange Park, FL 32073

Register: Gate Food Store, 904-824-3869. 2700 Ponte Vedra Blvd.

Start Point: Guana River State Park.

Event Info: Daily, 8-dusk. Closed Christmas. Rated 1. One brochure lists all 12 State Parks. Complete the event in each one and receive a certificate.

Safety Harbor - 10km Walk (YR441) **Jan 1-Dec 31**
Sponsoring Club: AVA-219, Suncoast Sandpipers Volkssport Club
POC: Al & Mary Barbieri, 813-584-7975. 131 Bluff View Dr #409, Belleair Bluffs, FL 34640

Start Point: Paradise Restaurant, 443 Main St. From N or S on US 19 to Sunset Point/Main St. Travel E 2.5 miles to Start (on the left). From Tampa, SR60 W to Clearwater. Right on Bayshore 2.5 miles to Main St. Left 4 blocks. Start is on right.

Event Info: Rated 1+. Suitable for strollers and wheelchairs with some difficulty and assistance. Closed Thanksgiving & Christmas. Mon-Sat open at 7. Sunday open at 8.

Sanibel Island - 10km Walk (YR521) & 25/45km Bike (YR649) **Jan 1-Dec 31**
Sponsoring Club: AVA-755, Fort Myers Meandering Manatees
POC: Maxine Johnson, 813-997-6384. 666 Brigantine Blvd, N Ft Myers Fl 33917

Start Point: Sanibel Seashell Industries, 813-472-1603. 905 Fitzhugh St. After causeway, go right on Periwinkle and then right on Fitzhugh to start.

Event Info: Mon-Sat, 10-5. Sun, 12-5. Closed on Sunday June-October. Call start to verify Sunday hours. Sanibel Causeway is a toll bridge ($3.00).

Tallahassee - Two 10km Walks (YR335 & YR596) & 25/36km Bike (YR442) **Jan 1-Dec 31**
Sponsoring Club: AVA-661, Tallahassee Volkssport Club
POC (YR335): Larry Tepe, 904-668-0565. 3679 Barbary Dr, Tallahassee FL 32308
POC (YR596): Kermit/Diane Brown, 904-386-3250. Same address
POC (YR442): Ron Brown, 904-224-6756. Same address

Start Point: Holiday Inn, 1302 Apalachee Pkwy. This is the registration for all events. Directions to bike start/finish will be provided at registration.

Event Info: Trails are rated 1+. Suitable for wheelchairs & strollers.

Tampa - 10km Walk (YR163) **Jan 2-Dec 31**
Sponsoring Club: AVA-219, Suncoast Sandpipers Volkssport Club
POC: Jeanie Martin, 813-986-3909. 11712 Thonotosaassa Rd, Thonotosassa, FL 33592

Start Point: Chris's Cookies, Harbour Island shops, 1st level. Take I-275 to exit 25. Follow signs to Convention Center. Left lane to Harbor Island. Park in garage under the shops.

Event Info: Daily, 7:30-3. Closed Christmas and New Years. Rated 1. Suitable for strollers & wheelchairs.

Winter Park - 11km Walk (YR394) **Jan 1-Dec 31**
Sponsoring Club: AVA-629, Mid-Florida Milers
POC: Jim Davern, 407-295-7146. 2077 Oneta Court, Orlando, FL 32818

Start Point: Florida Hospital Medical Center, Information Desk. 601 East Rollins St. From I-4 take Exit 43, Princeton St. east to the 1st light. Turn left on Orange Ave to the 3rd light. Turn right on King St for 1/2 block. Turn right into Parking Bldg, take ticket & park. Take elevator to 3rd floor. Turn right from elevator, walk overpass & take escalator down to main floor. Follow signs to main lobby.

Event Info: Daily, dawn to dusk. Rated 1+. Not suitable for strollers or wheelchairs. Pets must be leashed.

Winter Park - 25km Bike (YR395) **Jan 1-Dec 31**
Sponsoring Club: AVA-629, Mid-Florida Milers
POC: Jim Davern, 407-295-7146. 2077 Oneta Court, Orlando, FL 32818

Start Point: Winter Park Hospital Wellness Center, Information Desk. 2005 Mizell Ave. From I-4 take exit 45, Fairbanks Ave, east for 3.5 miles. Turn right on Lakemont Ave. At the 1st light, turn left on Mizell Ave. In two blocks Mizell dead ends at the Wellness Center.

Event Info: Mon-Fri, dawn to dusk. Sat & Sun, 8-6. Rated 1. Participants must sign waiver. Helmets are recommended.

GEORGIA

Decatur - 10km Walk (YR847) **Jan 2-Dec 31**
Sponsoring Club: AVA-178, Georgia Walkers
POC: Duncan Brantley, 404-961-0109. 6524 Revena Drive, Morrow, GA 30260

Start Point: Decatur/Dekalb Family Branch YMCA, 404-377-0241. 1100 Clairmont Ave

Event Info: Mon-Sat, 8-4; Sun, 1-4.

Helen - 10km Walk (YR603) **Jan 1-Dec 31**
Sponsoring Club: AVA-290, Alpine Helen Volkswanderung Club
POC: Jean Paul, 706-878-2810 after 6 P.M. 3114 hwy 225 North, Sautee GA 30571

Start Point: Helen/White County Convention & Visitor Bureau, Chattahoochee St. (next to Police Department)

Event Info: Daily, 9-12:30. Must be off trail by 4. Rated 3. Not recommended for strollers or wheelchairs. Pets must be leashed.

Kennesaw - 11km Walk (YR858) **Jan 1-Dec 31**
Sponsoring Club: AVA-684, Roswell Striders
POC: Linda Nickles, 404-641-3760. 38 Hill St, Suite 100, Roswell, GA 30075

Start Point: Kennesaw Mountain National Battlefield Park Visitor's Center, 900 Kennesaw Mountain Dr.

Event Info: Rated 3. Not suitable for wheelchairs nor most types of strollers.

Peachtree City - 10km Walk (YR508) **Jan 1-Dec 31** Credit Only Event
Sponsoring Club: AVA-178, Georgia Walkers
POC: Duncan Brantley, 404-961-0109. 6524 Revena Dr, Morrow GA 30260

Start Point: Kroger Grocery Store (Pharmacy Dept), Braelinn Village Shopping Ctr, 564 Crosstown Dr.

Event Info: Daily, dawn to 3 hours before dusk. Rated 1. Pets must be leashed.

Roswell - 10km Walk (YR096) **Jan 1-Dec 31** Credit Only Event
Sponsoring Club: AVA-178, Georgia Walkers
POC: Duncan Brantley, 404-961-0109. 6524 Revena Dr, Morrow GA 30260

Start Point: Courtyard by Marriott, 500 Market Blvd. From I-285 take Hwy 400 N to exit 7A, Holcomb Bridge Road. Bear right and take first right on Market Way to Courtyard by Marriott.

Event Info: Daily, dawn to 3 hours before dusk. Rated 1. Okay for strollers, no wheelchairs.

Roswell - Two 10km Walks (YR307 & YR651) **Jan 2-Dec 30**
Sponsoring Club: AVA-684, Roswell Striders
POC: Linda Nickles, 404-641-3760. 38 Hill St, Suite 100, Roswell GA 30075

Start Point: Community Activity Bldg, 404-641-3760. Roswell Area Park, 10495 Woodstock Rd.

Event Info: Both trails are rated 2. Closed Sundays & holidays.

Stone Mountain Park - 10km Walk (YR387) 25km Bike (YR384) & Swim (YR051) **Jan 1-Dec 31** Credit Only Events
Sponsoring Club: AVA-178, Georgia Walkers
POC: Duncan Brantley, 404-961-0109. 6524 Revena Dr, Morrow GA 30260

Start Point: Pedal Power Inc, 1944 Rockbridge Rd, #105. From Atlanta take I-285 to Exit 30B (Stone Mountain Freeway). Proceed to US Hwy 78 about 8 miles to West Park Place. Turn left into the right lane for an immediate right turn onto Rockbridge Road.
Start Point is in the shopping center on your left between a restaurant and Drug Emporium.

Event Info: Mon-Sat, 10-3. Closed Sundays & normal holidays. Trails are rated 2. Suitable for strollers & wheelchairs. Bikers must wear helmets and sign the bike waiver.

HAWAII

Honolulu - 12km Walk (YR166) **Jan 1-Dec 31**
Sponsoring Club: AVA-456, Menehune Marchers
POC: Terry Puuohau, 808-261-3774. PO Box 31102, Honolulu HI 96820

Start Point: New Otani Kaimana Beach Hotel, 2863 Kalakaua Ave.

Event Info: Daily, 8-3:30. Rated 1+. Suitable for strollers. Wheelchairs with difficulty.

Honolulu - 10km Walk (YR097) **Jan 1-Dec 31**
Sponsoring Club: AVA-456, Menehune Marchers
POC: Bob Iverson, 808-947-3359. PO Box 31102, Honolulu, HI 96820

Start Point: McDonald's of Manoa Market Place, 2915 East Manoa Rd. Take Bus #6 (University-Woodlawn) from Ala Moana Center to Manoa Market Place McDonald's.

Event Info: Daily, dawn to dusk. Rated 2. Strollers may encounter difficulty. No wheelchairs.

IDAHO

American Falls - 11km Walk (YR118) **May 29-Sept 4**
Sponsoring Club: AVA-650, American Falls Volkssport Club
POC: Max Newlin, 208-548-2672. 3592 Park Lane, American Falls, ID 83211

Start Point: Massacre Rock State Park Visitor Center. 3592 Park Lane. Located at exit 20 on I-86, 10 miles west of American Falls.

Athol - 10km Walk (YR310) **Apr 1-Oct 1**
Sponsoring Club: AVA-325, Panhandle Pacers
POC: Valerie Olson, 208-263-1441 ext 123. PO Box 1448, Sandpoint, ID 83864

Start Point: Farragut State Park, E 13400 Ranger Road. From I-90 East or West, in Coeur d'Alene, ID turn north at US95 towards Sandpoint and Canada. Drive north approximately 20 miles to Athol. When you come to State Hwy 54, turn east and go approximately 4 miles to park entrance and visitor's center.

Event Info: Trail is rated 3.

Boise- 11km Walk (YR089) & 12km Walk (YR613) **Jan 1-Dec 31**
Sponsoring Club: AVA-766, Treasure Valley Volkssports
POC: Juliann Fritchman, 208-345-8259. 3033 E Rivernest Dr, Boise ID 83706 or Barbara Silverstein, 208-939-7292. 3096 Holl Dr, Eagle, ID 83616

Start Point: Boise Family YMCA, N 11th St & W State St.

Event Info: Mon-Fri, 6-9:30; Sat, 7-5:30; Sun, 12-4:30. Closed major holidays. Trails are rated 1+. Suitable for strollers and wheelchairs. Pets must be leashed.

Coeur d'Alene - 10km Walk (YR733) **Apr 1-Oct 31** Credit Only Event
Sponsoring Club: AVA-475, Coeur d'Alene Volkssport Club
POC: John Huber, 208-667-6525 or Clyde Kaffenberger, 208-762-4440.

Start Point: Idaho State Police, 208-667-8682. 602 West Prairie Ave. I-90, Exit #12. North on US-95 to Prairie Ave. One block west to ISP HQs. (Large bldg on left).

Event Info: Daily, dawn to dusk. Rated 2+. Not suitable for strollers or wheelchairs. Pets must be leashed. Water & restrooms are NOT available on the walk.

Coeur d'Alene - 10km Walk (YR780) **Apr 1-Oct 31**
Sponsoring Club: AVA-475, Coeur 'd Alene Volkssport Club
POC: Larry Srobel, 208-664-4904. PO Box 535, Coeur d'Alene, ID 83814

Start Point: The Coeur d'Alene Resort, 115 S 2nd St

Event Info: Daily, dawn to dusk. Registration cabinet is near the Adventures Office in the lobby. Office is open 8-8. Rated 3 if doing Tubbs Hill. Alternate which eliminates Tubbs Hill is rated 1+. Suitable for strollers or wheelchairs if using alternate route. Leashed pets.

Sandpoint - 10km Walk (YR732) **Mar 15-Nov 30** Credit Only Event
Sponsoring Club: AVA-729, Selkirk Striders
POC: Lane or Ruby Lowe, 208-263-9639. 1812 Hickory St, Sandpoint, ID 83864

Start Point: Sandpoint West Athletic Club, 208-263-2792. 1905 Pine St. (corner of Pine & Lincoln)

Event Info: Daily, 6 A.M. to dusk. Closed major holidays. Rated 1. Pets are not allowed in city parks. Alternate route available for pet owners. Call POC for information. Suitable for strollers & wheelchairs.

ILLINOIS

Belleville - 10km Walk (YR226) **Jan 1-Dec 31**
Sponsoring Club: AVA-047, Illinois Trekkers Volkssport Club
POC: Richard Parle, 618-632-8390. 111 Stacy Dr, Fairview Heights, IL 62208

Start Point: Pilgrim's Inn, Shrine of Our Lady of the Snows, 9500 Hwy 15.

Event Info: Daily, dawn to dusk. Rated 1+.

Collinsville - 10km Walk (YR249) **Jan 3-Dec 31**
Sponsoring Club: AVA-047, Illinois Trekkers Volkssport Club
POC: Andrew Knopik, 618-482-5225. 3012 N 60th St, Fairmont City, IL 62201

Start Point: Cahokia Mounds Historical Site, Interpretive Center.

Event Info: Rated 1.

Chicago (Frankfort) - 10km Walk (YR831) **Jan 1-Dec 31**
Sponsoring Club: AVA-722, Wewalkits Volksmarching Club
POC: Tom O'Donnell, 708-339-8909. 3901 West 155th St, Markham, IL 60426

Start Point: Always Open Convenience Store, 6 West Elwood. From I-80 take exit 145A (Rt 45 LaGrange Rd/96th Ave). Go south to Frankfort. Just past stoplight at Rt 30, turn left onto White St (Historic Area). Start is on corner of White & Elwood.

Event Info: Daily, 8 A.M.-6 P.M. Suitable for strollers, no wheelchairs. Pets must be leashed.

Chicago (Oak Forest) - 10km Walk (YR828) **Jan 1-Dec 31** & 25km Bike (YR830) **Apr 1-Oct 31**
Sponsoring Club: AVA-722, Wewalkits Volksmarching Club
POC: Ken Stoffregen, 708-422-3034. %Color Key Printing, 9517 S Cook Ave, Oak Lawn, IL 60453

Start Point: The Bayberry Pantry, 6078 West 159th St. From I-57, exit at 167th St West. Right at stoplight (Cicero Ave). Left at 159th St. Start is on corner of 159th and Arroyo Dr.

Event Info: Daily, 8-6. No restrooms at start/finish. Both events are rated 2+. Pets must be leashed. Bikers must sign waiver. Helmets are recommended.

Edwardsville/Glen Carbon - 11km Walk (YR903) **May 7-Dec 31**
Sponsoring Club: AVA-682, S.M.T.M. Volkssport Society
POC: Gary Staley, 618-288-2804. 1300 New Florissant Rd, Florissant, MO 63033-2122

Start Point: Hardee's, 4207 S SR 159. Glen Carbon is located just south of I-70 between IL Hwy 157 & 159. From I-70, exit IL Hwy 159 (exit 12) and go north about one mile. Hardee's is on your left.

Event Info: Trail is rated 1. Suitable for strollers & wheelchairs. Pets must be leashed.

Hillsboro - 10km Walk (YR232) **Jan 2-Dec 31** Credit Only Event
Sponsoring Club: AVA-146, Railsplitter Wanderers
POC: Roger Mollett/Randy Mollett, 217-546-8137/532-5455. 837 S. Columbia Ave, Springfield IL 62704

Start Point: Red Rooster Inn, 217-532-6332. 123 East Seward St. From Rt 127 turn east on Seward St. Go around the Courthouse. Inn is just east of courthouse.

Event Info: Mon-Sat, 8-5; Sun, 8-1:30. Closed New Years & Christmas. Pets must be leashed. Rated 1.5. Difficult for strollers or wheelchairs.

Lockport - 10km Walk (YR625) **Jan 1-Dec 31**
Sponsoring Club: AVA-722, Wewalkits Volksmarching Club
POC: Tom O'Donnell, 708-339-8909. 3901 W 155th St, Markham, IL 60426

Start Point: White Hen Pantry, 1134 State St. Exit I-80 at Briggs St North to Division St. Left (west to State St, then right to the White Hen or exit I-55 at Joliet Rd South to Rt 53 to Rt 7 Lockport, then (after railroad tracks) turn right on State St to White Hen.

Event Info: Dail, 8-6. Rated 2. Not recommended for strollers or wheelchairs.

Oak Lawn - 10km Walk (YR593) **Jan 1-Dec 31**
Sponsoring Club: AVA-722, Wewalkits Volksmarching Club
POC: Ken Stoffregen, 708-422-3034. c/o Color Key Printing, 9517 S Cook Ave, Oak Lawn, IL 60453

Start Point: Oak Lawn Community Pavillion, 708-857-2420. 9401 South Oak Park Ave. Exit I-294 at 95th St East. Turn left (north) at stop light on Oak Park Ave (approximately 1/2 mile). Pavillion is one block on right.

Event Info: Daily, 8-6. Rated 1+. Not suitable for wheelchairs. Pets must be leashed.

Petersburg - 10km Walk (YR012) **Jan 2-Dec 31** Credit Only Event
Sponsoring Club: AVA-146, Railsplitter Wanderers
POC: Greg O'Toole, 217-636-8597. RR2, Country Lake Estates #24, Athens, IL 62613

Start Point: Lincoln's New Salem State Historic Site, 217-632-4000. RR 1 (Hwy 97). From I-55 South, take exit 109 and follow signs. From I-55 North, take US 36 West to SR 4. Go north to Rt 97 and follow it to start.

Event Info: Call to verify hours of operation. Closed Thanksgiving (Thurs & Fri) and Christmas. Rated 3.5 and is not suitable for strollers or wheelchairs. Pets must be leashed.

Rock Island - 10km Walk (YR731) **Jan 1-Dec 31**
Sponsoring Club: Mississippi River Ramblers
POC: Ralph Krippner, 309-797-8157. 1109 3rd St, Moline, IL 61265

Start Point: US Army Corps of Engineering, Mississippi River Visitor's Center, 309-797-8157. Lock & Dam 15, Arsenal Island. Take exit 11B on I-280 to downtown Rock Island. Follow signs to Arsenal.

Event Info: Mid May-mid Sep, 9-9. Rest of year, 9-5. Closed Christmas & New Year's. Trail is rated 1. Suitable for strollers & wheelchairs. Pets must be leashed. Headphones may not be worn on the island.

Springfield - 10km Walk (YR058) **Jan 1-Dec 31**
Sponsoring Club: AVA-IL, Illinois Volkssport Association
POC: Ken Stoffregen, 708-422-3034. 9517 S Cook Ave, Oak Lawn, IL 60453

Start Point: Best Inns of America Motel, 217-522-1100 Reservations Only. 500 N 1st St.

Event Info: Daily, 8:30-3:30. Closed Thanksgiving, Christmas & New Year's. Rated 1. Pets are not allowed inside historic building through which trail passes.

INDIANA

Anderson - 10km Walk (YR149-Blue) & 11km Walk (YR453-Red) **Jan 1-Dec 31**
Sponsoring Club: AVA-045, White River Ramblers
POC: Robert M. Kiefert, 317-286-7083. 501 S Umbarger Rd, Muncie IN 47304

Start Point: Shadyside Marina, 317-649-9025. 1117 Alexandria Pike. Take I-69 to SR 32W (mile post 32), then SR 32W to Anderson. Right at the SR 9/SR 32 intersection. Left at Lindberg Rd (1st light) to Alexandria Pike. Right (0.4 mi) on Alexandria Pie to Marina.

Event Info: Daily, 8-dusk. Closed major holidays. Call ahead if in doubt. Trails are rated 1+. Suitable for strollers.

Auburn - 10km Walk (YR750) **Jan 2-Dec 31**
Sponsoring Club: AVA-374, Auburn Duesey Walkers
POC: Hilda Kennedy, 219-925-0441. 1700 Woodview Drive, Garrett, IN 46738

Start Point: A-C-D Museum, 219-925-1444. 1600 S Wayne St. Take I-69 to exit 129 also SR 8. Go east on SR 8 to Van Buren St. South on Van Buren to the Auburn-Cord-Duesenberg Museum or follow signs for the museum.

Event Info: Daily, 9-4. Finish by 6. Closed Thanksgiving, Christmas & New Year's. Rated 1. Suitable for strollers & wheelchairs. Pets must be leashed.

Batesville - 10km Walk (YR354) **Jan 2-Dec 30**
Sponsoring Club: AVA-737, Town & Country Wanderers
POC: Pat Wenning, 812-934-6006. 30 SR #129 South, Batesville, IN 47006

Start Point: Southeastern Indiana YMCA, SR 30 #129. From I-74 exit toward Batesville. Follow SR 229 to SR 46. Turn left to SR 129. Turn right & YMCA is first left off of SR 129.

Event Info: Mon-Sat, 8-dusk. Closed major holidays & Sundays. Rated 1+. Portion of trail not suitable for strollers. Alternate handicap and/or inclement weather track is available. Pets must be leashed.

Columbus - 10km Walk (YR266) **Jan 1-Dec 31**
Sponsoring Club: AVA-357, Columbus Wellness Walkers
POC: Charles Chinn, 812-376-3828. 3121 13th Street, Columbus, IN 47201

Start Point: Tipton Lakes Racquet Club, 812-342-4495. 4000 W. Goeller Blvd. From I-65 exit #68 (SR46) go west one mile to first traffic light (Goeller Blvd) turn left then right at first corner (Mimosa). Start is on your right.

Event Info: Mon-Fri, 6 A.M.-10 P.M.; Sat & Sun, 6 A.M.-9 P.M. Closed all national holidays. Pets must be leashed. Portions of trail are not suitable for wheelchairs or strollers. Bypass option available for strollers & wheelchairs.

Ft Wayne - 10km Walk (YR907) **Jan 1-Dec 31**
Sponsoring Club: AVA-062, Three Rivers Strollers
POC: Bob Geldien, 219-493-2473. 3914 Scarborough Dr, New Haven, IN 46774

Start Point: Veteran's Hospital, 219-426-5431. 2121 Lake Avenue.

Event Info: Daily, dawn to dusk. Rated 1+. Not suitable for wheelchairs. Strollers will have some difficulty. Pets must be leashed.

Indianapolis - 10km Walk (YR091) **Jan 1-Dec 31**
Sponsoring Club: AVA-089, Indy "G" Walkers
POC: Clarence Wright, 317-357-8464. PO Box 16001, Ft Harrison IN 46216

Start Point: Eagle Creek City Park, 71st Street Gatehouse. Off I-65 or I-465 on the Northwest side.

Event Info: PARK FEE REQUIRED. Daily, 9-dusk. Closed Thanksgiving & Christmas. Rated 3. No strollers or wheelchairs. Pets must be leashed. No water available November through April.

Indianapolis - 10km Walk (YR259) **Jan 1-Dec 31**
Sponsoring Club: AVA-089, Indy "G" Walkers
POC: Clarence Wright, 317-357-8464. PO Box 16378, Indianapolis, IN 46216

Start Point: White River State Park Visitors Center, the "Pumphouse", 801 W Washington St.

Event Info: Mon-Fri, 8-5; WEEKENDS: Apr-Oct, 12-5; Nov-Mar, CLOSED. Also closed 1/2, 1/16, 4/14, 5/2/, 5/29, 7/4, 9/4, 10/9, 11/7, 11/10, 11/23, 11/24, 12/25 & 12/26. Rated 1. Suitable for strollers but wheelchairs will have problems with curbs. Pets must be leashed.

Marion - 11km Walk (YR373) **Jan 1-Dec 31**
Sponsoring Club: AVA-487, Marion Fussganger
POC: Bob or Jean Marrs, 317-662-7798. 1124 West 3rd St, Marion, IN 46952

Start Point: Holiday Inn, 317-668-8801. Downtown at 3rd & Shunk.

Event Info: Daily, 8-6. Trail is rated 1.

Marshall - 10km Walk (YR909) **Jan 1-Dec 31**
Sponsoring Club: AVA-615, Wabash Wanderers
POC: Karen Summers, 317-474-5630 or Susan Tapia, 317-474-0881. 1323 S 19th, Lafayette, IN 47905

Start Point: Turkey Run State Park Inn, 317-597-2211

Muncie - 10km Walk (YR092-White River) **Jan 1-Dec 31**
Sponsoring Club: AVA-045, White River Ramblers
POC: Robert M. Kiefert, 317-286-7083. 501 S Umbarger Rd, Muncie IN 47304

Start Point: Hotel Roberts, 317-741-7777. 420 S. High St. Take I-69 to SR32 exit. Go east to the center of Muncie, right on High St. Hotel is 3 blocks down on your left.

Event Info: Daily, dawn to dusk. Rated 1+. Suitable for strollers.

Muncie - 10km Walk (YR906-Cardinal) **Jan 1-Dec 31**
Sponsoring Club: AVA-045, White River Ramblers
POC: Robert Kiefert, 317-286-7083. 501 S. Umbarger Rd, Muncie, IN 47304

Start Point: Family Kitchen Restaurant, 1617 N. Wheeling. Take I-69 North to the SR 332 (McGalliard Rd) exit. Go east on SR332 to Wheeling Ave (6th stop light..about 9 miles) and turn right. Start is on your right just after the first stop light.

Event Info: Daily, dawn to dusk. Rated 1+. Suitable for strollers. Pets must be leashed.

South Bend - 10km Walk (YR291) **Jan 1-Dec 31**
Sponsoring Club: AVA-723, Hoosier Hikers
POC: Janice Bella, 219-277-9682. PO Box 11101, South Bend IN 46634

Start Point: Jamison Inn, 1404 N Ivy Rd.

Event Info: Daily, dawn to dusk. Rated 2. Difficult for strollers. Not recommended for wheelchairs. No dogs allowed.

West Lafayette - 10km Walk (YR908) **Jan 1-Dec 31**
Sponsoring Club: AVA-615, Lafayette Wabash Wanderers
POC: Karen Summers, 317-474-5630 or Susan Tapia, 317-474-0881. 1323 S 19th, Lafayette, IN 47905

Start Point: Snowbear Frozen Custard, 317-743-8024. 620 West Stadium Ave.

Event Info: Mon-Sat, 10am-11 P.M.; Sun 11-10.

IOWA

Akron - 10km Walk (YR504) **Apr 1-Dec 31**
Sponsoring Club: AVA-160, Prairie Wanderers
POC: Marlene Krause, 712-568-2600. RR 1, Box 39, Akron IA 51001

Start Point: Casey's General Store, 79 South St. Corner of Iowa Hwys 3 & 12. From I-29 take the Akron/Spink exit #31. Go east on SD Hwy 48 for 13 miles. Turn right at the stop sign onto Hwy 12 for 0.7 miles to Casey's located on the left.

Event Info: Daily, 7-11. Rated 2+.

Cresco - 10km Walk (YR772) & 28/60km Bike (YR773) **May 1-Oct 31**
Sponsoring Club: AVA-812, Northeast Iowa Volkssport Association
POC: Ward Budweg, 319-864-7112. Box 348, Postville, IA 52162

Start Point: Cresco Motel, 319-547-2240. 620 2nd Ave Se (Hwy 9 East)

Event Info: Daily, dawn to dusk. YR772 is rated 2. YR773 is rated 1. Bikers must sign waiver. Only one event credit even if doing both bike trails.

Decorah - 10km Walk (YR774) **May 1-Oct 31**
Sponsoring Club: AVA-812, Northeast Iowa Volkssport Association
POC: Ward Budweg, 319-864-7112. Box 348, Postville, IA 52162

Start Point: Vesterhiem Norwegian-American Museum Gift Shop, 319-382-9681. 502 W Water

Event Info: Daily, 9-5:30. Rated 2.

Des Moines - 10km Walk (YR021) **Jan 1-Dec 31**
Sponsoring Club: AVA-250, Greater Des Moines Volkssport Assn.
POC: Angie Anderson, 515-241-5902/277-9534. 1804 27th, Des Moines, IA 50310

Start Point: Des Moines Botanical Center, 909 E River Dr

Event Info: Daily, 10-5. Closed major holidays. Rated 1+. Please no pets.

Indianola - 10km Walk (YR813) **May 27-Sept 4**
Sponsoring Club: AVA-250, Greater Des Moines Volkssport Assn.
POC: Mary Jo Lippold, 515-274-2651. 5608 Franklin, Des Moines, IA 50310

Start Point: Lake Ahquabi State Park, 6 miles south of Indianola at the concessionaire stand at the beach.

Event Info: Rated 3+. Not suitable for strollers or wheelchairs. Walking sticks are recommended.

McGregor - 10km Walk (YR812) **May 27-Sept 4**
Sponsoring Club: AVA-250, Greater Des Moines Volkssport Assn.
POC: Ward Budweg, 319-864-7112. PO Box 348, Postville, IA 52162

Start Point: Pikes Peak State Park, Hwy 340, 1 1/2 miles past south end of McGregor's Main St. at concessionaire stand at the park.

Event Info: Rated 4.

Polk City - 10km Walk (YR810) **May 27-Sept 4**
Sponsoring Club: AVA-250, Greater Des Moines Volkssport Assn.
POC: Mary Jo Lippold, 515-247-7491. 5608 Franklin, Des Moines, IA 50310

Start Point: Big Creek State Park, two miles north of Polk City. Approximately 8 miles from I-35 at the concessionaire stand at the beach.

Event Info: Rated 1. Suitable for strollers & wheelchairs.

Solon - 10km Walk (YR811) **May 27-Sept 4**
Sponsoring Club: AVA-250, Greater Des Moines Volkssport Assn.
POC: Catherine Johnson, 319-337-5989. 242 Ferson Ave, Iowa City, IA 52246

Start Point: Lake Macbride State Park, Hwy 382 West of Solon. Approximately 10 miles north of I-80 at the concessionaire stand at the park.

Event Info: Rated 2.

Strawberry Point - 10km Walk (YR814) **May 27-Sept 4**
Sponsoring Club: AVA-250, Greater Des Moines Volkssport Assn.
POC: Ward Budweg, 319-864-7112. PO Box 348, Postville, IA 52162

Start Point: Backbone State Park, 2 miles south of Strawberry Point at Backbone Drive-Inn.

Event Info: Daily, 10:30-9. Rated 3+.

KANSAS

Abilene - 11km Walk (YR282) **Apr 1-Dec 31** Credit Only Event
Sponsoring Club: AVA-234, Sunflower Sod Stompers of Topeka
POC: Terri Tyler, 913-233-4385/Betty Augustine, 316-327-4124. PO Box 2576, Topeka, KS 66601

Start Point: West's Plaza Country Mart, 1900 N Buckeye; 913-263-2285. From I-70 exit 275. Proceed south on K-15 or N. Buckeye approximately 2 blocks to the Country Mart which on on the right.

Event Info: Daily, dawn to dusk. Rated 1. Suitable for strollers but difficulty with surfaces & curbing. Closed Christmas & Easter. Pets must be leashed.

Arkansas City - Four 10km Walks
      (YR934) **Jan 3-Mar 31**   (YR933) **Apr 1-Jun 30**
      (YR932) **Jul 1-Sep 30**   (YR931) **Oct 1-Dec 31**
Sponsoring Club: AVA-760, Friends of Nature Volkssport Club
POC: Donald W Sinclair, 316-358-3131. 304 N Main, Grenola KS 67346

Start Point: Chaplin Nature Center, Visitors Center, 316-442-4133. Rt 1, Box 216. On US Hwy 166 west of Arkansas City at mile marker 17, turn N on unpaved road. Continue two miles to Start on right.

Event info: Tue-Sat, 9-5; Sun, 1-5; closed Mondays. Rated 2. Strollers & wheelchairs will find some difficulty. No pets allowed in the Nature center.

Atchison - 10km Walk (YR778) **Jan 2-Dec 31**
Sponsoring Club: AVA-037, Kansas Jaywalkers
POC: Phil Koerin, 913-651-0811. 1305 Lawrence Ave, Leavenworth, KS 66048

Start Point: Atchison Tourism Bureau, 800-234-1854. 200 South 10th.

Event Info: Mon-Fri, 9-5; Sat, 10-4; Sun, noon-4. Must finish before office closes. Closed Easter, Thanksgiving, Christmas & New Years. Rated 2+. Suitable for strollers. Pets must be leashed.

Bonner Springs - 10km Walk (YR358) **Jan 1-Dec 31**
Sponsoring Club: AVA-795, Tiblow Trailblazers Walking Club
POC: Doris Elliott-Watson, 913-422-4076. 231 Sheidley Ave., Bonner Springs KS 66012.

Start: Piggly Wiggly Supermarket, 112 Oak St. From I-70 take exit 224. Left on Hwy 7 2.5 miles to Bonner Springs exit. Turn right 1/2 mile to Piggly Wiggly.

Event Info: Daily, 7-9. Closed Christmas. Rated 1+. Suitable for strollers. Wheelchairs may experience some difficulty. Pets must be leashed. Event has three trails. Only one event credit even if doing all trails.

Fort Leavenworth - Two 10km Walks (YR043-city & YR263-historic) **Jan 1-Dec 31**
Sponsoring Club: AVA-037, Kansas Jaywalkers
POC: Marian Wiehe, 816-330-3357. PO Box 3136, Ft. Leavenworth KS 66027

Start Point: Leavenworth Riverfront Community Center, 123 Esplanade; 913-651-2132.

Event Info: Mon-Fri 6 A.M.-9 P.M.; Sat 9am-7 P.M. ; Sun 1 P.M. -6 P.M. Closed all Federal holidays. Alternate Start for historic walk is at Hoge Barracks on Grant Ave. City walk is rated 1+. Suitable for strollers & wheelchairs. Historical walk is rated 2. Suitable for wagons & strollers but not recommended for wheelchairs.

Lawrence - Two 10km Walks (YR322 & YR691) **Jan 2-Dec 31**
Sponsoring Club: AVA-771, Free State Walkers
POC: Judith Galas, 913-842-4958. 1125 Vermont, Lawrence, KS 66044

Start Point: Eldridge Hotel, 701 Massachusetts. From I-70 take the east Lawrence exit. After you go through the toll booth, turn left at Hwy 59 and go toward Lawrence. Cross the river & continue on Vermont St. to 7th St. Turn left at 7th. The start is on the next corner.

Event Info: Trails are rated 1+. Daily, dawn to dusk. Closed Christmas.

Lenexa - 10km Walk (YR013) & 25km Bike (YR080) **Jan 1-Dec 31**
Sponsoring Club: AVA-331, Heart of America Volkssport Club
POC: Richard Porch, 913-888-1563/Dick Haberkorn, 913-492-5382. PO Box 4472, Shawnee Mission, KS 66204

Start Point: Lenexa Community Center, 13420 Oak St; 913-541-0209. Exit 95th St off of I-35. West on 95th to Pflumm. Right on Pflumm to Oak.

Event Info: Daily, 8-dusk. Closed Thanksgiving & Christmas. Both events are rated 1+. Suitable for strollers.

Lindsborg - 10km Walk (YR269) **Apr 1-Dec 31**
Sponsoring Club: AVA-234, Sunflower Sod Stompers of Topeka
POC: Terri Tyler, 913-233-4385/Betty Augustine, 316-327-4124. PO Box 2576, Topeka, KS 66601

Start Point: Viking Motel, 446 Harrison/I-135 Business Loop. 913-227-3336. (Room information or directions only). One mile NE on Business Loop I-135 & SR 4.

Event Info: Daily, dawn to dusk. Rated 1. Suitable for strollers but some difficulty with surfaces & curbing. Pets must be leashed.

Topeka - 10km Walk (YR008) **Jan 1-Dec 31**
Sponsoring Club: AVA-234, Sunflower Sod Stompers of Topeka
POC: Terri Tyler, 913-233-4385/Margaret Harney, 913-272-4572. PO Box 2576, Topeka KS 66601

Start Point: Holiday Inn City Centre, 914 Madison at intersection of 10th Ave & I-70. 913-232-7721 (Room information or directions only).

Event Info: Daily, dawn to dusk. Rated 1. Suitable for strollers but some difficulty with curbs. Pets must be leashed.

Wichita - 12km Walk (YR511) & 27km Bike (YR512) **Jan 1-Dec 31**
Sponsoring Club: AVA-211, Wichita Skywalkers
POC: Jerry Kasperek, 316-729-8349. 9042 Harvest Ct, Wichita, KS 67212-4066.

Registration: Family Inn, 221 E Kellogg. Intersection of Kellogg (US 54) and Broadway in downtown Wichita. Drive to start.

Start Point: Sedgwick County Park Office, on North Shore Blvd midway between 13th & 21st.

Event Info: Park hours are 7 A.M.-10 P.M. daily. Trails are rated 1. Suitable for strollers. Pets must be leashed. Bikers must sign waiver.

Wichita - 10km Walk (YR072) & 30km Bike (YR086) **Jan 1-Dec 31**
Sponsoring Club: AVA-211, Wichita Skywalkers
POC: John Wickham, 316-788-6406. 1101 Briarwood Rd, Derby KS 67037-3701

Start Point: Family Inn, 221 E Kellogg. Intersection of Kellogg (US 54) and Broadway in downtown Wichita.

Event Info: Daily, dawn to dusk. Trails are rated 1. Suitable for strollers. Pets must be leashed. Bikers must sign waiver. Helmets are recommended.

KENTUCKY

Covington - 10km Walk (YR078-Historic) & Two 11km Walks (YR624-Devou Park & YR787-Two State)
Jan 1-Dec 31
Sponsoring Club: AVA-548, Northern Kentucky Trotters
POC: Carol Fairbanks, 606-491-2664. 600 Garrard St, Covington KY 41011

Start Point: Holiday Inn-Riverfront, 606-291-4300. 3rd and Philadelphia Sts. I-75 N or S to Covington/5th Street exit (#192). Go East on 5th to first light. Turn left on Philadelphia and go to 3rd street where Holiday Inn is located.

Event Info: Daily, dawn to dusk. YR078 is rated 1+. YR624 is rated 3 and YR787 is rated 1+. Trails are suitable for strollers or wheelchairs. Pets must be leashed.

Ft Campbell - 10km Walk (YR265) **Jan 1-Dec 31**
Sponsoring Club: AVA-716, Striding Eagles
POC: Roy Matthews, 502-798-4664. Community Rec Div, Ft Campbell KY 42223

Start Point: ESTEP Wellness Center, 502-798-4023. 14th & Kentucky Ave., Bldg 2270.

Event Info: Mon-Fri, 6-4; Sat, 9-1; Sun, 12-3. Not recommended for strollers or wheelchairs.

Louisville (Vinegrove) - 11km Walk (YR580) **Jan 1-Dec 31**
Sponsoring Club: AVA-694, Derby City Walkers, Inc.
POC: Herb Zimmerman, 502-574-3365(day)/456-6126(eve). 1363 Tyler Park Dr, Louisville KY 40204

Start Point: Otter Creek Park Lodge, 502-583-3577. 850 Otter Creek Park Rd. Take 31W to Hwy 1638. Turn right and go two miles to the park.

Event Info: Daily, 7-5. Rated 3. Not suitable for strollers or wheelchairs. Pets must be leashed. Carry water during walk.

Louisville - 10km Walk (YR083) **Jan 2-Dec 31**
Sponsoring Club: AVA-694, Derby City Walkers, Inc.
POC: Herb Zimmerman, 502-574-3365(days) or 502-456-6126(eves). 11363 Tyler Park Dr, Louisville, KY 40204

Start Point: Iroquois Golf Club House, 1501 Rundill Road; 502-363-9520. From I-264 take the Southern Parkway exit. Turn south on the parkway and continue to the park entrance. Once on the park road, bear right up the hill to the Golf Course.

Event Info: Daily, 7-5. Closed Christmas & New Years. Rated 2+. Not suitable for strollers or wheelchairs.

Louisville - 11km Walk (YR087) **Jan 2-Dec 31**
Sponsoring Club: AVA-694, Derby City Walkers, Inc.
POC: Pat O'Connor, 502-896-4127. 119 McArthur Drive, Louisville, KY 40207

Start Point: Downtown YMCA, 555 South Second Street; 502-587-6700. From Cincinnati, southbound I-71, exit on Third Street & River Road. Go south on Third to York and turn left. At the next light turn left onto Second Street. YMCA is on the right about 2 1/2 blocks down. From Indianapolis, southbound on I-65, exit on Third Street & River Road. Follow same directions given above. From Northbound I-65, take the Muhammad Ali Boulevard exit and go west to Third Street. Go south on Third to York and turn left. Proceed as above.

Event Info: Daily, 7-5. Closed Thanksgiving & Christmas. Rated 1. Suitable for wheelchairs & strollers.

LOUISIANA

Baton Rouge - Four 10km Walks
YR557 **Jan 2-Mar 31**	YR125 **Apr 1-Jun 30**
YR172 **Jul 1-Sep 30**	YR206 **Oct 1-Dec 31**

Sponsoring Club: AVA-651, Red Stick Walkers
POC: Peggy Fleniken, 504-275-6189. 11221 Tams Dr, Baton Rouge LA 70815

Start Point: Independence Park Tennis Center, 504-923-2792. 7500 Independence Blvd. From east or west on I-12 take exit 2B onto Airline Hwy. Continue north on Airline Hwy to Goodwood Blvd (5th traffic light). Turn left onto Goodwood. Continue on Goodwood to East Airport Dr (3rd traffic light). Turn right onto East Airport Dr. Go one block to Independence Blvd. Turn left and go 1/2 mile. Start is on your right.

Event Info: Mon-Fri, 8-10; Sat, 8-6; Sun, 8-8. Closed Christmas & Thanksgiving. Rated 1. Not suitable for strollers or wheelchairs. Alternate route available in nearby mall for strollers & wheelchairs. City Information: Convention Bureau 1-800-LA-ROUGE.

Baton Rouge - Four 10km Walks
(YR539) **Jan 2-Mar 31**	(YR154) **Apr 1-Jun 30**
(YR175) **Jul 1-Sep 30**	(YR176) **Oct 1-Dec 31**

Sponsoring Club: AVA-651, Red Stick Walkers
POC: Peggy Fleniken, 504-275-6189. 11221 Tams Drive, Baton Rouge LA 70815

Start Point: Baton Rouge Area Convention & Visitors Bureau, 1st Floor, Louisiana State Capitol Bldg, 900 North Third Street; 1-800-LA ROUGE. From I-10, exit onto I-110 (northbound). Proceed to the North Street exit (1D) on the left. Caution: stay in the left lane to exit. Proceed to Fourth St (4th traffic light) and turn right. Go to Spanish Town Rd and turn left. Go to Third St and turn right. Go to State Capitol Rd.

Event Info: Daily, 8-4:30. Closed Easter, Thanksgiving & Christmas. Rated 1. Wheelchairs & strollers will have some difficulty maneuvering curbs.

New Orleans - 10km Walk (YR076) **Jan 1-Dec 31**
Sponsoring Club: AVA-473, Crescent City Volkssport Club
POC: Heinz Kloth, 504-455-6413. 3005 Kent Ave., Metairie, LA 70006

Start Point: Fritzel's Bar, 504-561-0432. 733 Bourbon Street.

Event Info: Daily 11-3.

MAINE

Bath - 10km Walk (YR673) **Apr 1-Nov 30**
Sponsoring Club: AVA-193, Southern Maine Volkssport Association
POC: Harriet Tyner, 207-443-2733 (eves). RR #1, Box 1360, Woolwich ME 04579

Start Point: Holiday Inn, 207-443-9741. 139 Western Ave.

Event Info: Daily, dawn to dusk. Rated 1. Suitable for strollers & wheelchairs. Pets must be leashed.

Greenville - 10km Walk (YR788) **May 1-Oct 22**
Sponsoring Club: AVA-800, Wandering Maine-iacs
POC: David Muzzy, 207-854-5424. PO Box 6403, Portland, ME 04102-6403

Start Point: Indian Hill Motel, 207-695-2623. South Main St. (RT 15).

Event Info: Daily, 7 to dusk. Rated 2. Not suitable for wheelchairs. Strollers may have difficulty in some sections. Pets must be leashed. No smoking in fields or wooded areas.

Portland - 11km Walk (YR029) **Jan 1-Dec 31**
Sponsoring Club: AVA-193, Southern Maine Volkssport Association
POC: John Tibbetts, 207-774-8306 (eves). 1544 Congress St., Portland ME 04102

Start Point: Ramada Inn, 207-774-5611. 1230 Congress St.

Event Info: Daily, dawn to dusk. Rated 1+. Okay for strollers & wheelchairs. Leashed pets.

South Freeport - 10km Walk (YR672) **Apr 1-Oct 31**
Sponsoring Club: AVA-193, Southern Maine Volkssport Association
POC: Richard Wise, 207-797-8726. 16 Heather Road, Portland ME 04103

Start Point: Super 8 Motel, 207-865-1408. 218 Rte 1.

Event Info: Daily, dawn to dusk. Rated 1+. Okay for strollers but not wheelchairs. Leashed pets.

South Portland - Three 11km Walks:
(YR864) **Apr 1-Jun 30**   (YR865) **Jul 1-Sep 30**   (YR866) **Oct 1-Nov 31**
Sponsoring Club: AVA-800, Wandering Maine-iacs
POC: Sylvia Allen, 207-774-8524. 887 Spring St, Westbrook, ME 04092

Start Point: Shop 'n Save Supermarket, 50 Cottage Rd.

Event Info: Daily, 8-dusk. Rated 1+. Strollers may have difficulty. An alternate handicap route is available. Pets must be leashed.

MARYLAND

Annapolis - 11km Walk (YR264) **Jan 2-Dec 31**
Sponsoring Club: AVA-595, Annapolis Amblers
POC: Gene & Roberta Ganske, 410-544-2243. 1234 Timber Turn, Arnold, MD 21012 or Bob & Mary Graham, 410-757-2155. 13 Ashcroft Court, Arnold, MD 21012

Start Point: Regina's Continental Delicatessen & Restaurant, 410-841-5565 or 410-268-2662. 26 Annapolis St. Take I-95 to Baltimore. Exit at I-895, through the tunnel to exit 14 and then exit 14A (Route 3). Follow Route 3 to I-97, Annapolis. I-97 merges into US 50/301. Exit US 50/301 at MD 70 South, Rowe Blvd. From the west, this is identified as exit 24. Turn left at first traffic light onto Melvin Ave, 2 blocks to Annapolis St, turn right, one block to start on left.

Event Info: Open daily by 8 A.M. Must finish by 2 P.M. on Sunday, 4 P.M. on Mon & Sat, 5 P.M. on Tues, Thurs, & Fri, and by 9 on Wed. Call ahead if in doubt about hours. Closed New Year's, Easter, Memorial Day, July 4th, Labor Day, Thanksgiving and Christmas. Rated 2. Suitable for large wheeled strollers. Dogs are not encouraged due to USNA restrictions.

Baltimore - 10km Walk (YR362-Monuments) & 12km Walk (YR130-Ft McHenry) **Jan 3-Dec 31**
Sponsoring Club: AVA-418, Star Spangled Steppers
POC: Mary Kowalski, 410-282-4953. 8163 Gray Haven Rd, Baltimore MD 21222

Start Point: Baltimore City Life Museum, 800 E. Lombard St. Enter at rear of building.

Event Info: May-Oct, 10-5; Nov-Apr, 10-4. Sundays open at Noon. Closed Mondays, and major holidays. Both trails are rated 1. Suitable for strollers & wheelchairs.

Brandywine - 10km Walk (YR885) & 27km Bike (YR886) **Apr 22-Oct 31** Bike is a Credit Only Event
Sponsoring Club: AVA-021, Washington DC Area Volksmarching Club
POC: Bob Leek, 301-843-8332. 3204 Bethesda Rd, Waldorf, MD 20601

Register: Cedarville Grocery, 301-888-1273. 11800 Cedarville Rd. Follow MD 5 from Capital Beltway (I-95) 12 miles south. Turn left on Cedarville Rd, drive four miles to grocery on left.

Start Point: Cedarville State Forest Park, approximately 3 miles from registration.

Event Info: Mon-Sat, 8-8; Sun, 8-1. Open 1/2 day (am) on Memorial Day, July 4th & Labor Day. Closed other holidays. Call if in doubt. Walk is rated 2. Not suitable for wheelchairs and may cause great difficulty for strollers. Bike is rated 2+. Bikers must sign waiver. Pets are not allowed. During Sept & Oct, there are some managed hunting areas in the park. We recommend you wear orange or other bright clothing during these months. There is no hunting on Sunday.

Columbia - 10/16km Walk (YR216) & 25km Bike (YR370) **Jan 2-Dec 31**
Sponsoring Club: AVA-264, Columbia Volksmarch Club
POC: Don Weinel, 410-997-0136. 5423 Chatterbird Place, Columbia, MD 21045

Start Point: Feet First, Lake Village Green, Twin Rivers Rd. 410-992-5800. From I-95, take Rt 175 west for 5 miles to Rt 29 interchange at which point Rt 175 becomes Little Patuxent Pkwy (LPP). Follow LPP through 2 traffic lights. After the 2nd light, bear right and follow Governor Warfield Pkwy. Proceed to Twin Rivers Rd (2nd light) and bear right. Follow Twin Rivers Rd for about 1/2 mile and turn left on Lynx Lane. Start is in the courtyard behind Giant Food, on the left.

Event Info: Walk has a 6km option. Only one event credit even if doing both distances. Suitable for strollers, but not wheelchairs. Trail is rated 1+. Bike is rated 1. Feet First is closed New Year's, Easter, Thanksgiving and Christmas. Please phone ahead for seasonal hours.

Easton - 10km Walk (YR882) **Jan 2-Dec 31**
Sponsoring Club: AVA-595, Annapolis Amblers
POC: Gene & Roberta Ganske, 410-544-2243. 1234 Timber Turn, Arnold, MD 21012

Start Point: The Chaffinch House, 410-822-5074. 132 S. Harrison St. From US 50 in the Easton area, exit onto MD 322. Exit 322 at MD 33 (Bay St). At the end of Bay St, turn right onto Washington St. Turn left on Brooklets Ave. Go one block and start is on the far corner.

Event Info: Daily, 8-dusk. Call ahead for holiday hours. Rated 2. Suitable for large-wheeled strollers but not wheelchairs. Pets must be leashed.

Frederick - 10km Walk (YR740) **Jan 2-Dec 31**
Sponsoring Club: AVA-264, Columbia Volksmarch Club
POC: Don Weinel, 410-997-0136. 5423 Chatterbird Place, Columbia, MD 21045

Start Point: Frederick's Visitor's Center, 301-696-1350. 19 East Church St. From I-70 take exit 54, Market St/MD Rt 355. At end of ramp turn left and follow Market St toward downtown Frederick. At Church St turn right. The Start/Finish is on your left. Park in the garage just before the Visitor's Center.

Event Info: Trail is rated 1+. Suitable for strollers but not wheelchairs. Center is closed on New Year's, Easter, Thanksgiving & Christmas.

Gaithersburg - Two 10km Walks (YR889 & YR890) **Jan 2-Dec 31**
Sponsoring Club: AVA-419, Seneca Valley Sugarloafers
POC: Ed Branges, 301-340-9418. 1830 Greenplace Terr, Rockville MD 20850-2942

Start Point: YMCA of Gaithersburg, 301-948-9622. 10011 Stedwick Rd. I-270 to exit 11A (Rt 124 east) to Stedwick Rd next to Montgomery Village Shopping Center.

Event Info: Mon-Sat, 6:30-dusk; Sun, 10-dusk. Closed New Year's, ML King Day, Easter, Thanksgiving & Christmas. Trails are rated 1+. Suitable for strollers & wheelchairs. Pets must be leashed.

Gaithersburg - Two 10km Walks (YR339 & YR735) **Jan 1-Dec 31**
Sponsoring Club: AVA-419, Seneca Valley Sugarloafers Volksmarch Club
POC: Ed Branges, 301-340-9418. 1830 Greenplace Terr, Rockville, MD 20850-2942

Start Point: Gourmet Grog Deli Store, 614 Quince Orchard Plaza I-270 to exit 10 (Rt 117) or exit 11B (Rt 124). Go two traffic lights to Quince Orchard Plaza.

Event Info: Daily, 10-sunset. Closed Christmas & Thanksgiving. Trails are rated 2 & 2+. Not suitable for strollers or wheelchairs. No pets allowed.

Havre de Grace - 10km Walk (YR131) **Jan 2-Dec 31**
Sponsoring Club: AVA-418, Star Spangled Steppers
POC: Richard & Carol Lindsley, 410-679-3594. 1223 Abinjud Dr, Abingdon MD 21009

Start Point: The Spencer Silver Mansion Bed & Breakfast, 200 S. Union St; 410-939-1097.

Event Info: B & B offers a discount to volksmarchers. Call for reservations. Daily, 10-4. Rated 1. Suitable for strollers & wheelchairs.

Laurel- 10km Walk (YR219) **Jan 1-Dec 31**
Sponsoring Club: AVA-190, Freestate Happy Wanderers
POC: Linda Hassell, 410-437-2164. 8256 Camion Rd, Pasadena, MD 21122

Start Point: Comfort Suites, 301-206-2600. 14402 Laurel Place. Take Rt 198 East off I-95 to US Rt 1 south 2 miles to Mulberry St to hotel on right.

Event Info: Daily, dawn to dusk. Trail is rated 1+. Not suitable for wheelchairs.

Rockville - Two 10km Walks (YR887 & YR888) **Jan 2-Dec 31**
Sponsoring Club: AVA-419, Seneca Valley Sugarloafers
POC: Ed Branges, 301-340-9418. 1830 Greenplace Terrace, Rockville, MD 20850

Start Point: Norbeck Deli Beer & Wine, 301-460-1400. 5514 Norbeck Rd. I-270 to exit 6, Rt 28 East to Bauer Dr & Rock Creek Village Shopping Center.

Event Info: Mon-Sat, 10-9; Sun, 10-7. Closed New Year's, Thanksgiving & Christmas. Rated 1+. Suitable for strollers & wheelchairs. Pets must be leashed.

Savage - 10km Walk (YR575) **Jan 2-Dec 31**
Sponsoring Club: AVA-190, Freestate Happy Wanderers
POC: Linda Hassell, 410-437-2164. 8256 Camion Rd, Pasadena, MD 21122

Start Point: Antique Center II @ Savage Mill, 301-470-4373. 8600 Foundry St. From I-95, take exit 38A Rt 32 East to US Rt 1. Right on 1 to next light (Howard St), turn right and go through the community following signs to the Mill off Fair St. Start point is upstairs in the New Weave Building.

Event Info: Daily, 9:30-3. Bldg closes at 5:30. Trail is rated 2. Not suitable for wheelchairs. Strollers may have difficulty.

Severna Park - 12/16km Walk (YR746), 12km Walk (YR884) & Two 27km Bikes (YR738 & YR883) **Jan 2-Dec 31**
Sponsoring Club: AVA-616, Chesapeake Bay Country Wanderers
POC: David Fluetsch, 410-647-3871. 487 Saint Bride's Ct, #211, Severna Park, MD 21146

Start Point: Severna Park YMCA at Baltimore-Annapolis Rd & Cypress Creek Rd. (Off of MD Rt 2.)

Event Info: Mon-Fri, 7-2:30; Sat, 8-2; Sun, noon-2. Must be off trails by dark. Closed major holidays. Walks are rated 1. Suitable for strollers. Bikes are rated 1+.

Wheaton - 10km Walk (YR144) & 25km Bike (YR233) **Jan 2-Dec 31**
Sponsoring Club: AVA-190, Freestate Happy Wanderers
POC: Linda Hassell, 410-437-2164. 8256 Camion Rd, Pasadena, MD 21122

Start Point: Wheaton Park Wine & Deli, 301-949-8191. 12039 Georgia Ave. Off I-495, take exit 31A (Georgia Ave/Rt 97) north for 2.8 miles. Turn right at Shorefield Rd then right into shopping center parking lot. Deli is on left end of strip.

Event Info: Mon-Sat, 10-5; Sun, 11-4. Call ahead to verify operating hours since deli is owner operated any may close Mon or Tues starting in March. Walk trail is rated 2. Not suitable for wheelchairs and strollers may have difficulty on the trails. Bike is rated 1+. CHILDREN UNDER 18 MUST WEAR A HELMET.

Westminster - 10km Walk (YR046) & 27km Bike (YR723) **Jan 2-Dec 31**
Sponsoring Club: AVA-476, Piedmont Pacers
POC: Steve Duex Sr. 410-848-4469. 916 Wampler Lane, Westminster, MD 21158

Start Point: The Westminster Inn, 410-876-2893. Green & Center Sts. Off of Rte 40 to Westminster turn at Center St opposite Mall through 1st light go 1/2 block and turn left into Inn Parking lot.

Event Info: Daily, 7-three hours before dusk. Finish by dusk. Walk is rated 1+. Bike is rated 2+. Closed New Year's, Memorial Day, Thanksgiving & Christmas. For any other major holidays, please phone ahead. Bikers must sign waiver & wear helmets. Walk is suitable for strollers. Pets must be leashed.

MASSACHUSETTS

Bedford - 10/13km Walk (YR928) 10/13km Ski (YR927) **Jan 2-Mar 31** Credit Only Events
Sponsoring Club: AVA-269, Walk'n Mass Volkssport Club
POC: Charlie Smith, 508-263-5093. 1 Mohawk Dr, Acton, MA 01720

Start Point: Pro-Motion Shop, 617-275-1113. 111 South St. From Rt 128 take Rts 4/225 west to Bedford. At approximately 1.5 miles, turn left on Loomis St. Follow Loomis to end at South Rd. Start is across the street.

Event Info: Mon, Wed & Fri, 10 A.M.-2 P.M.; Tues 11-2; Sat, 9-2; Sun noon-2. Call for verification of hours. YR927 is a ski event. It may NOT BE walked for credit. If there has been NO chance to ski the event, walking is allowed the last weekend. Only one event credit per year even if completing both the 10km and 13km trails. Trails are rated 1. Walk is suitable for strollers & wheelchairs. Pets must be leashed.

Boston - 11km Walk (YR730-Freedom Trail) **Mar 3-Dec 11**
Sponsoring Club: AVA-269, Walk'n Mass Volkssport Club
POC: Don Meltzer, 508-443-8513. 341 Old Lancaster Rd, Sudbury, MA 01776

Start Point: Boston National Historical Park Visitor Center, 15 State St. across from the Old State House. The Center can be reached from exit 25 on I-93 South; exit 22 on I-93 North; and the Expressway North exit at the eastern terminus of I-90 (to exit 22).

Alternate Sign-in Point: Howard Johnson Motor Lodge, Route 2 & Elm St. in Concord (23 miles west of Boston), from which walkers can drive to public transportation that will take them directly to the walk route and allow them to avoid downtown traffic & parking.

Event Info: Visitor Center is open 8-5 weekdays and 9-5 on Sat & Sun from Labor Day to Memorial Day; 8-6 weekdays & 9-6 Sat & Sun from Memorial Day to Labor Day. Rated 1. Suitable for strollers & wheelchairs. Pets must be leashed.

Boston - 11km Walk (YR836-Arnold Arboretum) **Apr 1-Dec 2**
Sponsoring Club: AVA-269, Walk'n Mass Volkssport Club
POC: Arlene Girouard, 617-325-9198. 22 Winton Street, Roslindale, MA 02131

Start Point: Larry's Mobil Station, 617-323-9859. 1225 Centre St. From Route 95/128 going either North or South, take Route 9 East (Exit 20A). Follow Rte 9 for 7 miles to the Riverway. Exit to your right onto the Riverway (Rt 1 south) toward Dedham & Providence. At the second rotary, turn right and stay on Rt 1 south for about one mile. Start is on the right one block after the Faulkner Hospital.

Event Info: Daily, 7-dusk. Rated 1. Suitable for strollers & wheelchairs. Leashed pets.

Chicopee - 10km Walk (YR926) **Jan 1-Dec 31**
Sponsoring Club: AVA-784, Connecticut Valley Volkssport Club
POC: Donna Harmer, 413-594-3161. 607 Front St, Chicopee, MA 01020

Start Point: Store 24, 413-592-6910. 201 Exchange St. Near junction of I-91 & I-90.

Event Info: Daily, dawn to dusk. Rated 1.

Concord - 11km Walk (YR223) **Apr 12-Dec 12**
Sponsoring Club: AVA-269, Walk 'n Mass Volkssport Club
POC: Jeanette Dose', 508-663-6756. 7 Shedd Rd, Billerica, MA 01862

Start Point: Howard Johnson Motor Lodge, 508-369-6100. Rt 2 and Elm St.

Event Info: Daily, dawn to dusk. Rated 1. Altitude 200 ft. Suitable for strollers & wheelchairs. Pets must be leashed.

Danvers - 10km Walk (YR245) **Jan 1-Dec 31**
Sponsoring Club: AVA-573, Two Town Walking Club
POC: Joe Piffat, 508-762-0494. 56 Ledgewood Dr, Danvers, MA 01923

Start Point: Econo Lodge, 50 Dayton St. (Rt 1 South); 508-777-1700. I-95, exit 50. Take 1st left onto Rt 1 South. Be sure you are on Rt 1 South. Take 2nd exit (Dayton Street) after you pass over Rt 62.

Event Info: Daily, dawn to dusk. Rated 1+. Suitable for strollers. Pets must be leashed.

Ipswich - 10km Walk (YR631) **Apr 1-Nov 27**
Sponsoring Club: AVA-573, Two Town Walking Club
POC: William Jenkins, 508-468-2104. 3 Arthur Ave, S. Hamilton MA 01982-1805

Start Point: Bruni Farms, Inc, Rt 133, Essex Road; 508-356-4877. FROM I-95 take exit 54 onto Rt 133 east toward Rowley. When Rt 133 joins Rt 1A, follow Rt's 133/1A through Ipswich center and stay on Rt 133 turning left as 1A continues straight. Look for start/finish 1/4 mile on left.

Event Info: Daily, dawn to dusk. Rated 1+. Suitable for strollers. Pets must be leashed.

Lexington - 25km Bike (YR295) **Apr 29-Nov 2** Credit Only Event
Sponsoring Club: AVA-269, Walk 'n Mass Volkssport Club
POC: Betty Foley, 508-443-4857. 807 Boston Post Rd, Sudbury MA 01776

Start Point: Bikeway Cycle, 617-861-1199. 3 Bow St. From Rt 128/95, take Rt 2A east toward Lexington for 3 miles. Turn right onto Rt 4/225 and go one mile. Bear left onto Massachusetts Ave. Keep to left lane. Turn left onto Bow St. Cycle shop is on the right. Parking in rear.

Event Info: Mon-Fri, 10-6; Sat, 10-4; Sun, 12-3. Helmets are mandatory and participants must sign a waiver. Rated 1. Carrying water is recommended.

Lowell - 10km Walk (YR674) **Apr 1-Dec 3**
Sponsoring Club: AVA-269, Walk 'n Mass Volkssport Club
POC: Larry Shelvey, 400 Butman Rd, Lowell, MA 01852 or Betty Foley, 508-443-4857.

Start Point: Lowell Nat'l Historical Park, 508-970-5000. 246 Market St. I-495, exit 36. Follow park signs.

Event Info: Daily, 8:30-3. Closed Jul 29-31. Rated 1+. Suitable for strollers. Leashed pets.

Salem - 10km Walk (YR060) **Jan 1-Dec 31**
Sponsoring Club: AVA-573, Two Town Walking Club
POC: William Jenkins, 508-468-2104. 3 Arthur Ave, S. Hamilton MA 01982

Start Point: Brothers Deli & Restaurant, 283 Derby St; 508-741-4648. From I-95 take exit 45. Take Rt 128 North towards Beverly/Gloucester. Take exit 26 and follow US National Park signs until you get on Rt 1A. Take right on Derby St. Deli is on left.

Event Info: Daily, dawn to dusk. Rated 1. Suitable for strollers. Pets must be leashed.

Salem - 10km Walk (YR246) **Jan 1-Dec 31**
Sponsoring Club: AVA-MA, Massachussets Volkssport Assn.
POC: William Jenkins, 508-468-2104. 3 Arthur Ave, South Hamilton, MA 01982-1805.

Start Point: US National Park Service Visitor Center, 508-741-3648, New Liberty St.

Event Info: Daily, 9:15-5. Rated 1. Suitable for strollers & wheelchairs. Leashed pets.

Sandwich - 10km Walk (YR608) **May 21-Oct 1**
Sponsoring Club: AVA-410, Empire State Capital Volkssporters
POC: Dan Schryver, 518-765-4630. PO Box 6995, Albany, NY 12206

Start Point: Dan'l Webster Inn, 149 Main St; 508-888-3622. Rt 6, exit 2. Take Rt 130 into Sandwich.

Event Info: Daily, dawn to dusk. Rated 1. Suitable for strollers. Pets must be leashed.

South Hamilton - 26km Bike (YR334) **Apr 1-Nov 27**
Sponsoring Club: AVA-573, Two Town Walking Club
POC: Mary Behrle, 508-922-8235 (eves). 21 Cobbler's Lane, Beverly MA 01915

Start Point: Bay Road Bike, 52 Railroad Avenue; 508-468-1301. From I95 north take exit 45 on to Rt 128 north towards Gloucester. On Rt 128 take exit 20A, Rt 1A north towards Hamilton. Pass Wenham Lake on left through Wenham. After Mobil Station take first left (Railroad Ave). Bike shop is on your left across from Post Office.

Event Info: Daily, 10-5. Call for Sunday hours. Rated 1+. Bike rental available.

Topsfield - 10km Walk (YR167) **Apr 1-Nov 27**
Sponsoring Club: AVA-573, Two Town Walking Club
POC: Mary Saratora, 508-777-0148. 9 Cole Rd, Danvers MA 01923

Start Point: Ipswich River Wildlife Sanctuary, 87 Perkins Row; 508-887-9264. I-95 exit 53, Rt 97 East, cross Rt 1, Left on Perkins Row.

Event Info: There is a fee for parking. Tues-Sun, 10-5. Closed Mondays & Thanksgiving. Rated 2. Not suitable for strollers or wheelchairs. Pets are not allowed. Spring or Fall time is recommended. Wet trails in the Spring. Need insect repellent in the Summer.

Williamstown - 10km Walk (YR867) **Apr 1-Nov 30**
Sponsoring Club: AVA-410, Empire State Capital Volkssporters
POC: Beryl Wolf, 518-383-2880/Lois Heyer, 518-477-6236. PO Box 6995, Albany, NY 12206-6995.

Start Point: The Williams Inn, 413-458-9371. Junction of Rtes 2 & 7.

Event Info: Volkssporters receive a discount on rooms & meals. Daily, 8-dusk. Rated 1. Suitable for strollers & wheelchairs with help.

MICHIGAN

Ionia- 10/13km Walk (YR536) **Jan 1-Dec 31** & 26/35km Bike (YR550) **Apr 1-Oct 31** Bike is a Credit Only Event
Sponsoring Club: AVA-461, Historic Pathwalkers
POC: John W. Pierce, 616-527-2413. 2215 Marquette Rd, Ionia, MI 48846

Start Point: Dan's Bicycle & Lock Shop, 116 S. Depot; 616-527-0471. Ionia is located halfway between Lansing & Grand Rapids, 7 miles N of I-96 (exit 67) or at the junction of M-21 & M-66. To reach Dan's Bicycle & Lock Shop, go two blocks east of M-66 on Main St (downtown business district) to Depot St. Turn south to last building on the east side.

Event Info: Mon-Fri, 9-6; Sat, 9-3. Hours are subject to change. Call to verify. Closed Sundays & major holidays. Walk is rated 2. Suitable for strollers & wheelchairs though not all corners are handicap accessible. Bike is rated 1. BIKERS MUST SIGN WAIVER. Pets must be leashed.

Lansing - 10km Walk (YR953) **Apr 1-Nov 13**
Sponsoring Club: AVA-461, Historic Pathwalkers
POC: John Pierce, 616-527-2413. 2215 Marquette Rd, Ionia, MI 48846-9513

Start Point: Michigania, 517-484-1137. 113 S Washington Square. From I-496, exit 6 (Walnut & Pine Streets. Take Walnut north (one-way) to Allegan St (south side of capitol) go east on Allegan (one-way) to Washington Square. Go north on Washington Square to start 1/2 block down on the east side.

Event Info: Mon-Fri, 9:30-6; Sat, 10-4. Rated 1. Suitable for strollers & wheelchairs although not all curbs have cuts. Pets must be leashed.

Marquette - 10/20km Walk (YR364) **Jan 1-Dec 31**
Sponsoring Club: AVA-340, Yooper Troopers
POC: Julie Ballaro, 906-372-2580. Outdoor Rec Ctr, 400 A Ave, Suite 109, K.I. Sawyer AFB MI 49842

Start Point: Marquette Welcome Center, US 41; 906-249-9066. The Welcome Center is a log cabin on your right, five minutes south of the city of Marquette.

Event Info: Daily, 9-4. Closed major holidays. Rated 1.

South Haven - 10km Walk (YR561) & 29km Bike (YR829) **Apr 1-Oct 31**
Sponsoring Club: AVA-722, Wewalkits Volksmarching Club
POC: Tom O'Donnell, 708-339-8909. 3901 West 155th St, Markham, IL 60426

Start Point: The Blueberry Store, 525 Phoenix St, 616-637-6322. Additional start cards & maps available across street at Arkins Gift Shop for early participants. Exit I-196 at exit 20 (Phoenix Road). Turn left (east) on Phoenix to Blueberry Store. Drive to Start Point for Bike at Kal-Haven bike trail. From Blueberry Store, take Blue Star Hwy (Bus. 196) north to trailhead.

Event Info: Call The Blueberry Store to check hours. $2.00 individual or $5.00 family pass fee required at Start Point for Bike. Passes can be purchased from rangers on the Kal-Haven trail. Bikers must sign waiver. Helmets are recommended.

MINNESOTA

Albert Lea - 10km Walk (YR119) **May 26-Sep 4**
Sponsoring Club: AVA-601, Minnesota State Parks
POC: Jerry Katzenmeyer, 507-373-5084. Myre Big Island State Park, Rt 3, Box 33, Albert Lea, MN 56007

Start Point: Myre Big Island State Park.

Event Info: Rated 2.

Bloomington - Two 10km Walks (YR807 & YR594) **Jan 1-Dec 31**
Sponsoring Club: AVA-793, Meandering Minnesotans
POC: Milt Luoma, 612-890-7560. 303 Concorde Pl, Burnsville MN 55337

Start Point: Super America, East 90th & Old Cedar Ave

Event Info: YR807 is rated 1. Suitable for strollers & wheelchairs. Pets must be leashed. YR594 is an indoor trail at the Mall of America. Rated 1.

Brainerd - 10km Walk (YR124) **May 29-Sept 4**
Sponsoring Club: AVA-601, Minnesota State Parks
POC: Paul Roth, 218-829-8022. 7100 State Park Rd SW, Brainerd, MN 56401

Start Point: Crow Wing State Park Picnic Shelter

Event Info: Rated 1+.

Burnsville - 10km Walk (YR016) **Jan 1-Dec 31**
Sponsoring Club: AVA-793, Meandering Minnesotans
POC: Milt Luoma, 612-890-7560. 303 Concorde Place, Burnsville, MN 55337

Start Point: Red Roof Inn, 612-890-1420. I-35 West & Burnsville Pkwy. From I-35W, exit at Burnsville Pkwy. Turn west on Burnsville Pkwy. Turn left onto Aldrich Ave (the frontage rd). Inn is on the right. From I-35E, exit at County Road 11 and turn North on Country Road 11 and follow it to Burnsville Pkwy. Turn left on Parkway to Aldrich Ave (about 2 1/3 miles). Turn left on Aldrich Ave (the frontage rd). Inn is on the right.

Event Info: Daily, dawn to dusk. Rated 1. Suitable for strollers & wheelchairs. Leashed pets.

Duluth - Two 10km Walks (YR808 & YR618) **Jan 1-Dec 31**
Sponsoring Club: AVA-793, Meandering Minnesotans
POC: Milt Luoma, 612-890-7560. 303 Concorde Pl, Burnsville, MN 55337

Start Point: St. Luke's Hospital, main entrance, Info Desk. 915 East First Street

Event Info: YR808 is rated 1+. Suitable for strollers & wheelchairs. Pets must be leashed. YR618 is rated 1.

Frontenac - 11km Walk (YR188) **May 6-Oct 22**
Sponsoring Club: AVA-601, Minnesota State Parks
POC: Harry Roberts, 612-345-3401. Rt 2, Box 134, Lake City MN 55041

Start Point: Park Office, Frontenac State Park.

Event Info: Rated 4.

Hutchinson - 10km Walk (YR546) **Mar 1-Oct 31**
Sponsoring Club: AVA-697, Central Minnesota Volkssports
POC: Rick Larson, 612-587-6846. 535 Hassan St South, Hutchinson MN 55350

Start Point: Citgo Quik Mart, Main St & 4th Ave. Located at intersection of Hwy 7 & Hwy 15.

Event Info: Daily, dawn to dusk. Rated 1+. Strollers & wheelchairs may experience some difficulty. Pets must be leashed.

Lake Bronson - 11km Walk (YR121) **May 26-Sep 4**
Sponsoring Club: AVA-601, Minnesota State Parks
POC: Garry Barvels, Park Manager 218-754-2200. Box 9, Lake Bronson MN 56734

Start Point: Lake Bronson State Park. Rated 2.

Event Info: Rated 2.

Le Sueur - 10km Walk (YR779) **Apr 1-Dec 31**
Sponsoring Club: AVA-161, Riverbend Striders
POC: Audrey & Earl von Holt, 507-625-5375. 1709 Linda Lane, North Mankato, MN 56003

Start Point: Super America, 612-665-6800. 205 North Main. 50 miles SW of Minneapolis on Hwy 169. Exits to Main St are Hwy 93 from the west or Hwy 112 from the north.

Event Info: Rated 3. Suitable for strollers & wheelchairs with assistance.

Mankato - Two 10km Walks (YR192 & YR769) **Jan 1-Dec 31**
Sponsoring Club: AVA-161, Riverbend Striders
POC: Audrey & Earl von Holt, 507-625-5375. 1709 Linda Ln, N. Mankato MN 56003

Start Point: Holiday Inn Downtown, 101 E Main St; 507-345-1234. Take Downtown Exit to Main St and Holiday Inn.

Event Info: If staying at the Holiday Inn, be sure to ask for the Volkssport Discount. Daily, dawn to dusk. YR192 is rated 3. YR769 is rated 2. Both difficult for strollers & wheelchairs.

Mankato - 25/35km Bike (YR770) **Apr 1-Oct 31**
Sponsoring Club: AVA-161, Riverbend Striders
POC: Earl & Audrey von Holt, 507-625-5375. 1709 Linda Lane, North Mankato, MN 56003

Start Point: Riverfront Inn, 507-388-1638. 1727 N Riverfront Dr. From Hwy 169, take Hwy 14 east exit. Exit right onto Riverfront Dr.

Event Info: If staying at the Inn, ask for the volkssport discount. Daily, 7:30-dusk. Rated 1+. Suitable for strollers & wheelchairs.

Marshall - 10km Walk (YR647) **Apr 1-Dec 31**
Sponsoring Club: AVA-160, Prairie Wanderers
POC: Shirley Luther, 605-692-5159 after 5. 1511 8th St S, Brookings SD 57006

Start Point: Burger King, 1229 E College; 507-532-3955. Marshall is located in western Minnesota at the junction of Minn. Hwys 19 & 23 and US 59. Follow Hwy 19 (E. College Dr) to BK. From Hwy 23, go West on 19 to BK; from Hwy 59, go east on 19 to BK.

Event Info: Daily 7-dusk. Closed Christmas & Easter. Rated 1.

McGregor - 10km Walk (YR122) **Jun 3-Sep 25**
Sponsoring Club: AVA-601, Minnesota State Parks
POC: Audrey Knutson, 218-426-3271. HCR 3, Box 591, McGregor, MN 55160

Start Point: Headquarters at Savanna Portage State Park.

Event Info: Rated 4.

Minneapolis - 10km Walk (YR016) **Jan 1-Dec 31**
Sponsoring Club: AVA-793, Meandering Minnesotans
POC: Milt Luoma, 612-890-7560. 303 Concord Pl, Burnsville MN 55337

Start Point: Red Roof Inn and Conoco, 612-890-1420. I-35W & Burnsville Pkwy.

Event Info: Daily, dawn to dusk. Rated 1.

Minneapolis - 10km Walk (YR806) & 25km Bike (YR721) **Apr 15-Nov 15**
Sponsoring Club: AVA-793, Meandering Minnesotans
POC: Robin Kilbury, 612-455-6878. 11235 Akron Ave, Inver Grove Heights, MN 55077

Start Point: Super America, 612-724-3388. 4740 Cedar Avenue South.

Event Info: Trails are rated 1. Bikers must sign waiver.

Minneapolis - 10km Walk (YR791-Heritage) 12km Walk (YR792-Lake) **Jan 1-Dec 31**
Sponsoring Club: AVA-114, Twin Cities Volksmarchers
POC: Carol Engel, 612-699-9026. 2053 Palace Avenue, St. Paul, MN 55105

Start Point: Park Inn International, 612-332-0371. 1313 Nicollet Mall.

Event Info: Daily, dawn to dusk. YR791 is rated 1+. YR792 is rated 2.

Monticello - 10km Walk (YR187) **Apr 22-Oct 22**
Sponsoring Club: AVA-601, Minnesota State Parks
POC: Mark Crawford, 612-878-2325. Rt 1, Box 128, Monticello MN 55362

Start Point: Lake Maria State Park

Event Info: Rated 3+.

Nerstrand - 10km Ski (YR815) **Jan 1-Mar 1**
Sponsoring Club: AVA-601, Minnesota State Parks
POC: Tony Tonga, 507-334-8848. 9700 170th Street East, Nerstrand, MN 55053

Event Info: This is a ski event. It may NOT be walked except on the last weekend IF there has been no chance to ski the event.

Spring Grove - 10km Walk (YR309) **May 1-Oct 30** Credit Only Event
Sponsoring Club: AVA-122, Syttende Mai Komiteen Folkemarsj Stiftelse
POC: Maribeth Anderson, 507-498-5669. PO Box 391, Spring Grove MN 55974-0391

Start Point: Ballard House, 163 W. Main.

Event Info: Daily. *Start* 10-2, finish by 5. Rated 1. Suitable for strollers or wagons. Pets must be leashed. No smoking in wooded areas.

St. Cloud - 25/34/49km Bike, (YR771) **Apr 1-Oct 31**
Sponsoring Club: AVA-697, Central Minnesota Volkssports
POC: Susan Nielsen, 612-255-1933. 1320 10th Avenue South, St. Cloud, MN 56301

Start Point: Granite City Mobile, 2510 2nd St South

Event Info: Only one event credit even if doing all trails.

St Cloud - 10km Walk (YR308) **Jan 1-Dec 31**
Sponsoring Club: AVA-697, Central Minnesota Volkssporters
POC: David Hunt, 612-253-4762. 221 26th Ave N, St Cloud MN 56303

Start Point: Best Western Kelly Inn, 1 Sunwood Plaza, Hwy 23 & South 4th Ave. From Hwy 23, (Division St) turn North on 4th Ave South, to the Inn on the right.

Event Info: Daily, dawn to dusk. Rated 1+. Alternate directions available for strollers & wheelchairs. Pets must be leashed.

St Paul - 10km Walk (YR526), 13km Walk (YR525) **Jan 1-Dec 31** 25km Bike (YR528) **Apr 1-Oct 31**
Sponsoring Club: AVA-114, Twin Cities Volksmarchers
POC: Carol Engel, 612-699-9026. 2053 Palace Ave, St Paul, MN 55105

Start Point: Super America, 612-690-4033. 2065 Randolph Ave

Event Info: Trails are rated 2.

St Paul (North) - 25/32/53km Bike (YR527) **Apr 1-Oct 31**
Sponsoring Club: AVA-114, Twin Cities Volksmarchers
POC: Gary DeVore, 612-738-1833. 1895 E conway, St. Paul, MN 55119

Start Point: Hardee's, 612-777-5602. 2600 Centennial Drive.

Event Info: Daily, dawn to dusk. Rated 2. Only one event credit even if doing all trails.

St Peter - 10km Walk (YR194) **Jan 1-Dec 31**
Sponsoring Club: AVA-161, Riverbend Striders
POC: Audrey & Earl von Holt, 507-625-5375. 1709 Linda Ln, N. Mankato MN 56003

Start Point: Americinn Motel, 700 N. Minnesota Ave; 507-931-6554. 12 miles north of Mankato on Hwy 169 (which is named Minnesota Ave within city limits).

Event Info: If staying at the Americinn Motel, be sure to ask for the Volksmarchers Discount. Daily, dawn to dusk. Rated 2+. Suitable for strollers. Could be difficult for wheelchairs.

Stillwater - 10km Walk (YR100) **Apr 29-Dec 31**
Sponsoring Club: AVA-MN, Minnesota Volkssport Association
POC: Don & Lucy Anderson, 612-439-3997. 6111 Paris Ave N. Apt 5A, Stillwater, MN 55082-6864

Start Point: Fina Service Station, 103 N Main.

Event Info: Trail is rated 2. Daily, dawn to dusk.

Taylors Falls - 10km Walk (YR123) **Apr 22-Sept 4**
Sponsoring Club: AVA-601, Minnesota State Parks
POC: Stephen Anderson, 612-465-5711. PO Box 254, Taylors Falls, MN 55084

Start Point: Interstate State Park.

Event Info: 100th anniversary of the park. Rated 3.

Tower - 11km Walk (YR623) **Jan 1-Dec 31**
Sponsoring Club: AVA-793, Meandering Minnesotans
POC: Milt Luoma, 612-890-7560. 303 Concorde Place, Burnsville, MN 55337

Start Point: Vermilion Fuel & Food, Hwy 169 (Main St)

Event Info: Trail is rated 2.

MISSISSIPPI

Bay St Louis - 10km Walk (YR332) **Jan 1-Dec 31**
Sponsoring Club: AVA-310, Magnolia State Volkssport Club
POC: Vernon Shockley, 601-467-5962. 1068 St. Joseph St, Waveland, MS 39576

Start Point: Bay St Louis Police Department, 601-467-9221. 310 Old Spanish Trail

Event Info: Daily, dawn to dusk.

Biloxi - 10km Walk (YR126) **Jan 1-Dec 31**
Sponsoring Club: AVA-310, Magnolia State Volkssport Club
POC: Kathleen Garlotte, 601-872-3059. PO Box 731, Biloxi, MS 39533

Start Point: Biloxi Visitor's Center, 710 Beach Blvd; 601-374-3105. From I-10 exit #46 south to Hwy 90. Go east on 90E. Start is located on the left at the corner of Main &6 Hwy 90.

Event Info: Rated 1. Mon-Fri, 8-5; Sat, 9-5; Sun, noon-5. Winter Hours: close at 4 on Sat/Sun. Suitable for strollers & wheelchairs. Pets are NOT encouraged. If taken they must be kept leashed.

Ocean Springs - 10km Walk (YR053) & 25km Bike (YR472) **Jan 1-Dec 31**
Sponsoring Club: AVA-310, Magnolia State Volkssport Club
POC: Neal Gambler 601-872-3059. PO Box 731, Biloxi MS 39533

Start Point: Master Grill, 601-875-5888. Corner of Hanley Rd. & Hwy 90.

Event Info: Daily, dawn to dusk. Trails are rated 2. Portions may not be suitable for strollers or wheelchairs. Pets are discouraged but if taken must be leashed. Bikers must sign waiver.

MISSOURI

Augusta - 10/20km Walk (YR212) & 25/44km Bike (YR213) **Jan 2-Dec 31**
Sponsoring Club: AVA-682, S.M.T.M. Volkssport Society
POC: Larry McKenna, 314-739-3597. 1300 New Florissant Rd, Florissant MO 63033-2122

Start Point: Augusta Winery, 314-228-4301. High & Jackson Streets.

Event Info: Closed Christmas. Rated 1+. Suitable for strollers. Wheelchairs with difficulty.

Ellisville - 10km Walk (YR551) & 12km Walk (YR014) **Jan 2-Dec 31**
Sponsoring Club: AVA-221, Die Ballwin Wanderfreunde
POC: Elsie Voyles, 314-527-3070. PO Box 1187, Ballwin, MO 63022-1187

Start Point: Video counter, Dierbergs Supermarket Clayton/Clarkson Ctr., at Clayton & Clarkson Roads. West St. Louis County.

Event Info: Daily, 7:30-10. Closed major holidays. Not suitable for strollers or wheelchairs. Pets must be leashed.

Hermann - 10km Walk (YR281) **Mar 1-Dec 31**
Sponsoring Club: AVA-018, Hermann Volkssport Association
POC: Tom Cabot, 314-486-2747. RR 1, Box 60A, Hermann, MO 65041

Start Point: Die Hermann Werks, 214 East 1st St.

Event Info: Mon-Fri, 9:30-5; Sat, 7-5; & Sun, 11-4. Closed Easter, Thanksgiving & Christmas. Rated 1. Suitable for strollers & wheelchairs. Pets must be leashed.

Independence - 10km Walk (YR032) **Jan 1-Dec 31**
Sponsoring Club: AVA-386, Jacomo Bushedwalkers
POC: Donald R. Francis, 816-228-0997. 816C NE Sunnyside School Rd, Blue Springs, MO 64014-2663

Start Point: Truman Home Ticket Office, 219 N Main St.

Jefferson City - 10km Walk (YR454) **Jan 1-Dec 31**
Sponsoring Club: AVA-MO, Missouri Volkssport Association
POC: Bill Thebo, 816-474-6191. 1904 East 28th Ave., N Kansas City MO 64116

Start Point: Coastal Mart, 1940 W Main.

Event Info: Daily, dawn to dusk. Rated 1+. Suitable for strollers & wheelchairs. Pets must be leashed.

Joplin - 10km Walk (YR535) **Jan 1-Dec 31**
Sponsoring Club: AVA-765, Dogwood Trailblazers
POC: Richard Miller, 417-782-7151. PO Box 8012, Joplin, MO 64802

Start Point: Murray's Market, First & Main.

Kansas City - 10km Walk (YR304) & 25km Bike (YR305) **Jan 1-Dec 31**
Sponsoring Club: AVA-644, Pace Setters Volkssport Club
POC: Peter & JoAnn Moroz, 816-246-0187 or Bobbi Pommer, 816-524-3067(eves)/816-251-7532(days). 208 NW Oldham Parkway, Lee's Summit, MO 64081

Start Point: Longview Lake, Longview Recreation Center Registration Counter, 816-672-2400. 3801 SW Longview Rd. Take I-470 to View High Drive Exit, go South on View High Dr to stop sign at View High & Third St. Go right (west) on Third to first entrance on left, then turn right into recreation center parking lot. Center is multi-story red brick building.

Event Info: Trails are rated 1. Suitable for strollers & wheelchairs with a little help. You will be driving from the rec center to the walk/bike start location. Closed major holidays.

Lemay - Four 11km Walks
    (YR919) **Jan 2-Mar 31**   (YR918) **Apr 1-Jun 30**
    (YR917) **Jul 1-Sep 30**   (YR916) **Oct 1-Dec 31**
Sponsoring Club: AVA-466, Missouri Marching Mules
POC: Shirley Thompson, 314-352-7118. 7910 Delmont, St Louis, MO 63123

Start Point: Hardee's, 314-892-1950. 2866 Telegraph Rd. From I-255, take exit #2, Route 231. Go 1/2 mile north.

Liberty - 10km Walk (YR609) **Jan 1-Dec 31**
Sponsoring Club: AVA-739, Clay-Platte Trackers of Kansas City
POC: Judy Sallee, 816-734-8294. 913 NE 108th Terrace, Kansas City, MO 64155

Start Point: Cody's Quick Stop, 405 East Mill; 816-792-4412. Take I-35N from Kansas City to Liberty (about 20 minutes). Exit on Hwy 152 East. Continue on to the Liberty Town Square. Turn right on Main St. Continue one block to Mill St. Turn left to Start/Finish.

Event Info: Daily, dawn to dusk. Rated 2+. Not recommended for strollers or wheelchairs. Pets must be leashed.

Marthasville - 10km Walk (YR915) & 25km Bike (YR914) **Jan 2-Dec 31**
Sponsoring Club: AVA-682, S.M.T.M. Volkssport Society
POC: Larry McKenna, 314-739-3597. 1300 New Florissant Rd, Florissant, MO 63033-2122

Start Point: Scenic Cyclist, 314-433-2909. 203 Depot St.

Event Info: Closed Tuesday. Rated 1+. Suitable for strollers, wheelchairs with difficulty.

Mound City - 10km Walk (YR958) **Jan 2-Dec 31**
Sponsoring Club: AVA-719, Missouri Riverbluff Ramblers
POC: Helen Caton, 816-232-3344. 315 S 6th St, St. Joseph, MO 64501

Start Point: Audrey's Motel, 816-442-3191. Hwy 59. Halfway between Kansas City & Omaha on I-29.

Event Info: Daily, dawn to dusk. Rated 2+. Not suitable for strollers or wheelchairs.

St Charles - 10km Walk (YR399) **Jan 1-Dec 31**
Sponsoring Club: AVA-682, S.M.T.M. Volkssport Society
POC: Larry McKenna, 314-739-3597. 1300 New Florissant Rd, Florissant MO 63033

Start Point: St. Joseph Health Center Information desk in main lobby. 300 First Capitol Dr

Event Info: Rated 1+. Suitable for strollers. Wheelchairs may have difficulty.

St Charles - 26km Bike (YR400) **Jan 2-Dec 31**
Sponsoring Club: AVA-682, S.M.T.M. Volkssport Society
POC: Larry McKenna, 314-739-3597. 1300 New Florissant Rd, Florissant MO 63033

Start Point: Touring Cyclist, 314-949-9630. 104 S. Main St.

Event Info: Closed New Years, Thanksgiving & Christmas. Rated 1+.

St Genevieve - 10km Walk (YR920) **Jan 2-Dec 31**
Sponsoring Club: AVA-466, Missouri Marching Mules
POC: Jerry Hoog, 314-296-3232. 3575 Lonedell, Arnold, MO 63010

Start Point: Rozier's Store, 314-883-2110. 305 Merchant St. From I-55, exit #150 to Merchant St. Turn right and go two blocks. Located in the center of downtown area.

St Joseph - 10km Walk (YR034) **Jan 2-Dec 30**
Sponsoring Club: AVA-719, Missouri Riverbluff Ramblers
POC: Helen Caton, 816-232-3344. 315 S 6th St, St. Joseph, MO 64501

Start Point: St. Joseph Museum, 816-232-8471. 1100 Charles St. 45 minutes north of Kansas City.

Event Info: Mon-Sat, 9-5; Sun, 1-5. Closed Dec 24 & 31 and major holidays. Rated 3. Suitable for strollers. Pets must be leashed.

St Louis - Four 10km Walks
(YR455) **Jan 1-Mar 31**	(YR948) **Apr 1-Jun 30**
(YR949) **Jul 1-Sep 30**	(YR950) **Oct 1-Dec 31**

Sponsoring Club: AVA-355, St. Louis-Stuttgart Sister City
POC: Clare Fulvio, 314-534-2655. 4453 West Pine #4, St. Louis, MO 63108

Start Point: Best Western Inn at the Park, 314-367-7500. 4630 Lindell Blvd. From I-64/40 take Kingshighway exit North to Lindell; right on Lindell 1.5 blocks to Hotel on right.

Event Info: Daily, dawn to dusk. Rated 1.

St Louis - Four 10km Walks
(YR030) **Jan 1-Mar 31**	(YR945) **Apr 1-Jun 30**
(YR946) **Jul 1-Sep 30**	(YR947) **Oct 1-Dec 31**

Sponsoring Club: AVA-355, St. Louis-Stuttgart Sister City
POC: Betty Hoffman, 314-867-6897. 1535 St. Ives Drive, St. Louis, MO 63136

Start Point: Courtyard Marriott, 314-241-9111. 2340 Market St. From I-55/I-70 take Memorial Dr to Market, 1.5 miles west to the hotel. Start is on south/left side of street.

Event Info: Daily, dawn to dusk. Rated 1.

St Louis - Four 10km Walks
(YR941) **Jan 1-Mar 31**	(YR942) **Apr 1-Jun 30**
(YR943) **Jul 1-Sep 30**	(YR944) **Oct 1-Dec 31**

Sponsoring Club: AVA-355, St. Louis-Stuttgart Sister City
POC: Ralph & Joyce Bass, 314-524-1234. 420 La Motte Lane, St. Louis, MO 63135

Start Point: McDonald's, 314-524-3030. 9131 W Florissant. From I-70, take Lucas & Hunt exit North, to West Florissant Rd. Left on W Florissant approx. 1/2 mile to restaurant on left.

Event Info: Daily, dawn to dusk. Rated 1.

St Peters - Two 10km Walks (YR210 & YR247) **Jan 2-Dec 31**
Sponsoring Club: AVA-682, S.M.T.M. Volkssport Society
POC: Flo Painter, 314-291-5268. 1300 N. Florissant Rd, Florissant MO 63033-2122

Start Point: Dierbergs Supermarket (video counter); 314-928-1117. 290 Mid Rivers Mall Dr

Event Info: Closed New Years, Christmas, Easter & Thanksgiving. Rated 2.

St Peters - 25km Bike (YR211) **Jan 2-Dec 31**
Sponsoring Club: AVA-682, S.M.T.M. Volkssport Society
POC: Flo Painter, 314-291-5268. 1300 N. Florissant Rd, Florissant MO 63033-2122

Start Point: Granada Cyclery, 3139 W Clay (North Outer Rd); 314-946-7442.

Event Info: Rated 2.

MONTANA

Bannack - 10km Walk (YR776) **May 27-Sept 4**
Sponsoring Club: AVA-519, Madison County Volkssport Club
POC: Elaine Mason, 406-683-6615. Box 264, Virginia City, MT 59755

Start Point: Bannack State Park Visitor Center, 406-834-3413. 25 miles west of Dillon.

Event Info: Daily, 10-6. $3.00 per car entry fee. Rated 3+. Elevation starts at 5,700 ft and will gain approximately 500 ft. Not suitable for strollers or wheelchairs. Carry your own water. No food is available at Bannack. Pets must be leashed.

☆ **Virginia City** - 10km Walk (YR105) **May 1-Sep 30**
Sponsoring Club: AVA-519, Madison County Volkssport Club
POC: Melinda Tichenor, 406-843-5454. PO Box 264, Virginia City MT 59755

Start Point: Ranks Drug Store, 406-843-5454; 211 W. Wallace. From I-15 turn off at Dillon, take 41 to Twin Bridges, then 287; I-90 turn off east of Butte at Whitehall, take 55 then 41 to Twin Bridges, then 287: From Bozeman, take 84 to Norris, then 287 turning right at Ennis to Virginia City; From West Yellowstone, take 27, turning left out of Ennis.

Event Info: Daily, in May & Sept, 8-6. Jun-Aug, 8-8. Rated 3. Elevation is 6,000 ft. Not suitable for strollers or wheelchairs. Carry your own water on the trail. Pets must be leashed.

NEBRASKA

Beatrice - 10km Walk (YR278) **Jan 1-Dec 31**
Sponsoring Club: AVA-492, Homestead Striders
POC: Jean Miller, 402-228-1783. 1918 Lincoln Blvd, Beatrice NE 68310

Start Point: Gas 'N Shop, 402-223-2522. 1116 N 6th St.

Event Info: Daily, dawn to dusk. Rated 1. Strollers & wheelchairs may have some difficulty. Pets must be leashed.

Fairbury - 10km Walk (YR402) **May 27-Sep 4** Credit Only Event
Sponsoring Club: AVA-492, Homestead Striders
POC: Jean Miller, 402-228-1783. 1918 Lincoln Blvd, Beatrice NE 68310

Start Point: Rock Creek Station Visitors Center, 402-729-5777.

Event Info: Daily, 9-5. Park fee required. Rated 2. Unsuitable for strollers & wheelchairs.

Fremont - 10km Walk (YR244) **Jan 1-Dec 31**
Sponsoring Club: AVA-510, Fremont Volkssport Club
POC: Mary M. Benderson, 402-721-1943 or Mary Moseman, 402-721-9413. 635 East 20th, Fremont, NE 68025-3072

Start Point: Holiday Lodge, 1220 East 23rd

Event Info: Daily, dawn to dusk. Rated 1.

Fremont - 10km Walk (YR513) **May 1-Oct 31**
Sponsoring Club: AVA-510, Fremont Volkssport Club
POC: Mary Benderson, 402-721-1943. 635 E 20th, Fremont NE 68025

Start Point: Touch & Go, 740 N Davenport Ave.

Event Info: Daily, dawn to dusk. Rated 1.

Kearney - 10km Walk (YR761) **Jan 1-Dec 31**
Sponsoring Club: AVA-818, Kearney Volkssport Club
POC: Janice Anderson, 308-234-6184. PO Box 506, Kearney, NE 68848-0506

Start Point: C-Store No 1, 308-234-6345. 3912 17th Avenue

Lincoln - Two 10km Walks (YR704-Historical & YR017) **Jan 1-Dec 31** YR017 is a Credit Only Event
Sponsoring Club: AVA-102, Lincoln Volkssport Club, Inc.
POC: Rose Quackenbush, 402-464-6972. 1519 N. 58th St, Lincoln NE 68505-1706

Start Point: Russ's IGA , 68th & 'O' St. (Sign-up only) Event starts at 33rd & 'J'. From I-80 West, ext 396 to 'O' St. Turn left on 'O' St to 66th. Turn left on 66th to the first intersection. Turn right and park in the shopping center lot. From I-80 East, exit 409 to Hwy 6. Turn left on Hwy 6 to 84th St. Turn left on 84th to 'O'. Turn right on 'O' to 68th. Turn right on 68th to the first intersection and park in the shopping center lot.

Event Info: Daily, 7-10:30. Rated 1+. Strollers & wheelchairs may have difficulty with curbs. Pets must be leashed.

Nebraska City - 10km Walk (YR554) **Jan 1-Dec 31**
Sponsoring Club: AVA-102, Lincoln Volkssport Club, Inc.
POC: Nebraska City Chamber of Commerce, 806 First Ave, Nebraska City, NE 68410 or Rose Quackenbush, 402-464-6972. 1519 North 58th St, Lincoln NE 68505-1706

Start Point: Apple Inn Motel, 506 South 11th St.

Event Info: Daily, 7-dusk. Rated 1+. Strollers & wheelchairs may have some difficulty with curbs. Pets must be leashed.

Omaha - 10km Walk (YR066) **Jan 2-Dec 30**
Sponsoring Club: AVA-016, Nebraska Wander Freunde
POC: Rita Eldrige, 402-558-4061. 4067 Valley St, Omaha NE 68127

Start Point: Chalco Hills Rec Area, 154th & Giles Rd. I-80, exit Hwy 50 North to Giles Rd. Turn West.

Event Info: Mon-Fri, 8-4; Sat & Sun, 10-2. Rated 1+

Omaha - Two 10km Walks (YR622 & YR093-Downtown) **Mar 1-Oct 31**
Sponsoring Club: AVA-016, Nebraska Wander Freunde
POC: Ed Beran, 402-556-1621. 4525 Oak St, Omaha NE 68106

Start Point: Nebraska Game & Parks/Visitor Center, 1212 Deer Park Blvd across from zoo. I-80, exit 13th St. Follow signs.

Event Info: Daily, 9-5. Trails are rated 2.

Seward - 10km Walk (YR775) **Jan 1-Dec 31**
Sponsoring Club: AVA-102, Lincoln Volkssport Club, Inc.
POC: Rose Quackenbush, 402-464-6972. 1519 North 58th St, Lincoln, NE 68505-1706

Start Point: Memorial Hospital, 300 N Columbia Ave.

Event Info: Daily, 7-dusk. Rated 1. Suitable for strollers & wheelchairs. Leashed pets.

Sidney - 10km Walk (YR383) **Jan 1-Dec 31**
Sponsoring Club: AVA-564, Panhandle Walkers
POC: Sandra Lyons, 308-254-4503. 1530 Manor Rd, Sidney NE 69162-1144

Start Point: Cheyenne County Community Ctr, Registration Desk, 627 Toledo; 308-254-7000.

Event Info: Mon-Fri, 6-10; Sat, 8-8; Sun, noon-6. During June, July & August, the Center will be closed on Sunday and will be open from 10-4 on Saturday. Closed on major holidays and may be closed all three days of a three-day weekend. Call ahead to make sure. Strollers may have some difficulty. Pets must be leashed.

York - 10km Walk (YR302) **Mar 1-Dec 31**
Sponsoring Club: AVA-666, Wellness Wanderers
POC: Yvonne Junge, 402-362-5247. 535 West 6th, York NE 68467

Start Point: Bosselman's Pump & Pantry #16, 109 Lincoln Ave. On I-80 exit 353.

Event Info: Daily, 6-11. Rated 1.

NEVADA

Carson - 10km Walk (YR936) **Jan 1-Dec 31** Credit Only Event
Sponsoring Club: AVA-683, Sierra Nevada Striders
POC: David Sampson, 702-746-1740. 5215 Mountcrest Lane, Reno, NV 89523-1806

Start Point: Downtowner Motor Inn, 1-800-364-4908. 801 North Carson St. From Reno, travel south on Hwy 395 to Carson City. From Tahoe, travel west on Hwy 50 to Hwy 395 then north on Hwy 395.

Event Info: Inn offers a 10% discount to all AVA walkers. Daily, 7-3, finish by 7. Bring your own water. Rated 1. Suitable for strollers & wheelchairs. Pets must be leashed.

Incline Village - Two 12km Walks (YR189 & YR190) **Apr 1-Dec 31** Credit Only Events
Sponsoring Club: AVA-683, Sierra Nevada Striders
POC: Dave Sampson, 702-746-1740. 5215 Mountcrest Ln, Incline Village, NV 89523

Start Point: Lake Tahoe, Fleet Feet, 930 Tahoe Blvd. (State Rt 28).

Event Info: Summer: Mon-Sat, 9-6; Sun, 11-5. Winter: Mon-Sat, 10-6; Sun, noon-5. Suitable for strollers & wheelchairs. Trails are rated 3. Strollers will have some difficulty. No wheelchairs. Pets must be leashed.

Las Vegas - 10km Walk (YR474) & 11km Walk (YR208) **Jan 1-Dec 31**
Sponsoring Club: AVA-296, Las Vegas High Rollers & Strollers
POC: Dick Lisk, 702-438-0145. PO Box 30153, N Las Vegas NV 89036-1753

Start Point: Best Western Mardi Gras Inn, 800-634-6501. 2500 Paradise Rd. Special rates for volkssporters.

Event Info: Daily, dawn to dusk. Trails are rated 1. Suitable for strollers & wheelchairs. Pets must be leashed. No picture taking in casinos.

Reno - 10km Walk (YR023), 12km Walk (YR935) & 25km/35km Bike (YR697) **Jan 1 - Dec 31**
Sponsoring Club: AVA-683, Sierra Nevada Striders
POC: Dave Sampson, 702-746-1740. 5215 Mountcrest Ln, Reno NV 89523

Start Point: National Automobile Museum, 702-333-9300. 10 Lake St South.

Event Info: Daily, 9:30-5:30. Closed Thanksgiving & Christmas. Bike rental available at BoBo's, 1200 S Wells (summer only). Trails are rated 1. Suitable for strollers. Leashed pets.

NEW HAMPSHIRE

Concord - 10km Walk (YR292) **Apr 1-Nov 30**
Sponsoring Club: AVA-247, Seacoast Striders
POC: Judy Schultz, 603-868-7348. PO Box 3151, Portsmouth NH 03802-3151

Start Point: Holiday Inn, 172 North Main; 603-224-9534. Exit 14, Rt 93.

Event Info: Daily, dawn to dusk. Rated 1. Suitable for wheelchairs and strollers.

Durham - 25km Bike (YR930) **Apr 1-Nov 30**
Sponsoring Club: AVA-247, Seacoast Striders
POC: Claudia Cauchon, 603-868-5088. 10 Ambler Way, Durham, NH 03824

Start Point: Burger King, 603-868-1332. 1 Mill Road

Event Info: Daily, 8:30 to dusk.

Nashua - 10km Walk (YR929) **Apr 1-Nov 30**
Sponsoring Club: AVA-247, Seacoast Striders
POC: Judy Schultz, 603-868-7348. PO Box 3151, Portsmouth NH 03802-3151

Start Point: Comfort Inn, 10 St Laurent Rd, 603-883-7700.

Event Info: Daily, dawn to dusk. Trail is rated 1. Suitable for strollers & wheelchairs.

Portsmouth - 10km Walk (YR132) **Apr 1-Nov 30**
Sponsoring Club: AVA-247, Seacoast Striders
POC: Judy Schultz, 603-868-7348. PO Box 3151, Portsmouth NH 03802-3151

Start Point: Howard Johnson's, Interstate Rte 1 Traffic Cir; 603-436-7600

Event Info: Daily, dawn to dusk. Rated 1+.

NEW JERSEY

Belmar - 10km Walk (YR737) **Jan 1-Dec 31** Credit Only Event
Sponsoring Club: AVA-776, Delaware Valley Volkssporters
POC: Ed Tognola, 908-747-5572 (eves). 121 Dorchester Way, Shrewsbury NJ 07702.

Start Point: Mayfair Hotel, 908-681-2629. 1001 Ocean Ave. I-195 East becomes 138 East to 35 North for .9 miles. Right on 10th to Ocean.

Event Info: Daily, dawn to dusk. Rated 1. Suitable for strollers & wheelchairs. Pets not allowed on boardwalk.

Princeton - 10km Walk (YR736) **Jan 1-Dec 31**
Sponsoring Club: AVA-776, Delaware Valley Volkssporters
POC: David Scull, 609-275-1721. 22 Bridgewater Dr, Princeton Junction NJ 08550

Registration: Best Western Palmer Inn, 609-452-2500. 3499 Rt 1 South (next to Pep Boys). Located on southbound Rt 1, 2.8 miles north of Jct I-295 and 1. Jughandle U-turn at Meadow Road.

Start Point: Turning Basin Park, 2.4 mile drive from registration.

Event Info: Daily, dawn to dusk. Rated 1. Suitable for strollers. Parts may be too uneven for wheelchairs. Pets must be leashed.

NEW MEXICO

Alamogordo - 10km Walk (YR067) **Jan 1-Dec 31** Credit Only Event
Sponsoring Club: AVA-014, Holloman Sun Runners
POC: Robert Turner, 800-545-4021 days 505-434-0405 eves. 3405 Fayne Ln, Alamogordo NM 88310

Start Point: J & J Mini Market, 1400 E 9th St. From US 54, 70, & 82, turn east on 9th St. Proceed to the corner of 9th & Washington.

Event Info: Daily, dawn-three hours before dark. Rated 1. Suitable for strollers & wheelchairs. Pets must be leashed.

Cloudcroft - 10km Walk (YR315) **Jan 1-Dec 31** Credit Only Event
Sponsoring Club: AVA-014, Holloman Sun Runners
POC: Robert Turner, 800-545-4021 days 505-434-0405 (eves). 3405 Fayne Ln, Alamogordo NM 88310

Start Point: The Aspen Motel & Restaurant, 505-682-2526. Hwy 82.

Event Info: Daily, 8-three hours before dark. Rated 5. 9,200 ft. altitude. We recommend that you stop frequently to avoid over-exertion. Participants with heart or blood pressure conditions should take special precautions. Pets must be leashed.

Dona Ana - 35/70km Bike (YR767) **Jan 1-Dec 31**
Sponsoring Club: AVA-108, Sun Country Striders, Ltd.
POC: Robert Macklin, 505-524-8032. 4276 Dona Ana Rd, Las Cruces, NM 88005-5339

Start Point: Larry's Food Store, 505-524-1768. Corner of Thorp (NM Hwy 320) & Ledesma Dr. Take exit 9 off I-25 and turn west onto NM Hwy 320 (Thorp Rd). Go for 0.4 miles. Turn right into parking lot.

Event Info: Daily, dawn to dusk. No bike rentals available. Rated 1.

Las Cruces - 11/22km Walk (YR010) **Jan 1-Dec 31**
Sponsoring Club: AVA-108, Sun Country Striders, Ltd.
POC: Don Weitz, 505-524-1368. 1655 Country Club Circle, Las Cruces, NM 88001-1553

Start Point: Las Cruces Hilton, 705 S Telshor Blvd; 505-522-4300. Take Exit 3 off I-25, turn onto Lohman Ave, turn right onto Telshor and turn left at the traffic light into parking lot.

Event Info: Daily, dawn to dusk. Rated 1+. Suitable for strollers.

Las Cruces - 10km Walk (YR385) **Jan 1-Dec 31**
Sponsoring Club: AVA-108, Sun Country Striders, Ltd.
POC: Eldon Cherry, 505-525-2714. 1000 Fawn Lane, Las Cruces NM 88001-2330

Start Point: Meerscheidt Rec Center, 1800 E Hadley Ave; 505-526-0550. Take Exit 6B off I-25 onto N Main and turn south onto N Solano Dr. Turn left onto E Hadley for 1/2 mile.

Event Info: Mon-Sat, 9-4:45. Closed Sundays. Rated 1. Suitable for strollers.

Mesilla - 10/20km Walk (YR766) **Jan 1-Dec 31**
Sponsoring Club: AVA-108, Sun Country Striders, Ltd.
POC: Barbara Garcia, 505-526-1675. 1500 Via Norte, Las Cruces, NM 88005-4923

Start Point: Adelina's, 505-527-1970. 1800 Avenida de Mesilla. From I-10, exit 140 onto Avenida de Mesilla for 0.8 miles and turn right into parking lot.

Event Info: Mon-Fri, 11-6; Sat & Sun, 11-5. Rated 1. Suitable for strollers. Only one event credit even if completing both trails. Pets must be leashed.

Organ - 10km Walk (YR102) **Jan 1-Dec 31**
Sponsoring Club: AVA-108, Sun Country Striders, Ltd.
POC: Doyle Piland, 505-523-7034. 1910 Camelot Dr, Las Cruces, NM 88005-1643

Start Point: Space Murals Museum and Gift Shop, 10002 US Hwy 70 E; 505-382-0977. Take Exit 6A off I-25 onto US Hwy 70 E for 11 miles and turn right into the parking lot next to a large water tank painted with murals.

Event Info: Mon-Sat, 9-7; Sun, 10-6. Rated 3+. No strollers or wheelchairs.

Silver City - 10/20km Walk (YR859) **Jan 1-Dec 31**
Sponsoring Club: AVA-108, Sun Country Striders, Ltd.
POC: Mary Wilmoth, 505-388-4655. 3636 Little Walnut, Silver City, NM 88061

Start Point: Copper Manor Motel, 505-538-5392. 710 Silver Heights Blvd. (US Hwy 180E)

Event Info: Daily, dawn to dusk.

NEW YORK

Albany - 11km Walk (YR248) **Jan 2-Dec 31**
Sponsoring Club: AVA-410, Empire State Capital Volkssporters
POC: Lois Heyer, 518-477-6236/Wayne Ubrich, 518-283-4606. PO Box 6995, Albany NY 12206

Start Point: Albany Urban Park Cultural Center, Visitors Center, 25 Quackenbush Sq; 518-434-5132.

Event Info: Daily, 10-4. Closed major holidays. Rated 1+. Suitable for strollers & wheelchairs with some assistance.

Apalachin - 10km Walk (YR239) **Jan 1-Dec 31**
Sponsoring Club: AVA-790, Fingerlakes Region Volkssports
POC: Gus Runte, 607-724-6879. 72 Aldrich Avenue, Binghamton, NY 13903

Start Point: Waterman Conservation Education Center, 607-625-2221. PO Box 288, Hilton Rd. Fron NYS 17, take exit 66. Turn right on Hwy 434. Go through one light & turn left on Hilton Road. Drive 1/8 mile to Waterman Center on the left.

Event Info: Daily, 10-4. Rated 2. No pets, strollers or wheelchairs.

Binghamton - 10/20km Walk (YR444) **Jan 1-Dec 31**
Sponsoring Club: AVA-790, Fingerlakes Region Volkssports
POC: Gus Runte, 607-724-6879. 72 Aldrich Avenue, Binghamton, NY 13903

Start Point: Roberson Center, 607-772-0660. 30 Front St. From I-81, take exit 4S. Proceed 2 miles on arterial Hwy 363 going through two traffic lights. Cross Chenango River. Turn right at third light onto Front St.

Event Info: Mon-Thurs 9-3; Fri 9-7; Sat 10-3; Sun 12-3. Rated 1. Only one event credit even if doing both trails. Suitable for strollers & wheelchairs.

Cooperstown - 10km Walk (YR386) **Apr 22-Dec 31**
Sponsoring Club: AVA-410, Empire State Capital Volkssporters
POC: Winifred Balz, 518-372-3663. PO Box 6995, Albany NY 12206-6995

Start Point: Clark Gymnasium, Susquehanna Ave. Additional start at: Cooperstown Chamber of Commerce, 31 Chestnut St when the gymnasium is closed. Cooperstown is 70 miles west of Albany.

Event Info: Daily, 7-2. Gym closed Sundays mid May-Sept. C of C hours are 10-5. Rated 1. Suitable for strollers & wheelchairs. Pets must be leashed.

Corbettsville - 12/14/25km Walk (YR692) **Jan 1-Dec 31**
Sponsoring Club: AVA-790, Fingerlakes Region Volkssport Club
POC: Gus Runte, 607-724-6879. 72 Aldrich Avenue, Binghamton, NY 13903

Register: Quickway Store, 607-775-2927. Conklin, NY. From I-81, take exit 1. Proceed on County Hwy 20 crossing Susquehanna River; turn left at light on Rte 7. Drive 1.6 miles to Quickway on right.

Start Point: After registering, drive 0.1 miles to KIWIS Historical Bldg., Ltd., 55 Corbettsville Rd; 607-775-4291.

Event Info: Daily, 8-6. Trails are rated 3. Elevation change is 500 ft. Not recommended for wheelchairs. Tough going for strollers. Pets must be leashed. Only one event credit even if doing all trails.

Cornwall - 10km Walk (YR252) Mar 1-Nov 30
Sponsoring Club: AVA-505, Volkssport Club of West Point
POC: Donna Gallo, 914-534-7164. PO Box 30, West Point, NY 10996

Start Point: The Open Pantry, 914-534-3659. 288 Main St. Take exits 16N/17S from NY Thruway; follow signs to Newburgh. Pick up Route 9W south to Cornwall exit; follow Route 218 to Cornwall.

Event Info: Rated 1+. Mon, 8-3; Tue & Wed, 8-6; Thurs & Fri, 8-7; Sat, 8-4; Sun, 10-3.

Deposit - 10/11/13km Walk (YR758), 300m Swim (YR760) & 25km Bike (YR759) **May 27-Oct 10**
Sponsoring Club: AVA-790, Fingerlakes Region Volkssport Club
POC: Gus Runte, 607-724-6879. 72 Aldrich Ave, Binghamton, NY 13903

Start Point: Scott's Oquaga Lake House, 607-467-3094. From NYS 17, take exit 82. Follow "Scott's" signs.

Event Info: Daily, 8-4. Walk trail has 3 options. 10km is rated 2, 11km is rated 2+ and 13km is rated 3. Suitable for strollers. Only one event credit allowed even if doing all three walks. Bike trail is rated 3. Single gear bike rental available. Swim is in a supervised area.

Ithaca - 10km Walk (YR922) **Jan 1-Dec 31**
Sponsoring Club: AVA-790, Fingerlakes Region Volkssport Club
POC: Gus Runte, 607-724-6879. 72 Aldrich Ave, Binghamton, NY 13903

Start Point: Cornell University, Plantation's Gift Shop, 607-255-3020. 1 Plantation's Rd.

Event Info: Mon-Fri, 8-4:30. Jan-Mar, closed on Sat & Sun. Apr, May & Sep-Dec, Sat, 10-5; closed Sunday. Jun-Aug, Sat & Sun 11-5. Rated 2.

Lockport - 10km Walk (YR146) **Apr 1-Nov 30**
Sponsoring Club: AVA-589, Niagara Frontier Volkssport Club
POC: Gail Davis, 716-741-2198. PO Box 99, Clarence Center NY 14032

Start Point: Friendly's, 2 Locks Plaza.

Event Info: Daily, dawn to dusk. Rated 1. Possible for strollers but not wheelchairs.

Lockport - Two 10km Walks (YR757 & YR937) **Apr 1-Oct 31**
Sponsoring Club: AVA-788, Niagara Escarpment Volkssport Assn.
POC: Dorothy N. Socie, 716-731-2630. 2181 Violet Circle, Niagara Falls, NY 14304-2901

Start Point: Best Western Lockport Inn, 716-625-6181 or 716-434-4751. 515 S. Transit Rd.

Event Info: Daily, dawn to dusk. YR757 is rated 1+. YR937 is rated 1.

Marathon - 11/23km Walk (YR052) **Jan 1-Dec 31**
Sponsoring Club: AVA-790, Fingerlakes Region Volkssports
POC: Gus Runte, 607-724-6879. 72 Aldrich Avenue, Binghamton, NY 13903

Start Point: Three Bear Inn, 800-322-8029/607-849-3258. 3 Broome St. From I-81, take exit 11. Proceed to town center to Inn.

Event Info: Daily, 8-5. 11km is rated 2. 23km is rated 3. Maximum elevation change is 500ft. Suitable for strollers. Only one event credit even if doing both trails.

☆ Niagara Falls - 10km Walk (YR214) & 15km Walk (YR862) **Apr 1-Nov 30**
Sponsoring Club: AVA-589, Niagara Frontier Volkssport Club
POC: Marge Brauer, 716-741-2700. 7110 Salt Rd, Clarence Center NY 14032

Start Point: Holiday Inn, 716-285-2521. 114 Buffalo Ave.

Event Info: Daily, dawn to dusk. Rated 1. Suitable for strollers & wheelchairs. Pets must be leashed. YR862 goes into Canada. A $.25 bridge toll will be required to cross the international border in each direction.

Niagara Falls - 10km Walk (YR422) **Apr 1-Oct 31**
Sponsoring Club: AVA-788, Niagara Escarpment Volkssport Association
POC: Dorothy N. Socie, 716-731-2630. 2181 Violet Circle #1, Niagara Falls, NY 14304-2901

Start Point: Schoellkopf Geological Museum, off North Robert Moses Pkwy; 716-278-1780.

Event Info: Rated 1. Apr-May 9-4:30; Jun-Aug 8-7; Sep & Oct 9-4:30.

Orchard Park - 10km Walk (YR734) Apr 1-Nov 30
Sponsoring Club: AVA-589, Niagara Frontier Volkssport Club
POC: Roger Black, 716-627-3104. 5817 Lake View Terr, Lake View NY 14085

Register: Bihr's Food Shop, 716-662-9948. 4906 South Buffalo St.

Start Point: Chestnut Ridge Park. Turn right on S. Buffalo Rd (Rt 277) and proceed about 1.8 miles to the park entrance on the right. Upon entering the park, follow signs to the casino parking lot where there should be ample parking. Refer to walk directions from here.

Event Info: Daily, dawn to dusk. Rated 2. Not for strollers or wheelchairs. Leashed pets.

Plattsburgh - 10km Walk (YR049) Apr 1-Oct 29
Sponsoring Club: AVA-084, Adirondack Wanderers
POC: Daniel W. Stockdale, 518-563-4336. 16 Chenango Rd, Plattsburgh, NY 12901

Start Point: Howard Johnson's Motor Lodge, I-87 & Rt 3, Exit 37.

Sakets Harbor - 10m Walk (YR938) Apr 1-Nov 30
Sponsoring Club: AVA-308, North Country Wanderers
POC: Pam Kennedy, 256 Clinton St, Watertown, NY 13601

Start Point: Ontario Place Hotel, 103 General Smith Dr.

Event Info: Trail is rated 1+.

Saratoga Springs - Two 11km Walks (YR169) Jan 2-Jun 30 & (YR325) Jul 1-Dec 31
Sponsoring Club: AVA-410, Empire State Capital Volkssporters
POC: Ron Hersh, 518-885-6281 or Beryl Wol, 518-383-2880. PO Box 6995, Albany NY 12206

Start Point: National Museum of Racing and Hall of Fame, 518-587-3241. Union Ave. & Ludlow St. Saratoga Springs is 30 miles north of Albany.

Event Info: Sun 12-4:30; Mon-Fri, 9-4:30; Sat, 10-4:30. Closed Thanksgiving, Christmas, Easter, & New Year's. Rated 1. Suitable for strollers & wheelchairs.

Schenectady - 11km Walk (YR250) Jan 7-Dec 31
Sponsoring Club: AVA-410, Empire State Capital Volkssporters
POC: Ellen McNett, 518-372-1270 or Wayne Ubrich, 518-282-4606. PO Box 6995, Albany NY 12206-6995

Start Point: Schenectady Museum & Planetarium, Nott Terrace Heights; 518-383-7890. Schenectady is located 20 minutes west of Albany & 30 minutes south of Saaratoga.

Event Info: Tues-Fri, 10-4:30; Sat & Sun, 12-5. Closed Mondays and major holidays. Pets must be leashed. Trails are rated 1+. Suitable for strollers & wheelchairs with assistance.

Syracuse - 10km Walk (YR367) Jan 1-Dec 31
Sponsoring Club: AVA-790, Fingerlakes Region Volkssport Club
POC: Gus Runte, 607-724-6879. 72 Aldrich Avenue, Binghamton, NY 13903

Start Point: YMCA, 315-474-6851. 340 Montgomery St. From I-81 take Adams St exit. Proceed on Adams to E Fayette St and turn left. Go to Montgomery St and turn left to YMCA.

Event Info: Daily, 8-4. Rated one. Suitable for strollers & wheelchairs.

Utica - 10km Walk (YR369) **Jan 1-Dec 31**
Sponsoring Club: AVA-790, Fingerlakes Region Volkssport Club
POC: Gus Runte, 607-724-6879. 72 Aldrich Avenue, Binghamton, NY 13903

Start Point: Radisson Hotel, 315-797-8010. 200 Genesee St. Exit 31 from I-90 To Genesee St. South to Hotel.

Event Info: Daily, 8-4. Rated 1+. Suitable for strollers & wheelchairs.

☆ **West Point** - 11km Walk (YR037) **Jan 1-Dec 31**
Sponsoring Club: AVA-505, Volkssport Club of West Point
POC: Farrell G. Patrick, 914-446-4709. PO Box 30, West Point NY 10996

Start Point: Hotel Thayer Gift Shop, Thayer Gate.

Event Info: Daily, 8-2. Rated 1+.

Windsor - 11/20km Walk (YR341) **Jan 1-Dec 31**
Sponsoring Club: AVA-790, Fingerlakes Region Volkssports
POC: Gus Runte, 607-724-6879. 72 Aldrich Avenue, Binghamton, NY 13903

Start Point: Country Haven Bed & Breakfast, 607-655-1204. 66 Garrett Rd. From NYS 17, exit 78/79 & proceed to Dunbar Rd; then right on Garrett Road to B & B.

Event Info: Daily, 8-5. Closed during Hunting Season (mid-Nov to mid-Dec). Rated 2+. No strollers or wheelchairs. Walking shoes recommended. Elevation change is 300 ft.

Youngstown - 10km Walk (YR253) **Apr 1-Oct 31**
Sponsoring Club: AVA-788, Niagara Escarpment Volkssport Association
POC: Dorothy N. Socie, 716-731-2630. 2181 Violet Cir #1, Niagara Falls NY 14304-2901

Start Point: Old Fort at Ft. Niagara State Park; 716-745-7611.

Event Info: Rated 2. Not suitable for strollers or wheelchairs. Apr-Jun, 9-4:30; Jul & Aug, 9-7; Sep & Oct, 9-4:30.

NORTH CAROLINA

Boone - 300m Swim (YR897) **Jan 1-Dec 31**
Sponsoring Club: AVA-464, High County Walkers
POC: Sonny/Lory Whitehead, 910-385-9105. PO Box 3484, Boone, NC 28607

Start Point: Watauga County Parks & Recreation Swim Complex, 704-264-0270. 231 Complex Drive.

Event Info: $2.00 pool usage fee. Daily, 12-4. Closed major holidays.

Boone - 10km Walk (YR898) **Jan 1-Dec 31**
Sponsoring Club: AVA-464, High Country Walkers
POC: Sonny & Lory Whitehead, 910-385-9105. PO Box 3484, Boone, NC 28607

Start Point: Visitor Information Center, 704-264-1299. 1700 Blowing Rock Rd.

Event Info: Daily, 9-5. Closed major holidays. Rated 2+. Difficult for strollers. Leashed pets.

Brevard - 10km Walk (YR600) **Jan 1-Dec 31**
Sponsoring Club: AVA-NC, Tarheel State Walkers
POC: Paul & Loretta Chasteen, 910-766-6446. PO Box 15013, Winston-Salem, NC 27012
Local POC: Carolyn Zinc, 704-884-7358

Start Point: Varner's Old Fashioned Soda Fountain, 704-884-4165. Broad St at Jordan.

Event Info: Mon-Fri, 805; Sat, 9-5. Closed Sunday and all major holidays. Rated 1+.

Buxton - 10km Walk (YR602) **Jan 1-Dec 31**
Sponsoring Club: AVA-NC, Tarheel State Walkers
POC: Paul & Loretta Chasteen, 910-766-6446. PO Box 15013, Winston-Salem, NC 27113

Start Point: Dillon's Corner, 919-995-5083. Hwy 12. From Raleigh take US Hwy 64 East to Hwy 12 South 45-50 miles.

Event Info: Daily, 6 A.M.-10 P.M. Closed Christmas. May close during bad weather. Rated 2+. Take bug repellent.

Chapel Hill - 10km Walk (YR314) **Jan 1-Dec 31**
Sponsoring Club: AVA-NC, Tarheel State Walkers
POC: Paul & Loretta Chasteen, 910-766-6446. PO Box 15013, Winston-Salem, NC 27113
Local POC: Sherry Salyer, 919-387-0619

Start Point: University of North Carolina Visitor Center, Morehead Planetarium (inside West entrance), 919-962-1630. East Franklin Street. Take exit 266 off I-40 (Hwy 86). This becomes Columbia St in Chapel Hill. Left on East Franklin. Planetarium is on right. Park in front & get parking permit.

Event Info: Mon-Sat, 10-5; Sun, 1-5.

Charlotte - 10km Walk (YR894) **Jan 1-Dec 31**
Sponsoring Club: AVA-NC, Tarheel State Walkers
POC: Paul/Loretta Chasteen, 910-766-6447. PO Box 15013 Winston-Salem, NC 27113

Start Point: Charlotte Visitor Center, 704-331-2700. 122 East Stonewall Street. Follow Visitor Center signs off I-77.

Event Info: Center will relocate around March 1. Call 1-800-231-4636 to check. Mon-Fri, 8:30-5; Sat, 10-4; Sun, 1-4. Closed New Year's, Thanksgiving, & Christmas.

Durham - 10km Walk (YR940) **Jan 2-Dec 31**
Sponsoring Club: AVA-786, Traingle Trailblazers
POC: Dan Rabideau, 919-676-8587. 12209 Glenlivet Way, Raleigh, NC 27613

Start Point: 9th Street Active Feet, Inc. 705 Ninth St.

Event Info: Daily, 10-7.

Elizabeth City - 10km Walk (YR895) **Jan 1-Dec 31**
Sponsoring Club: AVA-NC, Tarheel State Walkers
POC: Paul/Loretta Chasteen, 910-766-6446. PO Box 15013, Winston-Salem, NC 27113

Start Point: Main Street Cafe, 919-331-1505. 507-A East Main. From 17 Bypass, turn east on Main. The Cafe is on the right approximately 12 blocks down.

Event Info: Mon-Fri, 7:30-4:30; Sat 10-2. Closed Sunday & major holidays. Rated 1. Suitable for strollers & wheelchairs.

Ft Bragg - 10km Walk (YR892) **Jan 1-Dec 31**
Sponsoring Club: AVA-NC, Tarheel State Walkers
POC: Paul/Loretta Chasteen, 910-766-6446. PO Box 15013, Winston-Salem, NC 27113

Start Point: 82nd Airborne War Memorial Museum, 910-432-3443. Bldg 6841, Ardennes & Gela Sts.

Event Info: Tue-Sat, 10-4:30; Sun, 11:30-4. Closed Mondays, New Year's & Christmas. There is a mounted box near the door with maps & start cards for early walkers.

Morehead City - 10km Walk (YR896) **Jan 1-Dec 31**
Sponsoring Club: AVA-NC, Tarheel State Walkers
POC: Paul/Loretta Chasteen, 910-766-6446. PO Box 15013, Winston-Salem, NC 27113

Start Point: Visitors Information Center, 1-800-SUNNY NC. Hwy 70 Between 34th & 33rd.

Event Info: Summer hrs: Mon-Sat, 9-5; Sun 10-5. Check with Visitors Center for weekend hours after Oct and before April. Closed major holidays.

Mount Airy - 10km Walk (YR891) **Jan 1-Dec 31**
Sponsoring Club: AVA-NC, Tarheel State Walkers
POC: Paul/Loretta Chasteen, 910-766-6446. PO Box 15013, Winston-Salem, NC 27113

Start Point: Mount Airy Visitor Center, 910-789-4636. 615 N. Main. From Hwy 52, take Hwy 601 East (Rockford St) to Sout Main. Turn right then left on Cherry (immediately) turn left on Renfro (Bus 52). Just beyond Independence Blvd, take a sharp left on North Main.

Event Info: Mon-Sat 9-4; Sun 1-4. Closed major holidays. Rated 1+. Suitable for strollers but wheelchairs may have trouble with curbs. Pets must be leashed.

Raleigh - 11km Walk (YR728) **Jan 2-Dec 31**
Sponsoring Club: AVA-786, Traingle Trailblazers
POC: Dan Rabideau, 919-676-8587. 12209 Glenlivet Way, Raleigh, NC 27613

Start Point: Capitol Area Visitor Center, 301 N Blount St.

Event Info: Mon-Fri, 8-5; Sat, 9-5; Sun, 1-5. Rated 1+. Suitable for strollers & wheelchairs.

Raleigh - 10km Walk (YR597-Oakwood) **Jan 1-Dec 31**
Sponsoring Club: AVA-NC, Tarheel State Walkers
POC: Paul & Loretta Chasteen, 910-766-6446. PO Box 15013, Winston-Salem, NC 27113
Local POC: Dan Rabideau, 919-676-8587.

Start Point: Capital Area Visitor Center, 919-733-3456. 301 N Blount St.

Event Info: Mon-Fri, 8-5; Sat, 9-5; Sun, 1-5. Closed major holidays. Rated 1. Suitable for strollers.

Salisbury - 10km Walk (YR599) **Jan 1-Dec 31**
Sponsoring Club: AVA-NC, Tarheel State Walkers
POC: Paul & Loretta Chasteen, 910-766-6446. PO Box 15013, Winston-Salem, NC 27113
Local POC: Mary Anne Laningham, 704-633-1447

Start Point: Visitor Center at Railway Station, 704-638-3100. 215 Depot St.

Alternate Start Point: For Start Card & Map Only: Days Inn, 1810 Luthern Synod Dr. Exit 75 from I-85.

Event Info: Mon-Fri, 9-5; Sat, 10-4; Sun, 1-4. Closed major holidays.

Waynesville - 10km Walk (YR585) **Jan 1-Dec 31** Credit Only Event
Sponsoring Club: AVA-778, Greenway Walkers
POC: John Richardson, 704-452-0278. PO Box 1366, Waynesville NC 28786

Start Point: Mast General Store, 148 N. Main St; 704-452-2101.

Event Info: Mon-Sat, 10-5; Sun 1-5. Closed on New Year's, Easter, Thanksgiving, & Christmas. Free parking courtesy of Clyde Saving Bank on the corner of Miller & Montgomery. Rated 2. Wheelchairs may have some difficulty.

Waynesville - 10km Walk (YR601) **Jan 1-Dec 31**
Sponsoring Club: AVA-NC, Tarheel State Walkers
POC: Paul & Loretta Chasteen, 910-766-6446. PO Box 15013, Winston-Salem, NC 27113
Local POC: Mary Woodcock, 704-452-5066 (nights)

Start Point: Mast General Store, 704-452-2101. 148 N Main St.

Event Info: Mon-Sat, 10-5; Sun 1-5. Closed major holidays. Rated 1.

Wilmington - 10km Walk (YR893) **Jan 1-Dec 31**
Sponsoring Club: AVA-NC, Tarheel State Walkers
POC: Paul/Loretta Chasteen, 910-766-6446. PO Box 15013, Winston-Salem, NC 27113

Start Point: Visitor Information Center, 910-341-4030. 24 North Third St.

Event Info: Mon-Fri, 8:30-5; Sat, 9-4; Sun, 1-4. Closed Thanksgiving & Christmas. Rated 1+.

Winston-Salem - Two 10km Walks (YR073 & YR081) & 11km Walk (YR237) **Jan 1-Dec 31**
Sponsoring Club: AVA-284, Winston Wanderers
POC: Paul & Loretta Chasteen, 910-766-6446. PO Box 15013, Winston-Salem, NC 27113
Local POC: Karen Procter, 910-945-5506

Registration: Winston-Salem Visitor Center, 910-777-3796. 601 N Cherry St.

Alternate: For pick up of map & start cards: Salem Inn, 127 S Cherry St.

Start Point: YR081: Winston-Salem Visitor Center. YR073: Drive 3 miles to Historic Bethabara Park. YR 237: Drive 3 miles to Salem Lake.

Event Info: Mon-Fri, 9-5; Sat & Sun, 10-5. Closed major holidays. Trails are rated 2.

NORTH DAKOTA

Bismarck - 10km Walks (YR939) **Jan 1-Dec 31**
Sponsoring Club: AVA-406, Koda Manipe Volkssport Club
POC: Mike Starr, (home) 701-223-4355/(office) 701-224-5912. 1425 Portland SE, Bismarck, ND 58504

Start Point: Ramada Hotel, 701-223-9600. Memorial Hwy.

Event Info: Trail is rated 1+.

Fargo - Two 10km Walks (YR191 & YR762) **Apr 1-Nov 15**
Sponsoring Club: AVA-032, Red River Volkssport Association
POC: Donald Scoby, 701-235-3389. 3302 North 2nd St #22, Fargo ND 58102

Start Point: Townhouse Inn, 301 3rd Ave N. 1-800-437-4682.

Event Info: Daily, 6-dusk. Trails are rated 1. Suitable for strollers. YR191 is in Fargo, ND and YR762 is in Moorhead, MN.

Ft Ransom - 10km Walk (YR160) **May 1-Oct 15** Credit Only Event
Sponsoring Club: AVA-406, Koda Manipe Volkssport Club
POC: Wayne Beyer, 701-642-2811. 120 North 4th St, Wahpeton ND 58075

Start Point: Ft Cafe on Main St; 701-973-2301. Fort Ransom is 30 miles S of Valley City, 18 miles NW of Lisbon and 2 miles N of the town of Fort Ransom along the Waler Hjelle Pkwy.

Event Info: Pick up start cards at the Cafe and drive three miles to start the walk at Fort Ransom State Park. **Mandatory $2.00 State Park entry fee.** Mon-Sat, 7-3; Sun, 10-3. Rated 3. Advisable to bring your own water. Not suitable for strollers or wheelchairs. Pets must be leashed.

Medora - 10km Walk (YR645) **May 1-Sep 30**
Sponsoring Club: AVA-794, Theodore Roosevelt Medora Foundation
POC: Laurie Hatzenbuhler, 701-623-4444. PO Box 198, Medora ND 58645

Start Point: Badlands Motel Office, 701-623-4444. 501 Pacific Ave.

Event Info: Rated 1.

Wahpeton - 10km Walk (YR161) **Jan 1-Dec 31**
Sponsoring Club: AVA-406, Koda Manipe Volkssport Club
POC: Wayne Beyer, 701-642-2811. 120 North 4th St, Wahpeton ND 58075

Start Point: Comfort Inn, 209 13th St S; 701-642-1115. Wahpeton is located in southeastern North Dakota. 10 miles east of I-29 (Hwy 13), or 25 miles west of I-94 (Hwy 210).

Event Info: Daily, 7-6. Finish by 9. Rated 2.

OHIO

Berea - 27km Bike (YR856) **Jan 1-Dec 31** Credit Only Event
Sponsoring Club: AVA-049, Valley Vagabonds, Inc.
POC: Deva Simon, 216-777-6036. 13317 Tradewinds, Strongsville, OH 44136

Start Point: Elias Big Boy Restaurant, 216-234-3315. 442 W. Bagley Rd

Event Info: Rated 1+.

Cincinnati (Hyde Park) - 10km Walk (YR270) **Jan 7-Dec 31** Credit Only Event
Sponsoring Club: AVA-227, Queen City Skywalkers
POC: Ginny Drumm, 513-471-7029. 4432 Carnation Ave, Cincinnati, OH 45238-4902

Start Point: Bob Roncker's Running Spot, 513-321-3006. 1993 Madison Rd. I-71 to Dana (Exit 5). East to Madison, right into O'Bryonville to Roncker's.

Alternate Start (Sundays & Holidays Only): Graeter's, 2404 Erie Ave. Sun, 9 A.M.-10 P.M.; Holidays, noon-10.

Event Info: Mon-Fri, 11-7; Sat, 10-4. Both start locations are closed Thanksgiving, Christmas & New Year's. Rated 2. Not suitable for strollers or wheelchairs. Pets must be leashed.

Cincinnati (North College Hill) - 11km Walk (YR832) **Jan 1-Dec 31** Credit Only Event
Sponsoring Club: AVA-815, Mid-America Walking Association
POC: Ted Ballman, 513-385-1279. PO Box 53921, Cincinnati, OH 45253-0921

Start Point: Perkins Family Restaurant, 513-522-3008. 7124 Hamilton Avenue. From I-74, exit north (exit 14) on North Bend Rd and continue on North Bend as it makes a 90 degree right turn at eh Cheviot Road intersection. Proceed on North Bend past Colerain Ave to Hamilton Ave and turn left onto Hamilton to Start. From I-275 North, exit south (exit 36) onto Hamilton Ave and continue about 3 miles to Start. From I-75, exit West (exit 10B) on Galbraith Rd. Proceed on Galbraith, crossing Vine, Winton & Daly to Hamilton Ave. Right on Hamilton Ave to start.

Event Info: Daily, dawn to dusk. Extremely busy Sundays. Either start very early or be extremely patient while they assist their customers. Rated 2. Not suitable for strollers or wheelchairs. Pets must be leashed.

Cincinnati (White Oak) - 10km Walk (YR268) **Jan 2-Dec 31** Credit Only Event
Sponsoring Club: AVA-227, Queen City Skywalkers
POC: Ginny Drumm, 513-471-7029. 4432 Carnation Ave, Cincinnati, OH 45238-4902

Start Point: Union 76, 513-385-5954. 6050 Cheviot Rd. I-74 exit North Bend Rd. North on North Bend/Cheviot Rd to Union 76 (right side of street beyond White Oak Shopping Center).

Event Info: Mon-Sat, 7-10; Sun, 8-8. Closed major holidays. Rated 1+. Suitable for strollers. Pets must be leashed.

Cincinnati (Winton Woods) - 10km Walk (YR855) **Jan 1-Dec 31**
Sponsoring Club: AVA-098, Zinzinnati Wanderers, Inc.
POC: Jerry Bocock, 513-851-7310. 618 Waycross Rd, Cincinnati, OH 45240

Start Point: Winton Centre, Winton Woods, 513-521-PARK. 10245 Winton Rd. From I-275 take exit #39 (Winton Rd). Go south for about 3 miles to park entrance on the right. Take first left to Winton Centre. Contact Hamilton County Park Ranger Dispatcher.

Event Info: Daily, 8-dusk. Must be finished by dark. Vehicle permit is $3.00/annual or $1.00/day. Rated 2+. Not suitable for strollers or wheelchairs. Pets must be leashed.

Cincinnati - 11km Walk (YR303) **Jan 7-Dec 30**
Sponsoring Club: AVA-445, Norwood Highlanders
POC: Angeline Kremer, 513-761-1482. 507 W North Bend Rd, Cincinnati, OH 45224 or Ted Ballman, 513-385-1279. 3820 Woodthrush Dr, Cincinnati, OH 45251-5853

Start Point: Tischbein Pharmacy, 513-721-0233. Dixie Terminal Building, 4th & Walnut

Event Info: Mon-Fri, 8-5:30; Sat, 9-3. Closed Sundays and major holidays. Rated 2+. No pets allowed.

Cleveland - 10km Walk (YR538) & 11km Walk (YR178) **Jan 1-Dec 31**
Sponsoring Club: AVA-049, Valley Vagabonds, Inc.
POC: Deva Simon, 216-572-1675. 13317 Tradewinds, Strongsville OH 44136

Start Point: Elias Big Boy Restaurant, 442 W Bagley Rd in Berea. 15 miles SW of Cleveland. From East/West take I-480 to I-71 S, exit Bagley Rd W, 2.7 miles to W Valley Plaza.

Event Info: Mon-Fri, 6-midnight; Sat/Sun/Holidays 24 hrs. Closed Christmas. Trails are rated 1+. Pets must be leashed.

Columbus - 25km Bike (YR714) **Apr 1-Oct 29** Credit Only Event
Sponsoring Club: AVA-522, Heart of Ohio Hikers
POC: Max Rhoades, 614-451-2905. 599 Lummisford Lane N, Columbus OH 43214

Start Point: McDonald's Restaurant, 614-263-1586. 3095 North High St. McDonald's is in the NW corner of High St and W Weber. Two miles N of OSU.

Event Info: Mon-Sat, 6-dusk; Sun, 7-dusk. Rated 1+. Participants must sign waiver. No bikes are available for rent. Helmets are highly recommended.

Conneaut - 12km Walk (YR857) **Jan 1-Dec 31** Credit Only Event
Sponsoring Club: AVA-049, Valley Vagabonds, Inc.
POC: Deva Simon, 216-572-1675. 13317 Tradewinds, Strongsville, OH 44136

Start Point: Markko Vineyard, 216-593-3197. RD 2, South Ridge Rd. From I-90, exit #235. Go north on Rt 193 to Kingsville. Turn right on Main St. Bear right at first Y and then bear left about 100 ft onto South Ridge Rd. Follow South Ridge approximately 3 miles and you will see the vineyard on your left.

Event Info: Mon-Sat, 9-6. Closed Sundays & holidays. Rated 2. Suitable for strollers & wheelchairs. No restrooms or water on trail. Pets must be leashed.

Dresden - 10km Walk (YR954) **Mar 1-Dec 31**
Sponsoring Club: AVA-514, Westerville Boot-N-Leggers
POC: Tim Spurgeon, 614-891-0275. 3370 East Powell Rd, Westerville, OH 43051

Start Point: Dresden Village Association, 709 Main Street

Maumee - Two 10km Walks (YR329 & YR955) **Mar 12-Nov 22**
Sponsoring Club: AVA-532, Maumee Valley Volkssporters
POC: Kitty Hall, 419-885-4703. 4802 Wickford East, Sylvania, OH 43560

Start Point: Jacky's Depot, 419-893-0216. Allen & West Dudley Streets

Event Info: Mon-Sat, 10-6; Sun, 11-6.

Middletown - 10km Walk (YR199) **Jan 1-Dec 31** Credit Only Event
Sponsoring Club: AVA-229, Bulls Run Ramblers
POC: Robert Hawkins, 513-746-9394. 7754 Martz Paulin Road, Franklin, OH 45005

Start Point: Manchester Inn, 513-422-5481. 1027 Manchester Ave.

Event Info: Daily, dawn to dusk. Rated 1+. Okay for strollers & wheelchairs. Leashed pets.

Piqua - Two 10km Walks (YR333 & YR910) **Jan 1-Dec 31** Credit Only Event
Sponsoring Club: AVA-154, Pickawillany Walkers, Inc.
POC: Edward Mann, 513-773-1046. 512 Harney Dr, Piqua OH 45356

Start Point: Subway Sandwiches & Salads, 1563 Covington Ave. From I-75 S, take exit 82 (US 36). Turn left and follow 36 through Piqua to Sunset Dr and Covington Ave. Start is on left in the shopping center. From I-75 N, exit 82 (US 36) and turn right. Follow directions above.

Event Info: Summer, 10 A.M.-11 P.M.; winter, 11 A.M.-11 P.M.; Sun, 10 A.M.-11 P.M. Closed some holidays. Trails are rated 1+. Suitable for strollers. Pets must be leashed.

Sharonville - 11km Walk (YR301) **Jan 7-Dec 30**
Sponsoring Club: AVA-445, Norwood Highlanders
POC: Angeline Kremer, 513-761-1482. 507 West Northbend Rd, Cincinnati, OH 45224 or Ted Ballman, 513-385-1279. 3820 Woodthrush Dr, Cincinnati, OH 45251-5853

Start Point: Sharon Dippety. 3327 Creek Rd, Sharonville, OH 45241

Event Info: Mon-Sat, 11-dusk. Sundays & holidays, call for times. Rated 2. Suitable for strollers. Pets must be leashed.

Wapakoneta - 10km Walk (YR690) **Jan 1-Dec 31** Credit Only Event
Sponsoring Club: AVA-675, Four Seasons Pathfinders
POC: Jay Koenig, 419-738-3532. 105 Hamilton Rd, Wapakoneta OH 45895

Start Point: Holiday Inn, I-75 & Bellefontaine St, 419-738-8181.

Event Info: Daily, 8-dusk. Rated 1. Okay for strollers & wheelchairs. Pets must be leashed.

West Carrollton - 10km Walk (YR005) 25km Bike (YR004) **Jan 1-Dec 31** Credit only events
Sponsoring Club: AVA-OH, Ohio Volkssport Association
POC: Ed Low, 513-426-8008. 2286 Apricot Dr, Beavercreek, OH 45431

Start Point: Whitman's Bike Shop, 513-866-8022. 5641 Marina Dr. On I-75 take exit 47 right to West Carrollton. Right on Marina Dr. Start is on the left. From the South on I-75, exit 47 for Moraine-Kettering to first traffic light. One block beyond light to Winwood Ave, turn left. One block and turn left on Kettering Blvd. Stay to right to West Carrollton. When road merges, **use extreme caution** and go into right lane. Right on Marina Dr to Whitman's.

Event Info: Mon-Fri, 10-7; Sat, 10-5; Sun 11-4 (only open Sundays from Apr-Aug). Walk is rated 1+. Suitable for strollers. Pets must be leashed. Bike is rated 1+. Both events have alternate routes. Only one event credit per event is allowed, even if doing both the primary and alternate routes.

Westerville - 10km Walk (YR077) **Mar 1-Dec 31**
Sponsoring Club: AVA-514, Westerville-Boot-N-Leggers
POC: Duke Foell, 614-882-1623. 728 Waterton Dr, Westerville, OH 43081

Start Point: Westerville Athletic Club, 934 S State St

Wilmot - 10km Walk (YR376) **Jan 3-Dec 30**
Sponsoring Club: AVA-544, Gemutlich Wanderers
POC: Earl Franks, 216-359-2716. 501 N Market St, Shreve, OH 44676

Start Point: The Wilderness Center, Interpetive Bldg, 216-359-5235. 9877 Alabama Ave, SW

Event Info: Tues-Sat, 9-3; Sun, 1-3. You must finish by 5. Closed Mondays & New Year's Eve & Day, Presidents' Day, Thanksgiving, Christmas Eve & Day. Open Easter Sunday, Memorial Day, 4th of July & Labor Day but closed the Tuesday following these holidays. Rated 2+. Not suitable for strollers or wheelchairs. Pets are not allowed.

Xenia - Two 10km Walks (YR279 & YR956) & 30km Bike (YR280) **Jan 1-Dec 31**
Sponsoring Club: AVA-526, The Xenia Peg Legs
POC: Jean Scott, 513-372-6953/513-372-1802 after 7 P.M. 1737 Wilshire Dr, Xenia, OH 45385

Start Point: Friendly Ice Cream, 513-372-3108. 608 N Detroit St (Route 68)

Event Info: Daily, dawn to dusk. Closed Thanksgiving & Christmas. Walks are rated 1+. Suitable for strollers & wheelchairs. Pets must be leashed. Bike is rated 1+. Bikers must sign waiver and helmets are recommended.

Yellow Springs - 11km Walk (YR904) **Jan 1-Dec 31** & 10km Skate (YR905) **Apr 1-Oct 31** Credit Only
Events

Sponsoring Club: AVA-813, The Penny Pickers
POC: Maria Varandani, 513-767-7605. 1325 Corry St, Yellow Springs, OH 45387
POC: Craig Gauger, 513-879-3497. 552 W. Funderburg Rd, Fairborn, OH 45324

Start (WALK): BP Gas Station, SR 68 (4 Xenia Ave)/Corry St. From I-70, exit at SR 68 south to Yellow Springs. At the light you'll see the BP station.

Start (SKATE): C & O Bike & Skate Company, 513-767-2288. 197 Corry St (The Yellow Cabooses). Turn left at the light (Corry St) where the BP station is. The C&O Bike & Skate Co is on the left after SUBWAY.

Event Info Walk: Daily, dawn to dusk. Closed Christmas. Wheelchairs & strollers may have some difficulty. Rated 1+. Pets must be leashed

Event Info Skate: May 1-Sept 4, daily, dawn to dusk. Apr & Oct, weekends only. Call ahead first. Skates are available for rent. Trail has no restrooms or water available. Skaters must sign a waiver.

OKLAHOMA

Bartlesville - 10km Walk (YR718) & 25km Bike (YR719) **Jan 1-Dec 31**
Sponsoring Club: AVA-291, Green Country Wander-Freunde, Inc.
POC: Gary Hatfield, 918-335-0977. 3508 Woodland Rd, Bartlesville, OK 74006-4527

Register: Jan 1-Feb 28: Private Residence, 918-335-0977. 3508 Woodland Rd

Register: Mar 1-Dec 31: Visitor Information Ctr, 918-333-1800. 1400 SE Washington Blvd.

Event Info: Information Center is open Mon-Fri, 8-5; Sat, 9-5; & Sun, 10-3. Closed Easter, Thanksgiving & Christmas. Call to verify hours. After obtaining materials, you must drive to the start/finish point.

Lawton - 10km Walk (YR222) **Jan 1-Dec 31** Credit Only Event
Sponsoring Club: AVA-316, Holy Family Walkers
POC: George Snyder 405-357-2930. 1714 NW 49th St, Lawton OK 73505

Start Point: The Ramada Inn, 601 NW 2nd St; 405-355-7155. They offer discounts to our Walkers. From the south & east, exit I-44 at Exit 37. Go left to 2nd st, then right to Ferris. Inn is on your right. From the north, exit I-44 at Exit 39B and continue south 1/2 mile. Inn is on your left at Ferris (the first light). From the west follow US 62 through north Lawton to the Wichita Falls/Lawton exit. Take the right fork (Lawton/Bus 281) to the first traffic light (Ferris Ave). Inn is on your left.

Event Info: Daily, dawn to 3 hours before sunset. Rated 2. Wheelchairs will experience some difficulty with curbs. Pets must be leashed.

Norman - 11km Walk (YR262) **Jan 1-Dec 31**
Sponsoring Club: AVA-026, Wandergruppe Walking Club
POC: Al Heberlein 405-843-5731. 1008 NW 49th St, Oklahoma City OK 73118

Start Point: Thunderbird Lodge, 1430 24th Ave, SW; 405-329-6990. From I-35 exit at 108B (Lindsey). Travel about 3/4 of a mile east to the first light at 24th Ave. Turn right on 24th and about 1/3 mile down, the Lodge is on your right.

Event Info: Daily, dawn to dusk. Rated 1. Curbs & grassy areas may be difficult for strollers & wheelchairs. Pets must be leashed.

Oklahoma City - 10km Walk (YR064) **Jan 1-Dec 31** Credit Only Events
Sponsoring Club: AVA-232, Frontier Walkers, Inc.
POC: Carolyn Lewis, 405-946-4817/943-3196. 2913 NW 44th, Oklahoma City OK 73112

Start Point: Crystal Bridge Botanical Garden, Reno & Harvey Sts. Exit I-40 at Walker or Robinson Streets.

Event Info: Daily, 9-6. Closed Christmas. Trail is rated 2. Suitable for strollers but difficulty with curbs.

Oklahoma City - 11km Walk (YR350) **Jan 1-Dec 31** Credit Only Event
Sponsoring Club: AVA-232, Frontier Walkers, Inc.
POC: Chris Papahronis, 405-634-7222. PO Box 25233, Oklahoma City, OK 73125

Start Point: Conoco Food Mart, 405-842-2887. 6401 N. Western

Event Info: Daily, 6:30-11.

Oklahoma City - 10km Walk (YR518) & 25km Bike (YR059) **Jan 1-Dec 31**
Sponsoring Club: AVA-232, Frontier Walkers, Inc.
POC: Carolyn J. Lewis, 405-943-3196/946-4817. 2913 NW 44th St, Okla City, OK 73112

Start Point: Oklahoma City Sports Store, 405-749-1811. 9225 N May Ave.

Event Info: Mon-Fri, 9:30-9; Sat, 9-9; Sun, 11-6. Closed Christmas & Easter. Major holiday hours vary from above. Call before you make the trip.

Sulphur - 10/14km Walk (YR117) **Jan 2-Dec 31**
Sponsoring Club: AVA-026, Wandergruppe Walking Club
POC: Al Heberlein 405-843-5731. 1008 NW 49th St, Oklahoma City OK 73118

Start Point: Travertine Nature Center, Chickasaw National Recreation Area; 405-622-3165.

Event Info: 8-5 September-May; 8-9 June-August. Please call 405-622-3165 for information. Rated 1+. Pets must be leashed and are not allowed on the Springs Loop.

Tulsa - 10km Walk (YR009) **Jan 1-Dec 31**
Sponsoring Club: AVA-291, Green Country Wander-Freunde, Inc.
POC: Bob Pugh, 918-446-7924. 4743 S Waco, Tulsa, OK 74107

Start Point: Quik Trip Store No. 80, 918-742-7151. 2006 East 21st Street.

Event Info: Daily, dawn to dusk.

Tulsa - 10km Walk (YR079) **Jan 1-Dec 31**
Sponsoring Club: AVA-291, Green Country Wander-Freunde, Inc.
POC: Bob Pugh, 918-446-7924. 4743 S Waco, Tulsa, OK 74107

Start Point: Store just inside entrance of Keystone State Park, 918-865-4477.

Event Info: Park is 15 miles west of Tulsa. Daily, 8-dusk.

Tulsa - 25km Bike (YR148) **Jan 1-Dec 31**
Sponsoring Club: AVA-291, Green Country Wander-Freunde, Inc.
POC: David Hagar, 918-587-2795. PO Box 4764, Tulsa, OK 74159-0764

Start Point: The Wheel Bicycle & Emporium, 918-587-5927. 815 S Riverside Dr. On the east side of the 11th Street Bridge and Riverside Dr.

Event Info: Apr-Aug: Wed-Sun, 10-7. Sept-Mar: Wed-Sun, 10-6. Call to verify hours.

OREGON

Albany - 10km Walk (YR215-Historic) & 10/12km Walk (YR795-Parks, Lakes & Streams) & 10/14km Walk (YR377-N Albany) **Jan 1-Dec 31** Credit Only Events
Sponsoring Club: AVA-474, Albany Fitwalkers
POC: Chuck Boeder 503-967-9162. PO Box 1218, Albany OR 97321

Start Point: Pop's Branding Iron Restaurant, 901 Pacific Blvd. From South on I-5, exit 234B Pacific Blvd. From North on I-5, exit 233 (Hwy 20/Santiam Hwy). Turn west on Santiam Hwy. Stay in left lane and you will have to turn left on Pacific Blvd (no choice) . . . follow Pacific Blvd to Madison. Be in right lane. Pop's is on the right just before the BP Station.

Event Info: Daily, dawn to dusk. Closed after 3 P.M. on Christmas Eve and all day on Christmas Day. YR215 & 795 are rated 1. YR215 has a 5km option. Suitable for strollers and wheelchairs. May have some difficulty with curbs. YR377-Walk from Pop's for 14km or drive to North Albany for a 10km. Rated 3. Strollers may have problems. No wheelchairs.

Ashland - 11km Walk (YR063) **Jan 2-Dec 31** Credit Only Event
Sponsoring Club: AVA-486, Ashland Hillclimbers
POC: Linda Vanderlip 503-482-4674. 325 W. Nevada St, Ashland OR 97520

Start Point: Ashland Rexall Drug, 275 E Main St.

Event Info: Daily, 9 to 3 hours before dark. Closed New Year's, Memorial Day, July 4th, Labor Day, Thanksgiving & Christmas. Rated 3. Very difficult for strollers and wheelchairs. Pets must be leashed.

Astoria - 10km Walk (YR475) **Jan 1-Dec 31**
Sponsoring Club: AVA-679, Turnaround Trekkers
POC: Doris Larremore, 503-325-4734. PO Box 975, Seaside, OR 97138-0975

Start Point: Columbia Memorial Hospital, 2111 Exchange. Follow the signs from Hwy 101 or Hwy 30 to Astoria. Follow Hwy 30 through town. Turn south one block on 20th. Box is in lobby.

Event Info: Daily, dawn to dusk. Rated 2+. Not suitable for strollers or wheelchairs.

Baker City - Two 10km Walks (YR824-Historic & YR825-Flagstaff Hill) **Mar 15-Oct 15**
Sponsoring Club: AVA-474, Albany Fitwalkers
POC: Chuck Boeder, 503-967-9162. 2908 Millersburg Dr, NE, Albany, OR 97321

Start Point: Texaco Food Mart (Texaco Station), 500 Campbell St. Exit I-84 at #304. Turn west. Texaco is on the right about 1 block from I-84. Counter person has start box. **This is the registration point for YR825.** You must drive to start at: Interpretive Center at Flagstaff Hill.

Event Info: YR824 is rated 1. Strollers & wheelchairs may have difficulty with curbs.
YR825 has two trails available and each has a 5km option. Trail 1 is rated 2 and is suitable for strollers & wheelchairs. Trail 2 is rated 3+. No strollers or wheelchairs. Only one event credit event if doing both trails. Best to wear long pants. Carry your own water. Restrooms and water are not available until Center opens at 9. Pets must be leashed.

Bend - Three 10km Walks (YR661, YR515 & YR823) & 25km Bike (YR517) **Jan 1-Dec 31**
Sponsoring Club: AVA-493, Ponderosa Pathfinders
POC: Dianne Erdman, 503-389-4707. 905 NE Franklin, Bend OR 97701

Start Point: Private Home, 905 NE Franklin St. From Hwy 97 in Bend, turn E on NE Franklin. Go 6 blocks. Park on Larch behind the house.

Event Info: Daily, dawn to dusk. YR661 is rated 1+. YR515 is rated 4+. YR823 is rated 2+ and starts about three miles from registration site. Bike is rated 1+.

Canby - 10km Walk (YR797) **Jan 1-Dec 31**
Sponsoring Club: AVA-567, The Walking Connection
POC: Phyllis Stuart, 503-266-3747. 261 NE 4th, Canby, OR 97013

Start Point: Francesca's Coffee House & Candy Shop, 248 NW First St. From Oregon City take 99 East to Canby, turn right on N. Grant over railroad tracks to NW First St. Turn left on First to start point. From I-5 northbound, take exit #278 Aurora/Donald & follow signs to 99 East and Canby. Turn left on North Grant and right on NW FIrst to start. From I-5 southbound, take exit #282A, Canby/Hubbard and follow Truck Route signs to 99 E and Canby. Turn left on North Grant, cross railroad tracks and turn right on NW First to start.

Event Info: Closed Apr 16, May 29, July 5, Sept 4, Nov 23, & Dec 25 & 26. Rated 1.5. Suitable for strollers but not wheelchairs.

Cannon Beach - 10km Walk (YR434) **Jan 1-Dec 31**
Sponsoring Club: AVA-679, Turnaround Trekkers
POC: Mel Hickman, 503-436-1022(days) or 503-738-5859(eves). PO Box 975, Seaside, OR 97138

Start Point: Catch the Wind Kite Shop, 1st & Hemlock. Follow the signs from Hwy 101 or Hwy 26 to Cannon Beach. Take the first Cannon Beach exit and follow Hemlock to 1st Street. Hemlock is the main street through the business district of Cannon Beach.

Event Info: Trail is 2+. Winter/Fall hours: Jan 1-Memorial Day & after Labor Day are 10-5. Summer Hours: Memorial Day - Labor Day are 10-8. Closed Christmas & Thanksgiving.

Cape Perpetua - 10km Walk (YR437), 10/14km Walk (YR275) & 15km Walk (YR476) **Jan 1-Dec 31**
Events 437 & 476 are Credit Only Events
Sponsoring Club: AVA-695, Yachats Coastal Gems
POC: Shirley's, 503-547-3292. PO Box 896, Yachats OR 97498

Start at either: Cape Perpetua Visitor Center, 3 miles S of Yachats on Hwy 101, daily 9-5, May 1-Oct 1 and weekends 10-4, Oct 1-May 1, or Shirley's on Hwy 101 in downtown Yachats. Daily, 9-5:30, closed major holidays.

Event Info: YR275, 10km is rated 3 and 14km is rated 4 due to 600 ft elevation gain. YR437 is rated 3+. Has an 800 ft elevation gain in first 3 km. YR476 is rated 3+. Has a 1200 ft elevation gain during first 5km. None of the trails are suitable for strollers or wheelchairs. Pets must be leashed.

Charleston - 10km Walk (YR177) **Jan 1-Dec 31**
Sponsoring Club: AVA-507, South Coast Wavewalkers
POC: Ann Warner, 503-756-6212. 494 Lombard, North Bend, OR 97459

Start Point: Davey Jones Locker Grocery, across Charleston bridge.

Event Info: Rated 4+. Alternate trail is rated 2+. Only one event credit even if walking both trails. Not suitable for strollers or wheelchairs. Pets are not allowed.

Coos Bay - 10km Walk (YR420) **Jan 1-Dec 31**
Sponsoring Club: AVA-507, South Coast Wavewalkers
POC; Ann Warner, 503-756-6212. 494 Lombard, North Bend, OR 97459

Start Point: McKay's Market, 503-756-6212. corner of Central & 7th

Event Info: Rated 1. Suitable for strollers and wheelchairs but curbs lack cuts.

Enterprise - 10km Walk (YR798) **Jun 1-Oct 31** Credit Only Event
Sponsoring Club: AVA-600, Tough Trail Trompers
POC: Wendy Bumgardner, 503-692-3994 or Internet: w.bumgardnergenie.geis.com. Ruth Robbins, 503-656-3412. PO Box 1651, Tualatin, OR 97062-1651

Start Point: Wallowa Memorial Hospital, 401 NE 1st St. From the East or West, take Hwy I-84 to exit 261. Exit and go right approximately 1 mile. Be in the left hand lane for turn onto Hwy 82 to Enterprise. Enterprise is approximately 64 miles from I-84. You will enter town on North St. Continue on North St to NE 1st St. Turn left to hospital.

Event Info: Daily, dawn to dusk. Rated 2. Suitable for strollers but wheelchairs will need help on the hills. Pets must be leashed.

Eugene - Two 10km Walks (YR413 & YR677) & 25km Bike (YR414) **Jan 7-Dec 31**
Sponsoring Club: AVA-455, Eugene-Springfield Mossback Volkssport Club
POC: Frank W. Ross, 503-726-7169. 2398 N. 8th, Springfield OR 97477

Start Point: Run Pro, 525 High St; 503-343-1842. From I-5 exit 194B (West I-105), take first exit off I-105 with signs to City Center/Mall. Cross bridge and take exit to City Center/Hwy 99N. Stay in right lane, at bottom of ramp, turn right onto High Street. Start is approximately 1/2 block down.

Event Info: Mon-Fri, 10-6; Sat, 10-5; Sun, 11-4. Sunday hours subject to change. Please call ahead. Closed most holidays. Walks are rated 1+ and 2. Wheelchairs & strollers will have some difficulty on the trail rated 2. Pets are not permitted in the rhododendron garden. Bike is rated 1. Bikes & helmets can be rented at Pedal Power, located near start point.

Florence - 10km Walk (YR349) **Jan 1-Dec 31**
Sponsoring Club: AVA-695, Yachats Coastal Gems
POC: Shirley's, 503-547-3292. PO Box 896, Yachats OR 97498

Start Point: The Sportsman, 249 N Coast Hwy. (Hwy 101), 503-997-3336.

Event Info: Oct 1-Apr 30, Mon-Sat, 9-7; Sun 10-5. May-Sep 30, Mon-Sat 9-9; Sun 10-6. Closed major holidays. Rated 1+. Wheelchairs & strollers with some difficulty. Leashed pets.

Forest Grove - 10km Walk (YR050) **Jan 1-Dec 31** Credit Only Event
Sponsoring Club: AVA-225, Webfoot Walkers
POC: Wendy White, 503-357-3702. PO Box 813, Forest Grove, OR 97116

Start Point: Forest Grove Tuality Hospital, Main Lobby. 1809 Maple St. From I-5 exit at #292, Hwy 217. Continue north to Hwy 26W (Sunset Hwy). Go west for approximately 9 miles to the North Plains/Hillsboro exit. Exit, then go left on Glencoe Rd into Hillsboro. At 1st Ave and Baseline (Hwy 8), go right to Forest Grove. Maple St is approximately 1 mile from the city limit sign. Turn left to hospital.

Event Info: Daily dawn to dusk. Rated 1+. Okay for strollers & wheelchairs. Leashed pets.

Gaston - 10/13km Walk (YR755) **Jan 2-Dec 31** Credit Only Event
Sponsoring Club; AVA-225, Webfoot Walkers
POC: Wendy White, 503-357-3702. PO Box 813, Forest Grove, OR 97116

Start Point: Gaston Market, 222 Front Street. Located on Hwy 47 approximately 7 miles west of Forest Grove and approximately 19 miles east of McMinnville.

Event Info: Mon-Sat, 8-4:30; Sun, 9:30-3:30. Closed Easter, Thanksgiving, Christmas & New Years. No water or restrooms at start/finish. Only one event credit even if doing both trails. Trails are rated 2. Suitable for strollers but wheelchairs will need assistance. Dogs must be leashed.

Gervais - 10km Walk (YR794) **May 13-Nov 30** Credit Only Event
Sponsoring Club: AVA-425, Silverton Walk Abouts
POC: Pat Wurzel, 503-362-7651. 2410 Lancaster, Salem, OR 97301

Start Point: Willamette Mission State Park, 503-393-1172. 10991 Wheatland Rd, NE. From I-5, take exit 263 and follow the park signs approximately 5 miles to the park. Register at the Wildlife Viewing area (first turnout inside park-just past toll booth). The start table will be located in the turnaround area across from the US flag display. Then drive 1.4 miles inside the park to the Filbert Grove Day Use area for the trailhead.

Event Info: Daily, 8-7. Rated 1. Not suitable for wheelchairs and strollers would have a little difficulty. Pets must be leashed. If the Willamette River is high, call to see if park is open. $3.00 per car park use fee in effect May 13-Sept 24.

Gold Beach - 10km Walk (YR495) **Jan 1-Dec 31**
Sponsoring Club: AVA-507, South Coast Wavewalkers
POC: Ann Warner, 503-756-6212. 494 Lombard, North Bend, OR 97459

Start Point: McKay's Market, Hwy 101 in the middle of town.

Event Info: Rated 1-1+. Beach portion is an option. Suitable for strollers & wheelchairs if option is not taken.

Government Camp (Mt Hood) - 10km Walk (YR433) **May 1-Oct 31** Credit Only Event
Sponsoring Club: AVA-600, Tough Trail Trompers
POC: Wendy Bumgardner; 503-692-3994 or Internet: w.bumgardnergenie.geis.com. Ruth Robbins, 503-656-3412. PO Box 1651, Tualatin, OR 97062-1651

Start Point: Mt. Hood Inn, 87450 E Government Camp Loop. This is the registration only. Start is 4.4 miles west of Mt. Hood Inn on Hwy 26. Take & follow instructions provided at registration. From the North or South on I-5, take I-84 Eastbound exit 301 (The Dalles). From I-84 take Exit 16-A (Wood Village). Turn right on 238th St which becomes 242nd/Hogan Ave. In 2.7 miles, turn left on Burnside. At 3.5 miles from I-84, you will go through a light and Burnside becomes Hwy 26. At 41.3 miles turn left at the sign for Ski Bowl East & Government Camp. The Inn is 0.2 miles on the right.

Event Info: No IVV Books available at start. Daily, dawn to dusk. Rated 4. Please carry water & wear sturdy shoes. Not suitable for strollers or wheelchairs. Because snow pack varies, call 503-666-0771 for conditions on Pioneer Bridle Trail #795.

Government Camp - Two 10km Walks (YR568-White River Station & YR569-Barlow Crossing) **Jun 1-Oct 31** Credit Only Event
Sponsoring Club: AVA-743, Pathways to Adventure
POC: Judy Berry, 503-244-7073. 7065 SW Hunt Club Rd, Portland OR 97223

Register: The Brew Pub, 87394 E Govt Camp Rd. Follow Hwy 26 to Govt Camp. at Mt. Hood. Early Registration Box on porch. Pub opens at 11:30 A.M. for stamps.

Start Point: Walks are approx 20-25 minute drive from sign-in.

Event Info: Daily, dawn to dusk. YR568 is rated 2+. YR569 is rated 1+. Neither is suitable for wheelchairs.

Grants Pass - 10km Walk (YR633)) & Two 11km Walks (YR419 & YR783) **Jan 1-Dec 31**
Sponsoring Club: AVA-498, Rogue Valley Walkers
POC: Shirley E. O'Hare, 503-479-7989. 199 Gordon Way S, Grants Pass OR 97527

Start Point: Southern Oregon Medical Center (name will be changing to Three Rivers Medical Center), 1505 NW Washington Blvd.

Event Info: Daily, 7-dusk. Trails are rated 2. Not suitable for wheelchairs. Leashed pets.

Gresham - 10km Walk (YR519) **Jan 1-Dec 31**
Sponsoring Club: AVA-426, Oregon Telephone Pioneers Volkssport Club
POC: John Martinson, 503-760-6261. 421 SW Oak Street, Room 7S4, Portland OR 97204

Start Point: Quality Inn, 1545 NE Burnside St. From I-84, exit 16A, Wood Village and proceed south on 242nd Ave. Turn right on NE Division to Burnside. Turn left on Burnside and the start/finish is on the right. From MAX light rail system, get off in Gresh A.M. at Cleveland/8th, the last stop, and walk east 1/2 block to the Inn.

Event Info: Daily, 7-dusk. Rated 1+. Pets must be leashed.

Gresham - Two 10km Walks (YR612-Sunset & YR687-Mt Hood) & 25/43km Bike (YR713) **Jan 1-Dec 31**
Sponsoring Club: AVA-552, East County Windwalkers
POC: East County Windwalkers, 503-663-9222. PO Box 854, Gresham, OR 97030

Start Point: Mount Hood Medical Center, 24800 SE Stark St. Near I-84, 16 miles from downtown Portland. From I-84 E or W, exit Wood Village/Gresh A.M. (16A). Go south on 238th Dr (away from the Columbia River) and stay on 238th Dr as it curves and becomes 242nd. Turn left on Stark St which is the fourth stop light past the freeway. Turn right into the hospital entrance and park in an outlying spot.

Event Info: YR687 is suitable for strollers & wheelchairs if you use the option listed on the directions. Pets are not allowed on the Mt. Hood Community College campus. Walks are rated 1+-2. Bike is rated 2. Bikers must sign waiver. Helmets are recommended.

Hillsboro - 31km Bike (YR099) **Jan 1-Dec 31** Credit Only Event
Sponsoring Club: AVA-745, Tualatin Valley Volks
POC: Sheila Day, 503-324-6191. 41320 NW Lodge Rd, Banks OR 97106

Start Point: Tuality Community Hospital, 335 SE 8th Ave. Do NOT call Start Point. From Portland take Hwy 26 W to Hillsboro/Cornelius Pass Rd exit. Cornell Rd to Hillsboro, then 10th to Baseline, then 8th to Hospital.

Event Info: Daily, 8-dusk. Rated 1+. Remember to sign waiver. Bicycle helmets required for persons under age 16. Possible fines of up to $25 for non-compliance.

Hillsboro - 10km Walk (YR098) **Jan 1-Dec 31** Credit Only Event
Sponsoring Club: AVA-745, Tualatin Valley Volks
POC: Sheila Day, 503-324-6191. 41320 NW Lodge Rd, Banks OR 97106

Start Point: Hallmark Inn Restaurant/Lounge, 3500 NE Cornell Rd. Please do not call start point. From Portland take Hwy 26 W to Hillsboro/Cornelius Pass Rd exit. Cornell Rd into Hillsboro. Start across from Airport.

Event Info: Daily, 8-dusk. Rated 1. Suitable for strollers & wheelchairs. Leashed pets.

Klamath Falls - 10km Walk (YR368) **Apr 1-Dec 31**
Sponsoring Club: AVA-546, Pelican Pacers Volkssport Club
POC: Bonnie Wellington, 503-882-7190/Barbara Welch, 503-883-4118. PO Box 7599, Klamath Falls OR 97602

Start Point: Merle West Medical Center, 2865 Daggett Ave. Turn east off Hwy 97 at the intersection for Oregon Institute of Technology on Campus Drive. Continue to the top of the hill, turn right on Daggett. Start point is the Information desk in the lobby.

Event Info: Daily, 8-3 hours before sunset. Rated 3. Difficult for wheelchairs & strollers. Pets must be leashed.

Klamath Falls - 10km Walk (YR566) **Apr 1-Dec 31** Credit Only Event
Sponsoring Club: AVA-546, Pelican Pacers Volkssport Club
POC: Bonnie Wellington, 503-882-7190. PO Box 7599, Klamath Falls OR 97602

Start Point: Econolodge Motel, 75 Main St. Take City Center exit off of Hwy 97. Start point is in the lobby.

Event Info: Motels offer discounts to volkssporters. Daily, 8-3 hours before sunset. Rated 3. Not suitable for strollers or wheelchairs. Pets must be leashed.

Klamath Falls - 10km Walk (YR805) **Apr 1-Sept 30**
Sponsoring Club: AVA-546, Pelican Pacers
POC: Bonnie Wellington, 503-882-7190. PO Box 7599, Klamath Falls, OR 97602

Start Point: Gary's Grocery & Deli, 224 Nevada St.

Lafayette - 10km Walk (YR542) **Jan 1-Dec 31**
Sponsoring Club: AVA-700, Mac Trackers
POC: Velma Dennis, 503-864-2981. PO Box 923, Lafayette, OR 97127

Start Point: Bill's Market, 503-864-2428. 293 Bridge St. From Portland, take I-5 to Tigard exit. Then take 99 West through Tigard & Newberg to Lafayette. Market is on left side of Hwy at west end of town.

Event Info: Daily, dawn to dusk. Rated 2. Strollers & wheelchairs will have difficulty with approximately 2km of gravel road.

Lake Oswego - Two 10km Walks (YR405 & YR611) **Jan 1-Dec 31** Credit Only Events
Sponsoring Club: AVA-242, Columbia River Volkssport Club
POC: Julia Ferreira, 503-636-5520. 2161 Crest Dr, Lake Oswego OR 97034

Start Point: Finish Line Sports, 333 S. State St. Located 8 miles S of Portland & 6 miles N of West Linn on State Hwy 43 (I-205 exit 8 for West Linn or I-5 exit 299 for Macadam Ave).

Event Info: Mon-Fri, 10-7; Sat, 10-5 & Sun, 11-5. Closed major holidays. Trails are rated 2. Not suitable for wheelchairs. Okay for strollers. Pets must be leashed.

Lake Oswego - 11km Walk (YR793-Village) & 12km Walk (YR545-Lake) **Jan 1-Dec 31** Credit Only Event
Sponsoring Club: AVA-752, Lake Oswego Puddle Jumpers
POC: The Parsons, 503-620-4467. 5433 SW Red Leaf, Lake Oswego OR 97035

Start Point: Vienna Coffee Co, 503-620-4467. 406 "A" Avenue. From I-5 take exit 292. At the top of the ramp, turn left on Kruse Way to Boones Ferry. Turn left on Boones Ferry to Country Club Rd. Turn right and follow Country Club until it becomes "A" Ave. Follow "A" to 4th. Start is on the corner. Buses #35, #36, #37, and #78 serve Lake Oswego.

Event Info: Daily, 7-5. YR793 is rated 2 & YR545 is rated 2+. Suitable for strollers. A challenge for wheelchairs. Pets must be leashed.

Lake Oswego - 11km Walk (YR605) **Jan 1-Dec 31** Credit Only Event
Sponsoring Club: AVA-752, Lake Oswego Puddle Jumpers
POC: The Parsons, 503-620-4467. 5433 SW Red Leaf, Lake Oswego OR 97035

Start Point: Private Residence, 5433 SW Red Leaf St. From I-5 Northbound take exit 290 and turn right on Boones Ferry Rd. From I-5 Southbound take exit 290 and turn left on Boones Ferry Rd. Go approximately 1 mile to Pilkington Rd and turn right to Red Leaf. Turn left on Red Leaf. Start is the 1st house on the left. Please park on street.

Event Info: Daily, dawn to dusk. Rated 1+. Not suitable for strollers or wheelchairs. Pets must be leashed.

Lake Oswego - 10km Walk (YR578) **Jan 1-Dec 31** Credit Only Event
Sponsoring Club: AVA-752, Lake Oswego Puddle Jumpers
POC: The Parsons, 503-620-4467. 5433 SW Red Leaf St, Lake Oswego, OR 97035

Start Point: McDonald's, 503-620-4467. 16044 SW Boones Ferry Rd. From I-5 North or South, take exit 292, turn left on Kruse Way to Lower Boones Ferry Rd. Turn right on Lower Boones Ferry to start on left side approximately 1 mile.

Event Info: Daily, dawn to dusk. Rated 1+. Leashed pets. Okay for strollers & wheelchairs.

Lebanon - 10km Walk (YR415) & 28km Bike (YR416) **Jan 1-Dec 31** Credit Only Events
Sponsoring Club: AVA-474, Albany Fitwalkers
POC: Chuck Boeder, 503-967-9162. PO Box 1218, Albany OR 97321

Start Point: Lebanon Community Hospital, 525 Santiam Hwy. From I-5 southbound take exit 233. Turn east (on Hwy 20/Santian Hwy). Go 11 miles, hospital is on the left as you enter town. From I-5 northbound, exit 228 and go east on Hwy 34. Seven miles and turn left at Hwy 20/Santiam Hwy. Hospital is on right.

Event Info: Bike is rated 1. Bikers should wear helmets and must sign waiver. No water or restrooms are available on the bike route. Pets must be leashed and are not recommended on the bike. Walk is rated 1. Strollers & wheelchairs may have difficulty.

Lincoln City - Three 10km Walks (YR311-Around Town, YR312-Road's End & YR313-Siletz Bay) **Jan 1-Dec 31**
Sponsoring Club: AVA-727, Lincoln Fogchasers
POC: Lucille Fenske, 503-994-5998. PO Box 151, Neotsu, OR 97364

Start Point: Sea Gypsy Motel, 145 NW Inlet. One block west of Hwy 101.

Event Info: Daily, dawn to dusk. Trails are rated 2 except for YR313 which is rated 3 at high tide. YR311 is suitable for strollers & wheelchairs. YR312 & YR313 are on the beach.

Madras - 11/13km Walk (YR514) **Jan 1-Dec 31**
Sponsoring Club: AVA-493, Ponderosa Pathfinders
POC: Dianne Erdman, 503-389-4707. 905 NE Franklin, Bend OR 97701

Start Point: Mountain View Hospital, Emergency Room Desk. 470 NE "A" St. From Hwy 26 or 97, turn E on "B" St. Seven blocks to 12th St. Left on 12th one block to "A" St. Right on "A" two blocks to hospital.

Event Info: Daily, dawn to dusk. Rated 3+.

McMinnville - Two 10km Walks (YR571-Country & YR668-City) **Jan 1-Dec 31**
Sponsoring Club: AVA-700, Mac Trackers
POC: Traci Bruchok, 503-472-0772. 1412 East 3rd, McMinnville, OR 97128

Start Point: McMinnville Community Hospital. 603 S Baker St. Take I-5 from Portland to Tigard exit. Take Hwy 99 west through Tigard, Newberg & Lafayette to McMinnville. Follow Adams St (one way) to hospital at intersection of Adams & Baker.

Event Info: Daily, dawn to dusk. Both trails are rated 1. Strollers & wheelchairs will have some difficulty due to very narrow road shoulders on country walk.

Millersburg - 11km Walk (YR666) & 27km Bike (YR667) **Jan 1-Dec 31**
Sponsoring Club: AVA-474, Albany Fitwalkers
POC: Chuck Boeder 503-967-9162. PO Box 1218, Albany OR 97321

Start Point: Private Residence, 503-967-9162. 2908 Millersburg Dr, NE (about 1 mile off I-5). I-5 north or south bound exit 238, turn west at stop sign. Turn right at 1st side road (Morningstar). 1/10 mile turn left at Millersburg Dr. Start is the yellow & white house 1/2 mile down on the left. Start box is in a special room by garage.

Event Info: Daily, dawn to dusk. No restrooms available at start. Trails are rated 1.

Monmouth - 10km Walk (YR796) **Jan 1-Dec 31** Credit Only Event
Sponsoring Club: AVA-362, Willamette Wanderers
POC: Charlotte Copeland, 503-838-1641. 1575 Monmouth Independence Hwy, Monmouth, OR 97361

Start Point: Private Home, 1575 Monmouth Independence Hwy.

Event Info: Daily, dawn to dusk. Rated 1. Okay for strollers & wheelchairs. Leashed pets.

Mt Angel - 11km Walk (YR022) **Jan 1-Dec 31**
Sponsoring Club: AVA-349, Angel Trekkers
POC: Don West, 503-845-9306/503-845-6022. PO Box 66, Mt. Angel OR 97362

Start Point: Burger Time, 450 N. Main St. From I-5 N take the Woodburn exit #271 & follow State Hwy 214 to Mt. Angel, about 10 miles. From I-5 S take the Market St exit #256 at Salem and follow signs and State Hwy 213 east through Silverton to Mt Angel, about 16 miles.

Event Info: Mon-Sat, 7-dusk; Sun, 9-dusk. Closed Easter, Oktoberfest (9/14-17), Thanksgiving & Christmas. During Oktoberfest the start will be in front of City Hall at 1 Garfield St. Rated 2. Pets must be leashed. Suitable for strollers but not recommended for wheelchairs.

Newberg - Two 10km Walks, (YR356-Country & YR357-City) **Jan 1 - Dec 31** Credit Only Events
Sponsoring Club: AVA-496, Newberg Healthnuts
POC: Lyle Wilson, 503-538-3402. 610 S. Willamette, Newberg OR 97132

Start Point: Private residence: 812 N. Meridian. from I-5 take Exit 294. Proceed west on 99W for about 18 miles. In Newberg, the highway will make a sharp right and become one way. Continue 3 blocks on one way and turn right on Meridian. Start point is on the right just before the railroad tracks approx. 7 blocks down.

Event Info: Daily, 7 A.M. to dusk. Trails are rated 2. City walk contains a two block section of gravel. Not suitable for wheelchairs. Pets must be leashed.

Newport - Two 10km Walks (YR438-Center/Aquarium & YR665-Oceanfront) **Jan 1-Dec 31**
Sponsoring Club: AVA-727, Lincoln Fogchasers Volkssport Club
POC: Lucille Fenske, 503-994-5998. PO Box 151, Neotsu, OR 97364

Start Point: Oregon State University/Hatfield Marine Science Center, 2030 Marine Science Dr. Starts near the Oregon Coast Aquarium. Take Hwy 101 to South Beach, south side of the Yaquina Bay bridge from Newport. Exit Hwy 101 following signs to the Science Center. Self start box is located outside to the right of the Center entrance. For walk 665, register and pick up map before driving to the Yaquina Bay Lighthouse State Park.

Event Info: Daily, dawn to dusk. Trails are rated 2 & 3. Strollers & wheelchairs are not recommended. No IVV Books available at start.

North Bend - 11km Walk (YR494) **Jan 1-Dec 31**
Sponsoring Club: AVA-507, South Coast Wavewalkers
POC: Ann Warner, 503-756-6212. 494 Lombard, North Bend, OR 97459

Start Point: McDonald's, corner of Newmark & Broadway.

Event Info: Rated 1-2. Not suitable for wheelchairs & strollers would have difficulty.

Oregon City - 10km Walk (YR273) **Jan 1-Dec 31** Credit Only Event
Sponsoring Club: AVA-253, Valley Volkswalkers
POC: Pat Miller, 206-254-8009. 1609 SE 14th Court, Vancouver, WA 98684

Start Point: Willamette Falls Hospital, 1500 Division St. From I-205 take exit 9 (Oregon City). Go left on McLoughlin Blvd. Turn left on 14th Ave (by Union 76 station). At signal light turn left on Washington. Turn right on 15th and go up the hill until you see the hospital straight ahead at the flashing light. Please DO NOT park in the Hospital lot. Use street parking.

Event Info: Daily, dawn to dusk. Rated 3. Not suitable for strollers or wheelchairs due to stairs. Pets must be leashed.

Portland - Two 10km Walks (YR033 & YR409) **Jan 1-Dec 31**
Sponsoring Club: AVA-446, Rose City Roamers
POC: Carol Ottoson, 503-774-2072. 5960 SE Tibbetts, Portland OR 97206

Start Point: Providence Medical Center, 503-230-1111. 4805 NE Glisan. I-84 east, exit 3. Right on Glisan to 49th. Right to parking. Start box is adjacent to Securities desk.

Event Info: Daily, dawn to dusk. Trails are rated 1+. Each event has two routes available. Only one event credit even if doing both routes on each trail.

Portland - 10/14/24km Walk (YR410) & 10/12km Walk (YR411) **Jan 1-Dec 31**
Sponsoring Club: AVA-446, Rose City Roamers
POC: Carol Ottoson, 503-774-2072. 5960 SE Tibbetts, Portland, OR 97206

Start Point: Good Samaritan Hospital, 503-229-7711. 1015 NW 22nd Ave. I-405, exit 3 Vaughn St. Left on 23rd to Northrup. Left to 22nd. Right to Marshall. left to parking. Start in switchboard area adjacent to main lobby Info desk.

Event Info: Daily, dawn to dusk. Trails are rated 1+ to 3. Both events have multiple trails. You can receive only one event credit per event, even if doing all trails.

Portland - Three 10km Walks (YR256-Downtown, YR257-Forest & YR258-Pittock Mansion) **Jan 2-Dec 31**
Sponsoring Club: AVA-446, Rose City Roamers
POC: Carol Ottoson, 503-774-2072. 5960 SE Tibbetts, Portland OR 97206

Start Point: Food Front Cooperative Grocery, 2375 NW Thurman. I-405, exit 3. Vaughn St. Left on 23rd to Thurman. Right one block. Please do not park in their lot.

Event Info: Daily, 9-9. Closed New Year's, July 4th, Labor Day, Thanksgiving & Christmas. Trails are rated 1+ to 3+. Not suitable for strollers or wheelchairs.

Portland - Two 10km Walks (YR675 & YR676) **Jan 1-Dec 31**
Sponsoring Club: AVA-549, Cedar Milers Volkssport Club
POC: Shirley Corey, 503-646-7908. 10715 NW Jericho Ct, Portland, OR 97229

Start Point: Sunset Athletic Club, 503-645-3535. 13939 NW Cornell Rd. I-5 to US 26 West, exit Murray Rd, turn right. At Cornell Rd (1st light) turn left.

Event Info: Mon-Fri, 5:30-3 hour before dusk; Sat, 7-3 hours before dusk; Sun 9-3 hours before dusk. You must be off the trail by dusk. Remember that winter months have shorter daylight hours. Trails are rated 1+ and 3. Trail rated 1+ is suitable for strollers but wheelchairs might have difficulty. Trail rated 3 is not suitable for strollers or wheelchairs. Pets must be leashed.

Portland - Two 10km Walks (YR347 & YR406) & 25/35km Bike (YR346) **Jan 1-Dec 31** Credit Only Events
Sponsoring Club: AVA-242, Columbia River Volkssport Club
POC: Howard Bauer, 503-252-2683. 3333 NE 135th Ave, Portland OR 97230

Start Point: Videoland, 10302 NE Sandy Blvd. North on I-205, exit 23A, Sandy Blvd. Continue east on Sandy to NE 103rd, approximately 8 blocks. Southbound on I-205, take exit 23A, Sandy Blvd. Continue east on Sandy to NE 103rd, approximately 6 blocks.

Event Info: Daily, 10-10. $1.50 charge to take elevator to Grotto bluff on YR406. Trails are rated 1+.

Portland - 10km Walk (YR412) **Jan 1-Dec 31** Credit Only Event
Sponsoring Club: AVA-242, Columbia River Volkssport Club
POC: Allan Van Hoeter, 503-246-4619. 8330 SW 43rd Ave, Portland, OR 97219-3525

Start Point: Columbia Sportswear Outlet, 8128 SE 13th Ave. From Northbound on I-5, take Corbett St exit 298. Turn right on Corbett to SW Nebraska (approximately 1 mile). Turn left to SW Macadam (approximately 3 blocks). Turn right onto Macadam to Sellwood Bridge. Turn left onto Sellwood Bridge to SE 13th and Tacoma. Turn right on 13th - 1/2 block to start. From I-5 Southbound, take exit 299A, Lake Oswego, Johns Landing, Macadam exit south to Macadam to Sellwood Bridge. Continue as above.

Event Info: Mon-Fri, 9-6; Sat, 9-5; Sun, 12-5. Closed major holidays. Rated 1+. Suitable for strollers & wheelchairs. Pets must be leashed.

Portland - 11km Walk (YR366) **Jan 1-Dec 31** Credit Only Event
Sponsoring Club: AVA-738, Y.B. Normal Adventurers
POC: Gary Stong, 503-538-7462. 812 N. Meridian, Newberg OR 97132

Start Point: Tyron Creek State Park Nature Center, 11321 SW Terwilliger Blvd. From I-5 North take exit 297. Go South on Terwilliger Blvd. From the south on I-5 take exit 296A. Turn right onto Barber Blvd then right to Terwilliger Blvd. Follow State Park signs to park, about 3 miles.

Event Info: Daily, 7-sunset. Rated 3+. Sturdy shoes recommended. Walkers are urged to carry water. Not suitable for wheelchairs or strollers. Dogs must be leashed.

Portland - 10km Walk (YR615) & 25km Bike (YR840) **Jan 1-Dec 31** Credit Only Events
Sponsoring Club: AVA-552, East County Windwalkers
POC: East County Windwalkers, 503-774-3887 or 503-663-9222. 9242 SE Harney Ct, Portland OR 97266

Start Point: Portland Adventist Medical Center-Lobby, 10323 SE Market. Near I-205, 8 miles east of downtown. From I-205 North take exit 21A, Glisan St/Stark St. Stay in right lane through first light, turn left at third light (Washington St). Get into right lane and turn right at 96th Ave (the first street). Turn left onto Main, the first street past Mall 205. Turn right at 100th Ave and turn left into hospital parking lot. From I-205 South, take exit 20, Washington/Start St. Turn right at first light (Washington St). Turn right at 96th Ave and continue as above.

Event Info: Trails are rated 1+. Bikers must sign waiver. Helmets are recommended.

Portland - Two 10km Walks (YR173 & YR427) **Jan 1-Dec 31** Credit Only Events
Sponsoring Club: AVA-552, East County Windwalkers
POC: East County Windwalkers, 503-774-3887 or 503-663-9222. PO Box 854, Gresham, OR 97030

Start Point: Woodland Park Hospital, 10300 NE Hancock. From I-205 North take exit 21A, Glisan St. Turn right on Glisan and go to 102nd Ave. Turn left on 102nd for five or six blocks, past four stop lights to Hancock St. Turn right to the Hospital. From I-205 South, take exit 21A, Glisan St. Turn left on Glisan and go to 102nd Ave and continue as above. From the West, take I-84 to exit 7, Halsey/Gateway District. Continue to 102nd Ave, turn left and proceed to Hancock St. From the East, take I-84 to I-205 South and exit at Glisan St (Exit 21A) and follow directions above.

Event Info: Trails are rated 1-2.

Portland - 10km Skate (YR822) **Jan 1-Dec 31** Credit Only Event
Sponsoring Club: AVA-738, Y-B Normal Adventurers
POC: Gary Stong, 503-538-7462. 812 N. Meridian, Newberg, OR 97132

Start Point: ICU Skate Company, 503-497-9083. 115 SW Ash St. From I-5 south take the Front St exit. Continue on Front St to Ash. Turn left on Ash to start. From I-5 north, take 405 north exiting on 4th St. Continue on 4th, turn right on Ash.

Event Info: Summer hrs: Mon-Sat, 11-8; Sun 11-6. Winter hrs: 11-6. Jan-Mar closed on Sunday. Call ahead for hours due to closure for special events. Rated 1+. Suitable for strollers & wheelchairs. Pets must be leashed. Roller blade rentals Available.

Portland - 10km Walk (YR754) **Jan 1-Dec 31** Credit Only Event
Sponsoring Club: AVA-738, Y-B Normal Adventurers
POC: Gary Stong, 503-538-7462. 812 N. Meridian, Newberg, OR 97132

Start Point: Red Lion Jantzen Beach, 503-283-4466. 909 N Hayden Island Dr. On I-5 take Jantzen Beach Exit #308 just S of the Interstate Bridge. Hotel is on the east side of bridge.

Event Info: Daily, dawn to dusk. Rated 1+. Okay for strollers, no wheelchairs. Leashed pets.

Rockaway Beach - Two 10km Walks ((YR684 & 685) **Jan 1-Dec 31** Credit Only Events
Sponsoring Club: AVA-738, Y.B. Normal Adventurers
POC: Gary Stong, 503-538-7462. 812 N. Meridian, Newberg OR 97132

Start Point: Silver Sands Motel, 215 Pacific St. For reservations, 1-800-457-8972. From Portland take Hwy 26 to Hwy 6 and Hwy 6 to Tillamook. In Tillamook follow Hwy 101 N to Rockaway Beach. Turn west on 2nd St and go two block to the Motel.

Event Info: 8-dusk daily. Trails are rated 1+. Each route crosses two streams. Your feet will get wet. Not accessible for wheelchairs and difficult for strollers. Pets are welcome.

Roseburg - Two 10km Walks (YR164 & YR084) **Jan 2-Dec 31** Credit Only Events
Sponsoring Club: AVA-472, Umpqua Valley Walkers
POC: Leola Beck, 503-672-8518. 888 W. Indianola, Roseburg OR 97470

Start: Douglas Community Hospital, 748 West Harvard Ave. At I-5 exit 124.

Event Info: Daily, dawn to dusk. Rated 1+. Suitable for strollers & wheelchairs. No dogs allowed on veterans facility #94-084. Alternate route available.

Salem - 10km Walk (YR688) **Jan 1-Dec 31**
Sponsoring Club: AVA-362, Willamette Wanderers
POC: Mary Brillhart, 503-581-4385. PO Box 13982, Salem, OR 97309

Start Point: Execu-Lodge, 503-363-4123. 200 Commercial St.

Seaside - 10km Walk (YR300) **Jan 1-Dec 31**
Sponsoring Club: AVA-679, Turnaround Trekkers
POC: Pauline Vincent, 503-738-5960. PO Box 975, Seaside, OR 97138-0975

Start Point: Seaside Chamber of Commerce, 7 N. Roosevelt Dr. Stay on Hwy 101 to stop light at junction of Hwy 101 (Roosevelt Dr) and Broadway. Turn E off Hwy 101 and then left off Broadway into parking lot. Please park away from Chamber building.

Event Info: Rated 1. Jan 1-Apr 30 & Nov 1-Dec 31, 9-5 Mon-Fri; 10-4 on Sat; and 12-4 on Sun. 8 May 1-Sep 30, 8-6 Mon-Sat and 9-5 on Sun. Oct 1-31, 8-5 Mon-Sat & 9-5 on Sun. Closed New Year's, Thanksgiving, & Christmas. (Early start box available in entrance area of Chamber of Commerce.)

Silverton - 11km Walk (YR171) **Apr 15-Oct 31** Credit Only Event
Sponsoring Club: AVA-425, Silverton Walk Abouts
POC: Cathie Bittler, 503-845-9499. 14433 Marquam Rd, Mt. Angel, OR 97362

Start Point: Silver Fall's State Park. Roth's IGA, 918 North 1st St. Roth's is at north edge of town along Hwy 214.

Event Info: The Park is 14 miles SE of Silverton. $3.00 per car fee May 13-Sep 24. Daily, dawn to dusk. Rated 3+. Not suitable for strollers or wheelchairs. Pets not permitted.

Silverton - 11km Walk (YR106) & 25km Bike (YR686) **Jan 1-Dec 31** Credit Only Events
Sponsoring Club: AVA-425, Silverton Walk Abouts
POC: Dorothy Hettwer, 503-634-2498. 12481 Wilco Hwy NE, Mt Angel OR 97362

Start Point: Silverton Hospital, 342 Fairview St. Follow blue hospital signs at entrances to Silverton.

Event Info: Daily, dawn to dusk. Walk is rated 2+. Bike is rated 2. Strollers okay, no wheelchairs. Leashed pets. Bikers must sign waiver. Helmets are recommended.

Springfield - 11km Walk (YR800) & 28km Bike (YR801) **Jan 7-Dec 31**
Sponsoring Club: AVA-455, Eugene-Springfield Mossback Volkssport Club
POC: Frank Ross, 503-726-7169. 2398 North 8th, Springfield, OR 97477

Start Point: McKenzie Willamette Hospital, 1460 "G" St.

Event Info: Trails are rated 1. Suitable for strollers & wheelchairs.

St Paul - 10km Walk (YR218) **Jan 1-Dec 31** Credit Only Event
Sponsoring Club: AVA-567, The Walking Connection
POC: Marge Bergeron, 503-636-1025. 5276 West Sunset Dr, Lake Oswego, OR 97035.

Start: Champoeg State Park Visitor's Center, 8239 Champoeg Rd, NE. I-5 from North or South, exit 278. Follow signs (approx 6 mi) to Park Entrance. Turn west (right off of the Freeway if from the North, left if from the South) on Ehlen Rd which becomes Yergen Rd (3.6 miles). Turn right on Case Rd for 1.4 miles. Turn left on West Champoeg Rd for 1.0 miles to the park entrance.

Event Info: Seasonal Park fee. Daily, 9-4. Closed New Year's, Thanksgiving & Christmas. Rated 1+. Suitable for strollers but no wheelchair access. Pets must be leashed.

Stayton - 11km Walk (YR090) **Jan 1-Dec 22**
Sponsoring Club: AVA-479, Buffalo Quick Steppers
POC: Dale Goble, 503-769-6774. PO Box G, Stayton, OR 97383

Start Point: Buffalo Quick Print, 503-769-6774. 570 N 3rd Ave. 12 miles E of Salem. From I-5 north or south take the Hwy 22 (Stayton/Detroit Dam) exit and go east 12 miles to the Stayton/Sublimity exit. Turn right and go into town. After the 1st stop light you will be on 1st Ave. Go to the next light and turn left onto Washington. Go two blocks to Third Ave and turn right. Go two blocks to Buffalo Quick Print.

Event Info: Mon-Fri, 9-2. Finish by 5. Closed major holidays. Call ahead if there is a question about hours or days available. Rated 1+. Suitable for strollers & wheelchairs with alternate that allows bypass of unpaved areas.

Tigard - 10km Walk (YR056) **Jan 1-Dec 31** Credit Only Event
Sponsoring Club: AVA-253, Valley Volkswalkers
POC: Lee Byington, 503-643-4772. 5992 SW Heights Lane, Beaverton, OR 97007

Start Point: McDonald's, 12388 SW Scholl's Ferry Rd. From I-5 Northbound, follow signs to US 26 via I-405. Turn south on Hwy 217 to Scholl's Ferry Rd exit. Right onto Scholl's Ferry approximately 1 miles to N Dakota St (at the light). Left on N Dakota and left again on McDonald's access road. From I-5 Southbound, take exit 292. Go North on Hwy 217 (signs say Tigard/Beaverton) to Scholl's Ferry exit. Turn left onto Scholl's Ferry, crossing over Hwy 217. See above directions to McDonald's.

Event Info: Daily, dawn to dusk. May open late on Jan 1. Rated 1. Suitable for strollers & wheelchairs. Pets must be leashed.

Troutdale - 10km Walk (YR196) **Jan 1-Dec 31**
Sponsoring Club: AVA-552, East County Windwalkers
POC: East County Windwalkers, 503-663-9222 or 503-665-4942. PO Box 854, Gresham, OR 97030

Start Point: Burger, King, 366 SW Frontage Rd. Start box is near the water fountain. Westbound on I-84, take exit 17, Troutdale. Turn left at the stop sign. Turn right at 2nd stop sign. Burger King is immediately on your left. Eastbound on I-84, take exit 17, Troutdale to Frontage Rd. Burger King is about 1/2 mile down on the right.

Event Info: Rated 1+.

Waldport - Two 10km Walks (YR348 & YR436) **Jan 1-Dec 31** YR436 is a Credit Only Event
Sponsoring Club: AVA-695, Yachats Coastal Gems
POC: Shirley's, 503-547-3292. PO Box 896, Yachats OR 97498

Start Point: Ray's Food Place, 503-563-3542. North side of Hwy 34 about six blocks east of Hwy 101.

Event Info: Daily, 8-9. Closed Christmas. Variable hours on other holidays. Trails are rated 2. Strollers with difficulty. Not recommended for wheelchairs. Pets must be leashed.

Warrenton - 10km Walk (YR174) & 25km Bike (YR435) **Jan 1-Dec 31** Bike is a Credit Only Event
Sponsoring Club: AVA-679, Turnaround Trekkers
POC: Donna Byes, 503-861-1818(weekdays) or 503-738-0139 (evenings & weekends). PO Box 975, Seaside, OR 97138-0975

Start Point: KOA Campground, 1100 Ridge Rd. Traveling north from Seaside, or south from Astoria, follow the signs to Fort Stevens State Park. The KOA Campground is on Ridge Rd across from the main entrance to the park. Register here & drive to start point for the walk. Bike starts at KOA Campground.

Event Info: Daily, dawn-dusk. Walk is rated 2, bike 1+. Not suitable for strollers or wheelchairs. Recommended that you carry water. Bikers must wear a helmet and sign a release form.

Washburne - 10km Walk (YR664) **Mar 1-Nov 1**
Sponsoring Club: AVA-695, Yachats Coastal Gems
POC: Shirley's, 503-547-3292. PO Box 896, Yachats OR 97498

Start Point: Carl G. Washburne Memorial State Park. Midway between Yachats & Florence on Hwy 101. Register at Shirley's in Yachats (see Yachats listing for hours) or The Sportsman in Florence (see Florence listing for hours).

Event Info: Rated 2. Not recommended for strollers or wheelchairs. Pets must be leashed.

West Linn - 11km Walk (YR473) **Apr 1-Oct 31** Credit Only Event
Sponsoring Club: AVA-253, Valley Volkswalkers
POC: Marge Bergeron, 503-636-1025. 5276 West Sunset Dr, Lake Oswego, OR 97035

Start Point: Zupan Food Pavilion, 19133 Willamette Dr (Hwy 43). From Hwy 205 take exit 8 (Oregon City) to Hwy 43. Heading north on Hwy 43, drive 2.4 miles to signal lights at Hidden Springs Rd. Turn left, then right and proceed through Robinwood Center parking lot to Zupan Food Pavillion. Please park in outer area.

Event Info: Daily, 7-5:30. Rated 3. Strollers & wheelchairs not advisable. Leashed pets.

Winchester Bay - 11km Walk (YR846) **Jan 1-Dec 31** Credit Only Event
Sponsoring Club: AVA-507, South Coast Wavewalkers
POC: Ann Warner, 503-756-6212. 494 Lombard, North Bend, OR 97459

Start Point: Winchester Bay Market, 8th St & Hwy 101. From I-5 take Oregon Hwy 38 to US Hwy 101 at Reedsport, then south on Hwy 101 to Winchester Bay. From Coos Bay/North Bend, take Hwy 101 north to Winchester Bay. Turn left on 8th.

Event Info: Daily, 8-dusk. Rated 1+. Suitable for strollers, no wheelchairs. Leashed pets.

Yachats - Two 10km Walks (YR276 & YR752) **Jan 1-Dec 31** YR752 is a Credit Only Event
Sponsoring Club: AVA-695, Yachats Coastal Gems
POC: Shirley's, 503-547-3292. PO Box 896, Yachats OR 97498

Start Point: Shirley's, 271 Hwy 101, downtown.

Event Info: Daily, 9:30-5. Closed major holidays. YR276 rated 1. Suitable for strollers. Wheelchairs will have difficulty with gravel. YR752 is rated 2+. Not suitable for strollers or wheelchairs. Pets must be leashed.

Yamhill - 10km Walk (YR534) **Jan 1-Dec 31**
Sponsoring Club: AVA-700, McMinnville Mac Trackers
POC: Tammy McCarley, 503-472-5970. PO Box 710, Carlton, OR 97111

Start Point: T & E General Store, 110 N Maple. From I-5 North take Hwy 99 W . Exit at Tigard to Newberg. At stoplight at west end of Newberg, turn right on Hwy 240 to Yamhill. (Yamhill is on Hwy 47 between Forest Grove & McMinnville).

Event Info: Mon-Sat, 8 A.M.-9 P.M.; Sun, 9:30-7. Rated 2+.

PENNSYLVANIA

Chambersburg - 10km Walk (YR127) **Jan 2-Dec 30** Credit Only Event
Sponsoring Club: AVA-171, Cumberland Valley LeadFoot Club
POC: James Humelsine, 717-263-8633. PO Box 371, Shippensburg PA 17257-0371

Start Point: Olympia Ice Cream Parlor, 43 S Main. 1/2 block south and west of the intersection of US-11 South and US-30 West.

Event Info: Closed major holidays. Mon-Sat, 11-2 hrs before dusk; Sun, noon-2 hrs before dusk. Rated 1+. Suitable for strollers. Pets must be leashed.

Harrisburg - 11km Walk (YR745) **Jan 1-Dec 31**
Sponsoring Club: AVA-328, Susquehanna Rovers
POC: Shirley Disend, 717-564-0488. 409 Latshmere Dr, Harrisburg PA 17109

Start Point: Quality Inn - Riverfront, 525 S Front St.

Event Info: Daily, dawn to dusk. Rated 1+. Suitable for strollers & wheelchairs but some curbs lack cuts. Pets must be leashed.

Johnstown - 10km Walk (YR876) **Jan 1-Dec 31** Credit Only Event
Sponsoring Club: AVA-408, Altoona-Johnstown Summit Striders
POC: Sandra Zimmerman, 814-266-1854. 839 Leisure Ave, Johnstown, PA 15904

Start Point: Holiday Inn Downtown, 814-535-7777. 250 Market St.

Event Info: Daily, dawn to dusk. Closed Christmas & New Years. Rated 3+. Not suitable for strollers or wheelchairs. Pets must be leashed.

Kleinfeltersville - 10km Walk (YR484) & 28km Bike (YR483) **Mar 1-Oct 22**
Sponsoring Club: AVA-579, Penn Dutch Pacers Volksmarch Club, Inc.
POC: Russel Bechtold, 717-285-5855. 3471 Dawn View Dr, Lancaster, PA 17601

Start Point: Visitors Center at Middle Creek Wildlife Management Area.

Event Info: Tues-Sat, 9-2; Sun, noon-2. Finish by 4. Closed Mondays & holidays. Walk is rated 1+. Suitable for strollers & wheelchairs. Pets must be leashed. Bike is rated 2+. Bikers must sign waiver & a helmet and gloves are strongly recommended.

Lancaster - 11km Walk (YR137) & 25km Bike (YR488) **Jan 1-Dec 31**
Sponsoring Club: AVA-579, Penn Dutch Pacers Volksmarch Club, Inc.
POC: Russ Bechtold, 717-285-5855. PO Box 7445, Lancaster PA 17604-7445

Register: Your Place Country Inn, 2133 Lincoln Hwy E. Bike starts here. You must drive into Lancaster for the start of the walk trail.

Event Info: Daily, dawn to dusk. Walk is rated 1+. Suitable for strollers. Bike is rated 2+. Bikers must sign waiver. Helmets and gloves are recommended. DO NOT TAKE FACIAL PHOTOS OF OUR AMISH NEIGHBORS. Pets must be leashed.

Newport - 10km Walk (YR110) **Jan 1-Dec 31**
Sponsoring Club: AVA-328, Susquehanna Rovers
POC: Louise A. Clouser, 717-567-9537. RD4, Box 461, Newport PA 17074

Register: Sharar's Grocery, 19 South 2nd St

Start Point: Little Buffalo State Park. Access from Routes 322 & 34.

Event Info: Mon-Sat, 8-10; Sun, 9-9. Closed Christmas. Rated 3+. Not suitable for strollers or wheelchairs. Pets must be leashed.

Ohiopyle State Park - 10km Walk (YR471) & 25km Bike (YR470) **Mar 1-Oct 28** Credit Only Events
Sponsoring Club: AVA-408, Altoona-Johnstown Summit Striders
POC: Sandra Zimmerman, 814-266-1854. 839 Leisure Ave, Johnstown PA 15904

Start Point: Laurel Highlands Outdoor Ctr. behind Falls City Baptist Church, 800-472-3846. North of Rt 40 on PA 381.

Event Info: Daily, 9-4. Closed Easter. Walk is rated 3. Not suitable for strollers or wheelchairs. Overcrowded conditions may occur during summer weekends. Bike is rated 1. Bikes can be rented from Laurel Highlands Outdoor Ctr.

Philadelphia - 10km Walk (YR482) **Jan 1-Dec 31**
Sponsoring Club: AVA-238, Liberty Bell Wanderers
POC: Joan Lampart, 215-722-3095. 513 E. Alcott St, Philadelphia, PA 19120

Start Point: Holiday Inn, 4th & Arch St. 215-923-8660. Special rates for volkssporters.

Event Info: Daily, 8-dusk. Rated 1. Suitable for strollers. Wheelchairs would have a little difficulty. Pets must be leashed.

State College - 10km Walk (YR744) **Jan 1-Dec 31**
Sponsoring Club: AVA-726, Nittany Nomads
POC: Becky Nordberg, 814-238-1039. 110 Horseshoe Rd, Pennsylvania Furnace, PA 16865

Start Point: Best Western State College Inn, 814-237-8005. 1663 S. Atherton St. Business Rt 322, East of State College.

Event Info: Daily, dawn to dusk. Rated 2. Suitable for strollers. Pets must be leashed.

Valley Forge - 11km Walk (YR288) **Jan 1-Dec 31**
Sponsoring Club: AVA-641, Valley Forge Troopers
POC: Jean Schmidt, 610-539-8343. 417 S. Park Ave, Norristown, PA 19403

Start Point: Valley Forge National Historical Park, Visitors Center at the Book Store.

Event Info: Daily, 9-1:30. Finish by 4:30. Rated 1+. Suitable for strollers & wheelchairs. Pets must be leashed.

RHODE ISLAND

Bristol - 10km Walk (YR365) **Apr 1-Dec 31**
Sponsoring Club: AVA-410, Empire State Capital Volkssporters
POC: Beryl Wolf/Emily Koch, 518-383-2880/374-3588. PO Box 6995, Albany NY 12206

Start Point: Blithewold Gardens, 101 Ferry Rd (Rte 114); 401-253-2707. $4.00 admission fee required. Volks-marchers receive $1.00 off. From Providence, take Exit 2 off Rte 195 in Mass. Follow Rte 136S for 8.5 miles. Turn right onto Griswold Ave, follow to the end & take left onto Ferry Road. Start is on right. From Boston, take Rte 24. Take Mt. Hope Bridge exit, cross the bridge, bear left at fork onto Ferry Road (Rte 114). Start is on the left. From Newport, take Rte 114N. Cross the Mt. Hope Bridge, bear left at fork onto Ferry Road. Start is on left.

Event Info: Hours vary, call if in doubt. No pets. Rated 1. Strollers & wheelchairs with help.

Newport - Two 11km Walks (YR294 & YR729) **Apr 1-Dec 3**
Sponsoring Club: AVA-269, Walk'n Mass Volkssport Club
POC: John H. Woodhouse, Jr, 401-847-1502. 3 Haymaker Rd, Middletown, RI 02842

Start Point: Cliff Walk Manor, 82 Memorial Blvd; 401-847-1300.

Event Info: Daily, 8 to dusk. YR294 is rated 3. YR729 is rated 3.5 (an alternate course rated 2 is available). Not suitable for strollers or wheelchairs. Pets must be leashed & are not allowed in the bird sanctuary.

SOUTH CAROLINA

Columbia - 10km Walk (YR598) **Jan 1-Dec 31**
Sponsoring Club: AVA-NC, Tarheel State Walkers
POC: Paul & Loretta Chasteen, 910-766-6646. PO Box 15013, Winston-Salem, NC 27113.
Local POC: Pat Mahaney, 803-254-0479 (days) 803-783-3781 (nights)

Start Point: Visitor Center, 803-254-0479. 1012 Gervais St.

Alternate Start Point: The Governor's House Hotel, 1301 Main St.

Event Info: Mon-Fri, 9-5; Sat, 10-4. Closed Sunday & major holidays. If staying at the Governor's House, ask for the volksmarcher rate.

SOUTH DAKOTA

Brookings - 10km Walk (YR018) & 25km Bike (YR503) **Apr 1-Dec 31**
Sponsoring Club: AVA-160, Prairie Wanderers
POC: Fayne D. Bell, 605-692-5352 (after 5). 102-14th Ave S, Brookings SD 57006

Start Point: Brookings Hospital, 300 22nd Ave. From I-29 take exit 132 west onto Hwy 14 (6th St) to 22nd Ave. Turn south 3 blocks to hospital on left side of 22nd Ave at 3rd St.

Event Info: Daily, 7-9. Trails are rated 1.

Corona - 10km Walk (YR320) **Jun 3-Sep 24**
Sponsoring Club: AVA-417, South Dakota Parks & Recreation Volkssport Assoc.
POC: Jeff Nodsle, 605-432-6374. RR #1, Box 50, Corona SD 57227

Start Point: Hartford Beach State Park, RR1, Box 51; 605-432-4227.

Event Info: Rated 2. Not suitable for strollers or wheelchairs.

Custer State Park - 10km Walk (YR101) **May 20-Oct 31**
Sponsoring Club: AVA-417, South Dakota Parks & Recreation Volkssport Assoc.
POC: Jon Corey or Sally Svensom, 605-255-4515. HC 83, Box 70, Custer SD 57730

Start Point: Peter Nor Beck Visitor Center. Located on Hwy 16A near the State Game Lodge.

Event Info: Vehicle entrance fee is required. Daily, 8-8.

Dell Rapids - 10km Walk (YR502) **Apr 1-Dec 31**
Sponsoring Club: AVA-160, Prairie Wanderers
POC: Eunice McGee, 605-446-3484. RR 1, Box 53, Colton SD 57108

Start Point: The Rose Stone Inn, 605-428-3698. 504 East 4th St. From I-29 take exit 98 east 3 miles to Hwy 115 and continue 5 blocks to the Inn on the left.

Event Info: Daily, 7 to dusk. Rated 1+

Flandreau - 10km Walk (YR501) **Apr 1-Dec 31**
Sponsoring Club: AVA-160, Prairie Wanderers
POC: Connie Hove, 605-997-2738. RR 2, Box 76, Flandreau SD 57028

Start Point: The Trading Post, 510 E. Pipestone. From I-29 take exit 114 and go east on SD 32 through town to junction with 13. Trading Post is on the left.

Event Info: Mon-Sat, 6 to dusk. Rated 1.

Hot Springs - 10km Walk (YR764) **Apr 1-Sept 30**
Sponsoring Club: AVA-274, Black Hills Volkssport Assn.
POC: Reta Ringer, 605-745-5587. HCR 52, Box 168A, Hot Springs, SD 57747

Start Point: Mammoth Site, 605-745-6017. Hwy 18 truck by-pass within city limits.

Event Info: Apr 1-May 14, 9-2 finish by 5. May 15-Aug 31, 8-5 finish by 8. Sept 1-Sept 30, 9-2 finish by 5. Rated 2. Suitable for strollers but not wheelchairs. Guided tours are available at the Mammoth Site.

Mitchell - 10km Walk (YR186) **Apr 1-Dec 31**
Sponsoring Club: AVA-160, Prairie Wanderers
POC: Shirley Luther, 605-692-5159 after 5. 1511 8th St S, Brookings SD 57006

Start Point: Queen of Peace Hospital, 605-995-2000; 5th & Foster. Mitchell is located in south central South Dakota on I-90 and S.D. Hwys 37 & 38. From I-90 exit 332 north on Burr St to 5th Ave. Right to Foster. From Hwy 37 N or S, go east on 5th Ave to Foster. From East or West on Hwy 38, go north on Burr to 5th Ave then east to Foster.

Event Info: Daily, dawn-dusk. Rated 1.

Pierre - 10km Walk (YR768) **Jan 1-Dec 31**
Sponsoring Club: AVA-417, SDPRA Volkssport Assn.
POC: Gail Brink, 800-962-2034. 800 East Dakota, Pierre, SD 57501

Start Point: MON-FRI: Pierre Area Chamber of Commerce, 800-962-2034. 800 West Dakota. WEEKENDS: Ram Kota Inn, 920 W. Sioux (Hwy 14/34) at the MO River Bridge.

Event Info: Daily, dawn to dusk. Rated 1+

Rapid City - 10km Walk (YR045) **Jan 1-Dec 31**
Sponsoring Club: AVA-274, Black Hills Volkssport Association
POC: Douglas Kapaun, 605-348-5191. 3020 Sunny Hill Cir, Rapid City SD 57702

Start Point: Hotel Alex Johnson, 523 6th St; 605-342-1210.

Event Info: Rated 1.

Rapid City - 25km Bike (YR646) **Apr 1-Nov 30** Credit Only Event
Sponsoring Club: AVA-497, Bandit Hikers
POC: Heidi Lorence, 605-399-1665. 7545 Crossbill Circle, Rapid City, SD 57702

Start Point: Two Wheeler Dealer, 100 East Blvd. N; 605-343-0524. From I-90 exit 58. Drive S on Haines Ave. Left onto Omaha St. Left onto East Blvd. Start is on right.

Event Info: Mon-Fri, 9-8 (After Labor Day the store closes at 5:30); Sat, 9-5; Sun, 12-4. Rated 1. Bicycle rental available on limited basis. Rated 1.

Sioux Falls - 10km Walk (YR505) & 25km Bike (YR506) **Apr 1-Dec 31**
Sponsoring Club: AVA-160, Prairie Wanderers
POC: Sharon Hofstad, 605-338-9100. 1437 North Dr, Sioux Falls SD 57104

Start Point: S & A Conoco, 1322 N. Minnesota Ave. From I-29 take exit 81 east on Russell St to Minnesota. Start is located on SE corner.

Event Info: Mon-Fri, 7-8; Sat & Sun, 8-8. Walk is rated 1+. Bike is rated 1.

Spearfish - 10km Walk (YR035) **Jan 1-Dec 31**
Sponsoring Club: AVA-274, Black Hills Volkssport Association
POC: Cliff Hanson, 605-642-3232. 933 University, Spearfish SD 57783

Start Point: Big D Oil Company, 305 W Jackson Blvd; 605-642-5151.

Event Info: Rated 1.

Sturgis - 11km Walk (YR610) **May 1-Sep 30**
Sponsoring Club: AVA-028, Sturgis Ft. Meade Walkfest Association
POC: Ernest Miller, 605-347-3354. PO Box 504 S Junction Ave, Sturgis SD 57785

Start Point: Star-Lite Motel, 605-347-2506. S Junction 57785 near I-90 Exit 32.

Event Info: Daily, dawn to dusk. Closed Aug 1-15. Rated 3.

Sturgis - 10km Walk (YR532) **May 1-Sep 18**

Sponsoring Club: AVA-417, South Dakota Parks & Recreation Volkssport Assn.
POC: Tony Gullett, 605-347-5240. Box 688, Sturgis SD 57785

Start Point: Bear Butte State Park Visitor's Center; 605-347-5240. Follow Hwy 34 thru Sturgis from I-90. Turn left on SD79.

Event Info: May 1-Jun 1, 9-12. Finish by 4. Jun 1-Aug 31, 8-3. Finish by 7. Aug 31-mid Sep, 9-12. Finish by 4. This mountain is sacred to the Lakota & Cheyenne. Please follow the etiquette guidelines as posted. Rated 3+. Wheelchairs & strollers are not appropriate. Alternate route to the summit is rated 4+.

Watertown - 10km Walk (YR184) **Apr 1-Dec 31**

Sponsoring Club: AVA-160, Prairie Wanderers
POC: Richard & Eunice Solem, 605-874-2437. 711 3rd Ave South, Box 523, Clear Lake SD 57226

Start Point: Prairie Lakes West Hospital, 605-886-8491. 400 10th Ave. NW. From I-29, exit 117 west 3.7 miles to SD 20. Turn right (north) and go 1.5 miles to 10th Ave NW, then turn right again to hospital.

Event Info: Daily, 7-9. Rated 1+.

Yankton - 10km Walk (YR185) & 25km Bike (YR648) **Apr 1-Dec 31**

Sponsoring Club: AVA-160, Prairie Wanderers
POC: Helen Bechtold, 605-692-2902. 618 13th Avenue, Brookings SD 57006

Start Point: Rick's Lake Area Convenience Store. West Hwy 52. From Yankton, go west on SD 52 about three miles to start. Rick's is on the right side of the road.

Event Info: Daily 7-9. Trails are rated 1.

TENNESSEE

Clarksville - 12km Walk (YR523) **Jan 1-Dec 31**

Sponsoring Club: AVA-730, Clarksville Volksmarchers
POC: Dayton W. Herrington, 615-358-9161. PO Box 2294, Clarksville TN 37042

Start Point: Travel Lodge, 615-645-1400 (reservations only). Wilma Rudolph Blvd. Located 500 yards South of junction of I-24 and US Hwy 79 North.

Event Info: Daily, 8-5. Rated 1. Strollers & wheelchairs not recommended. Leashed pets.

Clarksville - 10km Walk (YR344) **Jan 1-Dec 31**

Sponsoring Club: AVA-730, Clarksville Volksmarchers
POC: Dayton W. Herrington, 615-358-9161. PO Box 2294, Clarksville TN 37042

Start Point: Ramada Riverview Inn, 615-552-3331 (Reservations only). 50 College St.

Event Info: Daily, 8-5. Rated 2+. Strollers & wheelchairs not recommended. Leashed pets.

Clarksville - 10km Walk (YR727) **Jan 1-Dec 31**
Sponsoring Club: AVA-020, Tuck-A-See Wanderers
POC: Vernon Hessey, 502-439-3716. PO Box 956, Oak Grove, KY 42262

Register: Clarksville/Montgomery County Tourist Information Center, 615-648-0001. Exit 4 off I-24. Go south 500 yards and turn left on Holiday Dr (next to Holiday Inn).

Start Point: After picking up your start card, you drive to Dunbar Cave to complete the walk.

Event Info: Center is open 8-5 during daylight savings time. The remainder of the year it is open Mon-Fri, 8-4; Sat & Sun, 9-4. Please call for schedule during Christmas holidays. Rated 2. Pets must be leashed.

TEXAS

Abilene - Two 11km Walks (YR193 & YR393) & 10km Walk (YR756) **Jan 1-Dec 31**
Sponsoring Club: AVA-757, Shoeleather Express
POC: Chris Scott, 915-698-5616/698-1313. 3117 Meander St, Abilene TX 79602-6624

Start Point: Quality Inn, 915-676-0222. 505 Pine St. Downtown. From I-20, exit 286A.

Event Info: Daily, dawn to dusk. Box is available 24 hrs a day. Trails are rated 1+. Suitable for strollers. Wheelchairs will experience difficulty. Pets must be leashed.

Austin - Two 10km Walks (YR068-Historical & YR069-Town Lake) & 25km Bike (YR082) **Jan 1-Dec 31**
Sponsoring Club: AVA-077, Colorado River Walkers
POC: Robin Rosenstock, 512-795-0286. 5909 Painted Valley, Austin, TX 78759

Start Point: Hyatt Regency Hotel, 208 Barton Springs Rd; 512-477-1234. Box is located at the Bellboy stand.

Event Info: Daily, dawn to dusk. All trails are rated 1. Suitable for strollers but wheelchairs may need assistance due to curbs & stairs. Bikers must sign a waiver. Leashed pets.

Boerne - Two 10km Walks (YR220-Town & YR234-Country) & 26km Bike (YR379) **Jan 1-Dec 31**
Sponsoring Club: AVA-652, Hill Country Hikers
POC: Barbara Hill 210-249-3535/537-4172. PO Box 1252, Boerne TX 78006

Start Point: Key to the Hills Motel, 1228 S. Main; 210-249-3562.

Event Info: Daily, dawn to dusk. Walks are rated 1 & 1+. Bike is rated 1.

Corpus Christi - 10km Walk (YR057) **Jan 1-Dec 31**
Sponsoring Club: AVA-179, Sparkling City Strollers
POC: Marjorie Louise Hays, 512-991-2383. 1014 Ronald Dr, Corpus Christi TX 78412-3548

Start Point: Sand & Sea-Budget Inn, 1013 N Shoreline Dr.

Event Info: Daily, dawn to dusk. Rated 1. Suitable for strollers. Wheelchairs may experience some difficulty. Pets must be leashed.

Dallas - 15km Walk (YR141) & 25km Bike (YR142) **Jan 1-Dec 31**
Sponsoring Club: AVA-034, The Dallas Trekkers
POC: Earl Anderson, 214-341-8654. 11460 Audelia Rd #187, Dallas TX 75243

Start Point: White Rock Lake Park, Johnston Bicycles, 9005 Garland Rd (at Emerald Isle)

Dallas - 10km Walk (YR085) **Jan 1-Dec 31**
Sponsoring Club: AVA-034, The Dallas Trekkers
POC: Earl Anderson, 214-341-8654. 11460 Audelia Rd #187, Dallas TX 75243

Start Point: Downtown Visitor's Center at Union Station, 401 S. Houston Street

Denison - 10km Walk (YR629) **Jan 1-Dec 31**
Sponsoring Club: AVA-767, Texoma Amblers
POC: Helen Jones, 903-893-6801/Pat Taylor 903-465-7170. 401 Iowa, Sherman TX 75090

Start Point: Central Fire Station, 700 West Chestnut.

Event Info: Daily, dawn to dusk.

DeSoto - 10km Walk (YR201) **Jan 1-Dec 31**
Sponsoring Club: AVA-034, The Dallas Trekkers
POC: Earl Anderson, 214-341-8654. 11460 Audelia Rd #187, Dallas TX 75243

Start Point: Albertsons Grocery Store, 901 N Polk St.

El Paso - 11km Walk (YR702) **Jan 1-Dec 31**
Sponsoring Club: AVA-769, Amigo Amblers
POC: Bill Hollis, 915-833-7048. 305 Sundown Place, El Paso, TX 79912

Start Point: Jordan's Shur Sav, 5300 Doniphan Dr. I-10 exit 11 Mesa. South to Doniphan. Go right. Jordan's is one mile on the right.

Event Info: Daily, 7-10. Rated 1. Suitable for strollers but not wheelchairs.

El Paso/Ft Bliss - 11km Walk (YR439) **Jan 1-Dec 31**
Sponsoring Club: AVA-769, Amigo Amblers
POC: Dave Wick, 915-757-3324. 406 B.T. Cassidy Dr, El Paso, TX 79924

Start Point: Ft Bliss Inn. US-54 to Fred Wilson. Go East. At light turn right. Left at 1st Street. Inn is on left.

Event Info: Daily, dawn-3 hours before dark. Rated 1. Suitable for strollers & wheelchairs.

Fredericksburg - 11km Walk (YR108-Town & Country), 10km Walk (YR107-Cemetery) & 13km Walk (YR001) **Jan 1-Dec 31**
Sponsoring Club: AVA-001, Volkssportverein Friedrichsburg
POC: Robert Deming, 210-997-6251 or Becky Lindig, 210-997-8056. PO Box 503, Fredericksburg TX 78624

Start Point: Comfort Inn, 908 S. Adams; 210-997-9811 (For reservations only)

Event Info: Daily, dawn to dusk. 10km & 13km are rated 1. Suitable for strollers & wheelchairs. 11km is rated 1+. Pets must be leashed.

Ft Hancock - 10km Walk (YR900) **Jan 1-Dec 31**
Sponsoring Club: AVA-769, Amigo Amblers
POC: Mary Seagrove, 915-595-2291. 2024 Pier Lane, El Paso, TX 79936

Start Point: Ft. Hancock Mercantile. I-10 exit 72. Go west towards town. Mercantile is 0.3 miles on right, just past the railroad tracks.

Event Info: Mon-Sat, 7 A.M.-8 P.M.; Sun, 8am-7 P.M. Rated 1+. Not for strollers or wheelchairs.

Ft Worth - 12km Walk (YR044) **Jan 1-Dec 31**
Sponsoring Club: AVA-019, Tarrant County Walkers, Inc.
POC: Sue Layton, 817-924-8450. 516 East Drew, Ft. Worth, TX 76110

Start Point: Hardwicke Interpretive Nature Ctr, 817-237-1111. 9600 Fossil Ridge Rd.

Event Info: Daily, 9-1:30. Must be off trail by 4:30. Closed Mondays & holidays. Rated 3.

Ft Worth - 11km Walk (YR363) **Jan 1-Dec 31**
Sponsoring Club: AVA-019, Tarrant County Walkers, Inc.
POC: Ernest LaCroix, 817-451-1291. 4920 Emerald Lake Drive, Ft. Worth, TX 76103

Start Point: Ramada Inn, 1700 Commerce St, 817-335-7000.

Event Info: Daily, 1 hour after dawn-3 hours before dusk. Rated 1.

Ft Worth - 10km Walk (YR630) **Jan 2-Dec 31**
Sponsoring Club: AVA-019, Tarrant County Walkers, Inc.
POC: Mac Mackechnie, 817-926-4477. 4225 Westmont Ct., Ft. Worth TX 76109

Start Point: Foster Park, Corner of Old Granbury Rd & Trail Lake. Phillip 66 Station.

Event Info: Daily, 7-6. Rated 1.

Galveston Island - Two 10km Walks (YR088 & YR562) **Jan 1-Dec 31**
Sponsoring Club: AVA-251, Friendswood Fun Walkers
POC: Rosemary Hopkins Creamer, 713-996-5735. PO Box 781, Friendswood TX 77546

Start Point: Galveston Island Visitor's Bureau (Moody Center) 2106 Seawall Blvd; 1-800-351-4237 or 409-763-4311.

Event Info: Mon-Sat, 9-5; Sun 12-5. Trails are rated 1. Wheelchairs & strollers may have difficulty with high curbs. Pets must be leashed.

Garland - 10km Walk (YR324) **Jan 1-Dec 31**
Sponsoring Club: AVA-034, The Dallas Trekkers
POC: Earl Anderson, 214-341-8654. 11460 Audelia Rd #187, Dallas TX 75150

Start Point: Audubon Park/Duck Creek Greenbelt Expressway Convenience Store, 3925 Broadway

Granbury - 10km Walk (YR382) **Jan 1-Dec 31**
Sponsoring Club: AVA-718, Hood County Hummers
POC: Ardyce Pfanstiel, 817-326-2164. 3621 Fairway DCBE, Granbury TX 76049-5338

Start Point: Lodge of Granbury, 400 E Pearl St.

Event Info: Daily, 8-3 hours before dark. Rated 1-2. Strollers and wheelchairs will encounter difficulty on parts of the trail. Pets must be leashed.

Hamilton - 10km Walk (YR428) **Jan 1-Dec 31** Credit Only Event
Sponsoring Club: AVA-205, Trotting Texas Turtles
POC: Karl/Beverly Kittinger, 817-547-1403. 712 Ridge St, Copperas Cove, TX 76522-3137

Start Point: Value Lodge Inn Motel, 817-386-8959. Hwy 281 North.

Event Info: Daily, 8-dusk. Not suitable for wheelchairs. Strollers will have difficulty with approximately 1/2 km. Pets must be leashed. Rated 1+

Hewitt - 12km Walk (YR429) & 26km Bike (YR448) **Jan 1-Dec 31**
Sponsoring Club: AVA-791, Chisholm Trail Blazers
POC: Jim Boardman, 817-666-7110. 101 Buckingham Place, Hewitt, TX 76643

Start Point: Citgo Service Station, Intersection of FM 2113 (Spring Valley Rd) and FM 1695. Two miles south on FM 2113 from I-35, exit 328.

Event Info: Daily, 7-dusk. Walk is rated 1. Bike is rated 2+. Bikers must sign waiver. Wearing a helmet is recommended.

Houston - 10km Walk (YR143) 11km Walk (YR071) **Jan 1-Dec 31** Credit Only Event
Sponsoring Club: AVA-015, Houston Happy Hikers
POC: Connie Bath, 713-665-2663. 2502 Watts, Houston TX 77030

Start Point: Holiday Inn Medical Ctr, 6701 S Main St. From 610 South Loop, take Main St north to the Holiday Inn. From US 59 take Greenbriar south to University, then left on University to Fannin and right on Fannin to the Holiday Inn.

Event Info: Special rates available to walkers. Daily, dawn to dusk. Rated 1. Suitable for strollers. Pets must be leashed.

Irving - 10km Walk (YR316) **Jan 1-Dec 31**
Sponsoring Club: AVA-681, Star Trekkers
POC: Gunhilt Money, 214-986-5086. 2828 Gamelake, Irving, TX 75060

Start Point: McDonald's Restaurant, 214-259-7881. 302 W. Irving Blvd.

Event Info: Daily, 7-dusk. Finish by dark. Closed Thanksgiving & Christmas. Pets must be leashed. Rated 1. Not suitable for wheelchairs. Strollers will have some difficulty.

Irving (Las Colinas) - 10km Walk (YR202) & 27km Bike (YR586) **Jan 1-Dec 31**
Sponsoring Club: AVA-681, Star Trekkers
POC: (Walk) Carol Talpey, 214-717-3988. 3916 Acapulco, Irving, TX 75062
POC: (Bike) Tim Allen, 214-252-5663. 2821 Keyhole Circle, Irving TX 75062

Start Point: The Ultimate Chocolate Cookie, 5205 O'Connor, Suite 100. South side of the Plaza in Williams Square at Velma.

Event Info: Mon-Fri, 7-5; Sat & Sun, 10-5. Please do not ride your bike in Williams Square. Helmets are recommended. No pets permitted. Walk is rated 2. Suitable for strollers.

Irving - 10km Walk (YR671) **Jan 1-Dec 31**
Sponsoring Club: AVA-681, Star Trekkers
POC: Allan Ortiz, 214-255-7648. 1518 McHam Street, Irving TX 75062

Start Point: 7-11 Village Shopping Center, 214-556-2540. 9400 N. MacArthur Blvd.

Event Info: Open daily at 7am. Must be finished by 2 hours before dusk. Rated 2. Suitable for strollers but not wheelchairs. Pets must be leashed.

Kerrville - Two 10km Walks (YR026-Town & YR027-Residential) **Jan 1-Dec 31**
Sponsoring Club: AVA-106, Kerrville Trailblazers
POC: Sybil Jean Davis, 210-896-7765. PO Box 2097, Kerrville, TX 78029

Start Point: Inn of the Hills, 210-895-5000. 1001 Junction Hwy. From IH-10 exit 505. South on Harper Rd., to Junction of Hwy 27 then turn left to Inn of the Hills.

Event Info: Daily, dawn to dusk. Rated 1. Strollers okay, no wheelchairs. Leashed pets.

McKinney - 10km Walk (YR229) **Jan 1-Dec 31**
Sponsoring Club: AVA-124, Plano Plodders Walking Club, Inc.
POC: Mike Dunahoo, 214-578-8415/Jerry Slayton, 214-424-6485. 2804 Bengal Lane, Plano, TX 75023

Start Point: Holiday Inn, Central Expressway at White Ave Exit 40B.

Event Info: Daily, dawn to dusk. Rated 1+. Strollers okay, no wheelchairs. Leashed pets.

Midlothian - 10km Walk (YR036) **Jan 1-Dec 31** Credit Only Event
Sponsoring Club: AVA-034, The Dallas Trekkers
POC: Earl Anderson, 214-341-8654. 11460 Audelia Rd #187, Dallas TX 75243

Start Point: Midlothian Police Dept, 101 E Ave F.

Event Info: Daily, 8-3 hours before dusk. Rated 1+. Strollers may have to be carried in some places. No wheelchairs.

New Braunfels - 11km Walk (YR614) **Jan 1-Dec 31**
Sponsoring Club: AVA-036, New Braunfels Marsch-und Wandergruppe
POC: Don Flick, 210-625-0742. PO Box 310778, New Braunfels TX 78131-0778

Start Point: Hotel Faust, 240 S Seguin Ave. Take I-35 to exit 187.

Event Info: Rated 1. Strollers okay but may have to be carried short distances. Pets must be leashed.

Ottine - 10km Walk (YR703) **Jan 1-Dec 31**
Sponsoring Club: AVA-088, Selma Pathfinders
POC: Mark Abolafia-Rosenzweig, 210-672-3266. Palmetto State Park, Rt 5, Box 201, Gonzales, TX 78629.

Start Point: Palmetto State Park, Park Hqs. From I-10 take the Hwy 183 exit south toward Gonzales. Turn right at Park Rd 11 and follow the road to the Park Hqs. located on the right side of the road in Ottine.

Event Info: Fee of $4.00 per car or $1.00 per person (if you walk in) will be charged. Daily, 8-5. Rated 1+. Suitable for strollers. Wheelchairs may experience difficulty.
Please do not smoke in wooded areas. Park is closed if the San Marcos River is flooding.

Pflugerville - 10km Walk (YR478), 28km Bike (YR516) & 300m Swim (YR477) **Jan 1-Dec 31**
Sponsoring Club: AVAA-077, Colorado River Walkers
POC: Robin Rosenstock, 512-795-0286. 5909 Painted Valley, Austin, TX 78759

Start Walk & Bike, Register for Swim: Police Station, 200 Main.

Start for Swim: Gilleland Creek Park Swimming Pool

Event Info: Walk & Bike daily, dawn to dusk. Pool is closed Mondays and certain holidays. Call for schedule (512-251-5082). Walk is rated 1. Suitable for strollers & wheelchairs. $2.00 swimming pool usage fee. Bikers & swimmers must sign a waiver.

Plano - 10km Walk (YR151) **Jan 1-Dec 31**
Sponsoring Club: AVA-124, Plano Plodders Walking Club, Inc.
POC: Mike Dunahoe, 214-578-8415/Jerry Slayton, 214-424-6485. 2804 Bengal Lane, Plano, TX 75023

Start Point: Brookshire's Food Store, 2060 W. Spring Creek Pkwy (Southeast corner).

Event Info: Rated 1+. Suitable for strollers but not wheelchairs. Daily, dawn to dusk. Closed Easter, Thanksgiving & Christmas. Pets must be leashed.

Salado - 11km Walk (YR450) & 25km Bike (YR652) **Jan 1-Dec 31**
Sponsoring Club: AVA-205, Trotting Texas Turtles
POC: Karl/Beverly Kittinger, 817-547-1403. 712 Ridge St, Copperas Cove TX 76522-3137

Start Point: Stagecoach Inn, IH 35; 817-947-5111. From IH-35 North, exit 284. Cross over 35 and continue to Main Street. Turn right on Main, cross Salado Creek, take first right onto Stagecoach Inn property. For IH-35 South, exit 284. At Exxon Station turn right and go one block to Main. Follow directions above.

Event Info: Daily, dawn to dusk. Walk is rated 1+. Suitable for strollers but wheelchairs will have difficulty. Bike is rated 1. No bicycle rental available. Pets must be leashed.

San Antonio - 10km Walk (YR544) **Mar 19-Nov 20**
Sponsoring Club: AVA-652, Hill Country Hikers
POC: Barbara Hill, 210-249-3575/537-4172. PO Box 1252, Boerne TX 78006

Start Point: Fiesta Texas Theme Park Hospitality Center.

Event Info: Weekends only, spring & fall, Daily during summer season. Start anytime after park opens until three hours before park closes. Check park schedule for times or call 210-697-5050. Rated 1+. Suitable for strollers and wheelchairs.

San Antonio -10km Walk (YR261) **Jan 1-Dec 31** Credit Only Event
Sponsoring Club: AVA-006, Texas Wanderers
POC: Lyn Ward, 210-651-6536. 9355 Blazing Star Trail, San Antonio, TX 78266-2311

Start Point: Ft. Sam Houston, Entrance way, Bldg T300, Stanley Rd. From I-35, exit 159A. Go North on N. New Braunfels to Stanley Road. Go right on Stanley.

Event Info: Rated 1. Suitable for strollers. Daily, dawn to dusk. Pets must be leashed and are not allowed in the quadrangle.

San Antonio - 12km Walk (YR461), 11km Walk (YR462) & 30km Bike (YR463) **Jan 2-Dec 31**
Sponsoring Club: AVA-088, Selma Pathfinders
POC: Phyllis Eagan, 210-496-1402. 17314 Springhill, San Antonio TX 78232

Start Point: San Jose Mission Hqs, S Roosevelt at San Jose Dr.

Event Info: Summer, 8-5; Winter, 9-6. Closed Christmas & New Years. Trails are rated 1. YR462 is suitable for strollers & wheelchairs. Pets must be leashed. They are not allowed in the mission grounds.

☆ San Antonio - 11km Walk (YR055) **Jan 1-Dec 31**
Sponsoring Club: AVA-006, Texas Wanderers
POC: Lyn Ward, 210-651-6536. 9355 Blazing Star Trail, San Antonio, TX 78266

Start Point: Holiday Inn Riverwalk North, 110 Lexington Ave; 210-223-9461. Start box is located at the Bell Captain's Station. From I-35, exit 157B. Go south on McCullough toward downtown, to St. Mary's. Go right to Lexington and then turn left.

Event Info: Daily, 8 to dusk. Rated 1. Not suitable for wheelchairs. Pets are not appropriate but must be leashed if brought.

San Marcos - 10km Walk (YR481) **Jan 1-Dec 31**
Sponsoring Club: AVA-411, San Marcos River Walkers
POC: Barbara Piersol, 512-396-4463. 100 E Laurel Ln, San Marcos TX 78666

Start Point: Aquarena Springs Inn, 1 Aquarena Springs Dr; 512-396-8901. NOTE: Start is at the Inn and not the Park. Buildings are located in the same area. I-35, exit 206, Aquarena Springs Dr.

Event Info: Daily, dawn to dusk. Rated 2. Some areas not suitable for strollers or wheelchairs. Pets must be leashed.

Shiner - Two 10km Walks (YR221 & YR228) **Jan 1-Dec 31**
Sponsoring Club: AVA-460, Shiner Half Moon Walkers
POC: Virginia Helweg, 512-594-3304. PO Box 294, Shiner TX 77984

Start Point: Howard's Diamond Shamrock, 1701 North Avenue East; 512-594-4200.

Event Info: Daily, 6-11. Trails are rated 1. Suitable for strollers difficult for wheelchairs.

Universal City - 10km Walk (YR510) & 11km Walk (YR156) & 26km Bike (YR147) **Jan 1-Dec 31** Credit Only Events
Sponsoring Club: AVA-044, Randolph Roadrunners
POC: Terry Larson, 210-659-5104. 113 Ft Wayne, Universal City TX 78148

Start Point: The Comfort Inn, 210-659-5851; 200 Palisades Dr. From IH-35 exit at the 171/172 mile marker (FM218/Pat Booker/Randolph AFB exit). On Pat Booker Road, follow signs to the Comfort Inn. Palisades Drive is on the right. Blockbuster Video is on the corner.

Event Info: Daily, dawn to dusk. Walks are rated 1. Suitable for strollers. Bikers must sign waiver. Pets must be leashed.

Uvalde - 10km Walk (YR709) & 25km Bike (YR710) **Jan 1-Dec 31**
Sponsoring Club: AVA-789, Tree City Troopers
POC: Clay Baulch, 210-864-4519. PO Box 56, Mountain Home, TX 78058

Start Point: Continental Inn Best Western, 701 E Main; 210-278-5671.

Vanderpool - 10km Walk (YR460) **Jan 1-Dec 31**
Sponsoring Club: AVA-088, Selma Pathfinders
POC: Phyllis Eagan, 210-496-1402. 17314 Springhill, San Antonio TX 78232

Start Point: Lost Maples State National Area, Ranger Station.

Event Info: Park is closed on weekdays the first three weeks of December and the month of January but is open weekends. Remainder of year, Mon-Fri, 8-5; Sat & Sun, 8-8; call 210-966-3413 for info. Rated 2. Optional trail is rated 4+. Not suitable for strollers or wheelchairs. Only one event credit even if doing both trails. Pets must be leashed. Please carry water.

Waco - Two 10km Walks (YR626 & YR627) & 25km Bike (YR628) **Jan 1-Dec 31** Credit Only Events
Sponsoring Club: AVA-791, Chisholm Trail Blazers
POC: Jim Boardman, 817-666-7110. 101 Buckingham Place, Hewitt, TX 76643

Start Point: Hilton Hotel, 817-754-8484. 113 S. University Parks Dr. I-35 to University Parks exit. Go W on University Parks to Hilton Hotel.

Event Info: Daily, dawn to dusk. Trails are rated 1.

Wichita Falls - Two 10km Walks (YR203 & YR109) **Jan 1-Dec 31**
Sponsoring Club: AVA-182, Buffalo Chipkickers Volksmarch Club, Inc.
POC: Chuck Samus, 817-691-0584 (eves). PO Box 8523, Wichita Falls TX 76307

Start Point: Econo Lodge, 817-761-1889. 1700 5th St.

Event Info: Daily, dawn to dusk. Trails are rated 1 & 1+. Suitable for strollers but wheelchairs may have some difficulty. Pets must be leashed.

UTAH

Ogden - 10km Walk (YR062-City) **Jan 2-Dec 30**
Sponsoring Club: AVA-436, Golden Spike Striders
POC: Myra Tams, 801-782-8580. 3897 N 1050 W, Ogden UT 84414-1323

Start Point: Ogden's Union Station, Gift Shop, 25th & Wall Ave; 801-629-8533. Exit I-15 at 21st Street near the Flying J Plaza (exit 346). Turn right at Wall Ave and drive to 25th St.

Event Info: Mon-Sat, 10-6. Call POC for after hours or on Sundays. Rated 2+.

Ogden - 10km Walk (YR198 River) & 25/50/75km Bike (YR112) **Jan 1-Dec 31**
Sponsoring Club: AVA-436, Golden Spike Striders
POC: Myra Tams, 801-782-8580. 3897 N 1050 W, Ogden UT 84414

Start Point: Kar Kwik Convenience Store, 1918 Washington Blvd; 801-392-2104. Exit I-15 at 21st Street near the Flying J Plaza (exit 346). Go east toward the mountains to Washington Blvd (Main city street). Turn left at light & drive to 19th St. Watch for the "Welcome to Ogden" sign that spans Washington over the Ogden River. Store is on the east side of street.

Event Info: Daily, 7-11. Not recommended in winter as snow may not be cleared. Trails are rated 2+. To make arrangements for bike rental, call Weber State University Wilderness Recreation Dept. 801-626-6373. Bike has three distances. Only one event credit allowed, even if completing all distances.

Provo - 10km Walk (YR327) **Jan 2-Dec 30**
Sponsoring Club: AVA-731, Gadabouts
POC: Mike Tams, 801-224-4557. 387 E 720 N, Orem UT 84057.

Start Point: Utah County Travel Council, Historic County Courthouse, 801-370-8390. 51 S University

Event Info: Mon-Fri, 8-5; Sat & Sun, 10-6. Rated 2+.

Provo Canyon - 10km Walk (YR326) **Apr 1-Oct 30**
Sponsoring Club: AVA-731, Gadabouts

POC: Mike Tams, 801-224-4557. 387 E 720 N, Orem UT 84057.

Start Point: Chevron Station on bike path to Bridal Veil Falls.

Salt Lake City - 10/11km Walk (YR075) **Jan 1-Dec 31**
Sponsoring Club: AVA-356, Footloose
POC: Carolyn Lai, 801-250-2755/560-9286. 2936 S Buccaneer Dr, Magna, UT 84044

Start Point: Shilo Inn, 801-521-9500. 206 S. West Temple St.

Event Info: Three routes available. Only one event credit even if doing all routes. Trails are rated 1 & 2+. Route 3 is not accessible for wheelchairs or strollers. Plan for harsh weather.

Salt Lake City - 10km Walk (YR653) **Apr 29-Oct 28**
Sponsoring Club: AVA-356, Footloose
POC: Carolyn Lai, 801-250-2755/560-9286. 2936 S Buccaneer Dr, Magna, UT 84044

Register: Shilo Inn, 801-521-9500. 206 S. West Temple St.

Start Point: Ft. Douglas Military Museum, 32 Potter St.

Event Info: Tues-Sat, 10-12 & 1-4. Closed on some holiday weekends. Rated 4+. Pets are not allowed on the shoreline trail. Alternate route available for pets, strollers & wheelchairs.

Tooele - 10km Walk (YR496) **Jan 1-Dec 31**
Sponsoring Club: AVA-356, Footloose
POC: Carolyn Lai, 801-250-2755/560-9286. 2936 S Buccaneer Dr, Magna, UT 84044

Start Point: Albertson's Customer Service Counter, 250 N Main.

Event Info: Two routes available. Only one event credit even if doing both routes. Daily, dawn to dusk. Trails are rated 1+ & 3.

VERMONT

White River Junction - 10km Walk (YR094) **Apr 1-Nov 30**
Sponsoring Club: AVA-341, Twin State Volkssport Association
POC: Pat Stark, 802-296-2192 (eves) 295-9353 X32 (days). PO Box 184, Wilder VT 05088

Start Point: Hotel Coolidge, (near the Amtrak Station) 800-622-1124. 7 S. Main St. From I-91 take exit 11 (White River Jct) and continue on Rt 5 North approximately 1 mile to the second stop light. Continue 3 blocks. Park in Town Lot across from hotel.

Event Info: Daily dawn to dusk. Rated 2+. Suitable for strollers but wheelchairs will have difficulty with long hill.

Middlebury - 10/11km Walk (YR707) **Apr 1-Nov 30**
Sponsoring Club: AVA-341, Twin State Volkssport Association
POC: Charlotte Phillips, 802-462-2019. PO Box 907, Middlebury VT 05753

Start Point: Middlebury Information Center, 2 Court St. Route 7 at Village Green.

Event Info: Mon-Fri, 9-5. Other times: Middlebury Inn across Washington St from Info Center. Finish is always at the Registration Desk of the Middlebury Inn. Rated 1+. Not suitable for wheelchairs due to stairs. Strollers will need assistance. Pets must be leashed.

VIRGINIA

Abingdon - 10/12km Walk (YR587) **Jan 1-Dec 31**
Sponsoring Club: AVA-VA, Virginia Volkssport Assn.
POC: Jim Geith, 804-851-1829. PO Box 7100, Hampton, VA 23666

Start Point: Abingdon Visitors Center, 335 Cummings St.

Alternate Start Point: Super 8 Motel, 298 Town Centre Dr. For either start, exit 17. Super 8 on left above Mc-Donald's. Visitors Center 1/2 mile on left across rom Heilig-Meyers Furniture.

Event Info: Super 8 offers special rates to volkssporters. Rated 1+. Pets must be leashed. Suitable for strollers & wheelchairs.

☆ Alexandria - 10km Walk (YR061) **Jan 3-Dec 31**
Sponsoring Club: AVA-151, Northern Virginia Volksmarchers
POC: Charlene Agne-Traub, 703-250-4008 or Bob McLean, 703-455-1878.
10260 Quiet Pond Terrace, Burke VA 22015

Start Point: Bavarian Alps Gift Store, 703-683-3994. 924 King St. From I-495/I-95 take Exit 1B, Rt 1 North to Old Town Alexandria. Bavarian Alps is located on right corner of Rt 1 (Patrick St.) and King St. (7 blocks from exit). Also accessible by Metro Train from National Airport to King Street Station.

Event Info: Tues-Sat, start 10-3; finish by 6. Sun start noon-2; finish by 5. Rated 1+. Suitable for strollers. Pets must be leashed.

Bristol - 10km Walk (YR588) **Jan 1-Dec 31**
Sponsoring Club: AVA-VA, Virginia Volkssport Association
POC: Jim Geith, 804-851-1829. PO Box 7100, Hampton VA 23666

Start Point: Bristol Convention & Visitors Bureau, 20 Volunteer Pkwy. Exit 1 or 3 in Virginia. Follow to corner of State St & Volunteer Pkwy. Visitors Center is on the Right.

Alternate Start Point: Holiday Inn Medical Center, US 11 W & I-81 (Exit 74B in Tennessee).

Event Info: Mon-Fri, 8:30-5. Closed major holidays. The Holiday Inn offers special rates to volkssporters. Rated 2. Suitable for strollers & wheelchairs. Pets must be leashed.

Charlottesville - Two 10km Walks (YR742 & YR743) **Jan 2-Dec 31** Credit Only Events
Sponsoring Club: AVA-792, Fuma Volksmarchers
POC: Fred Tucker, 804-589-5341. RR 1, Box 90, Palmyra, VA 22963

Start Point: Charlottesville/Albemarle Convention & Visitors Bureau, 804-977-1783. I-64, exit 121.

Event Info: Closed major holidays. Must drive short distance to start/finish. Trails are rated 1+. Suitable for strollers and wheelchairs. Pets must be leashed.

Fredericksburg - 10km Walk (YR115) **Jan 1-Dec 31**
Sponsoring Club: AVA-610, Germanna Volkssport Association
POC: Justin R. Hughes, 703-891-2968. PO Box 7674, Fredericksburg, VA 22404

Start Point: Fredericksburg Visitor Center, 703-373-1776. 706 Caroline St. Exit I-95 at Rt 3 East (Exit 130A) to the Visitors Center.

Event Info: Daily, 9-5. Closed major holidays. Rated 1+. Suitable for strollers & wheelchairs.

Gloucester - 10km Walk (YR875) **Jan 1-Dec 31** Credit Only Event
Sponsoring Club: AVA-365, Explorer Post 49
POC: Sam Tollett, 804-766-3065. 3 Delmont Court, Hampton, VA 23666

Start Point: Beaverdam Park Ranger's Station, Roaring Springs Rd. Follow your favorite route to US 17 South. Turn left at the traffic light on South Business 17 into Gloucester. Do not go off at the other South Business 17 into Saluda or any other town. Go one block and turn left on Route 616 (Roaring Springs Rd). Follow Rt 616 approximately 2.4 miles. Road will dead end in the park. From US 17 North, cross the York River Bridge. Approximately 14 miles from bridge, turn right at traffic light on S. Business 17. Follow directions from North to Route 616 and park.

Event Info: Daily, 8-dusk. Pets must be leashed. No water is available on the trail. Rated 2. Not suitable for strollers or wheelchairs.

Hampton (Ft Monroe) - 10km Walk (YR874) **Jan 1-Dec 31**
Sponsoring Club: AVA-142, Peninsula Pathfinders of Virginia
POC: Shirley Boyd, 804-722-5637. 11 Berkley Dr, Hampton, VA 23666

Start Point: Chamberlin Hotel Registration Desk, 804-723-6511. Take I-64 to Hampton. Exit at 268, Phoebus. Turn left at stop light onto Mallory St. Go approximately 2/10 mile. Turn right on E. Mellen St (SR East 143). Follow signs to Fort Monroe. Turn right on McNair Dr. Follow signs to Hotel.

Event Info: Daily, dawn to dusk. Rated 1+. Suitable for strollers or wheelchairs if they bypass portion that goes along top of the old fort. Pets must be leashed.

Jamestown - 11/15km Walk (YR286) & 26km Bike (YR489) **Jan 1-Dec 31** Bike is a Credit Only Event
Sponsoring Club: AVA-142, Peninsula Pathfinders
POC: James Geith, 804-851-1829. PO Box 7100, Hampton, VA 23666

Start Point: Gift Shop, Visitors Center Colonial National Historic Park.

Event Info: $8.00 per car to enter. Jan 1-Mar 31, 9-5; Apr 1-Jun 16, 9-5:30; Jun 17-Aug 20, 9-6; Aug 21-Oct 27, 9-5:30; Oct 28-Dec 31, 9-5. Closed Christmas. Trails are rated 1+. Pets must be leashed.

Kilmarnock - 10km Walk (YR872) **Jul 1-Sept 30** Credit Only Event
Sponsoring Club: AVA-365, Explorer Post 49
POC: Sam Tollett, 804-766-3065. 3 Delmont Court, Hampton, VA 23666

Start Point: Get & Zip Convenience Store. Take your favorite route to US 17 at Tappahannock. Turn on US 360 east. Follow US 360 approximately 7 miles to SR 3 East. Go approximately 35 miles to Kilmarnock. The Get and Zip (Amoco Station) is on your left shortly before McDonald's.

Event Info: Daily, dawn to dusk. Rated 1. Strollers & wheelchairs okay. Leashed pets.

Lexington - Two 10km Walks (YR589-City & YR901-Country) **Jan 2-Dec 31** Credit Only Events
Sponsoring Club: AVA-545, Hillbilly Hikers
POC: Kitra A. Burnham, 304-846-2201. 6 Front Street, Richwood, WV 26261

Start Point: Lexington Visitor Center, 703-463-3777. 102 E Washington St. Exit 188 West off I-81 or Exit 55 South off I-64. Follow signs to Visitor Center.

Event Info: Daily, 9-5. Closed major holidays. YR589 is rated 2+. YR is rated 1+. Suitable for strollers but not wheelchairs. Pets must be leashed.

Manassas - Two 10km Walks (YR340 & YR739) **Jan 3-Dec 31**
Sponsoring Club: AVA-306, Wood & Dale Wanderers
POC: Dick Reichert, 703-335-1428. PO Box 2422, Woodbridge VA 22193-2422

Start Point: Two Days Gifts, 9249 Center St.

Event Info: Mon-Sat, 10-5; Closed Sundays & major holidays. Trails are rated 1. Suitable for strollers. Pets must be leashed.

Matthews - 10km Walk (YR868) **Jan 1-Mar 31** Credit Only Events
Sponsoring Club: AVA-365, Explorer Post 49
POC: Sam Tollett, 804-766-3065. 3 Delmont Court, Hampton, VA 23666

Start Point: Little Sue Convenience Store. Take your favorite route to US 17 south. Turn left on Rt 198 east shortly after you enter Gloucester County. Continue on Rt 198 after it joins with Rt 14 East. Start is on your right at the first stop sign (where Rt 14 turns right). From US 17 North, cross the York River Bridge. Approximately 12 miles from the bridge, turn right at traffic light to 14 East. Follow 14 East approximately 17 miles to start.

Event Info: Daily, dawn to dusk. Rated 1. Strollers & wheelchairs okay. Leashed pets.

Norfolk - 10km Walk (YR469) **Jan 2-Dec 31**
Sponsoring Club: AVA-013, Gator Volksmarsch Club
POC: Daniel Horne, 804-523-1614. 1910 Shepherd's Gate, Chesapeake VA 23320

Start Point: MacArthur Memorial Theater Bldg, 804-441-2965. Bank St & City Hall Ave. From I-64 take I-264 W to exit 10. Straight to Bank St. Start is on left.

Event Info: Mon-Sat, 10-2; Sun, 11-2. Finish by 4:30 each day. Closed New Year's, Thanksgiving & Christmas. Rated 1. Strollers & wheelchairs okay. Pets must be leashed.

Richmond - 12km Walk (YR592-Three Mile Lock Park) & 11km Walk (YR591-Monument) **Jan 1-Dec 31**
YR591 is a Credit Only Event
Sponsoring Club: AVA-027, Lee Lepus Volksverband
POC: Dee Schrum, 804-768-0055. PO Box 2031, Petersburg VA 23803

Start Point: Virginia Historical Society, 804-358-4901. 428 N Blvd. From I-95, exit 78. Follow signs to Historical Society. Corner of North Blvd. & Kensington Ave. Park in rear.

Event Info: Mon-Sat, 10-5; Sun, 1-5. Closed holidays. 11km trail is rated 1+. Suitable for strollers and wheelchairs. 12km is rated 3. Suitable for strollers.

Roanoke - 10km Walk (YR911) **Jan 1-Dec 31** Credit Only Event
Sponsoring Club: AVA-792, Fuma Volksmarchers
POC: Pat Mead, 703-342-0013. 1109 Clearfield Rd SW, Roanoke, VA 24015

Start Point: Roanoke Valley Convention & Visitors Bureau, 800-635-5535. 114 Market St.

Event Info: Rated 1+. Suitable for strollers & wheelchairs.

Urbanna - 10km Walk (YR871) **Apr 1-Jun 30** Credit Only Event
Sponsoring Club: AVA-365, Explorer Post 49
POC: Sam Tollett, 804-766-3065. 3 Delmont Court, Hampton, VA 23666

Start Point: Virginia Street Cafe. From US 17 South, turn left on Rt 602 to Remlik and Urbanna. Stay on Rt 602 until you reach Urbanna. Rt 602 ends and Rt 227 starts here. The Cafe is on your left at the corner where Rt 227 turns right. From US 17 North, cross the York River Bridge. Approximately 30 miles from the bridge, turn right on Rt 616 (this turn is a short distance north of Saluda). At the T-intersection, turn right on Rt 602 to Urbanna. Rt 602 ends and Rt 227 starts in Urbanna. Cafe if on your left at the corner where Rt 227 turns right.

Event Info: Rated 1. Mon-Sat, 8-3; Sun 9-noon. Leashed pets. Strollers & wheelchairs okay.

Vienna - 10km Walk (YR869) & 25km Bike (YR870) **Jan 2-Dec 31**
Sponsoring Club: AVA-151, Northern Virginia Volksmarchers
POC: Dr. Charlene Agne-Traub, 703-250-4008. 10260 Quiet Pond Terrace, Burke VA 22015

Start Point: NOVA Cycling & Fitness, 703-938-7191. 124 Maple Ave. From I-495, use I-66 West exit 9 to Nutley St (Rt 243), exit 62 towards Vienna. Turn right on Maple Ave (Rt 123) and go 6/10 of a mile to start.

Event Info: Seasonal hours, usually: Mon-Sat, 11-6; Sun, noon-5. Closed Sundays in Jan & Feb. Trails are rated 1+. Bikers must sign waiver. Helmets are recommended.

Virginia Beach - 10km Walk (YR468) & 25km Bike (YR724) **Jan 1-Dec 31**
Sponsoring Club: AVA-013, Gator Volksmarsch Club
POC: Daniel Horne, 804-523-1614. 1910 Shepherd's Gate, Chesapeake VA 23320

Start Point: Virginia Beach Resort Hotel & Conference Center, 804-481-9000. 2800 Shore Dr. Use I-64 to Route 13 North (Northampton Blvd), exit 282. Go to Rte 60 East (Shore Dr).

Event Info: Daily, dawn to dusk. Trails are rated 2. Pets must be leashed. Bikers must sign waiver. Helmets are recommended.

Warsaw - 10km Walk (YR873) **Oct 1-Dec 31** Credit Only Event
Sponsoring Club: AVA-365, Explorer Post 49
POC: Sam Tollett, 804-766-3065. 3 Delmont Court, Hampton, VA 23666

Start Point: Warsaw Supermarket . Take your favorite route to US 17 at Tappahannock. Turn on US 360 East. Go approximately 6 miles to Warsaw. The Market is in the shopping center on your right as you come into town.

Event Info: Mon-Sat, 8-3; Sun 9-3. Rated 1. Strollers & wheelchairs okay. Leashed pets.

Williamsburg - 10km Walk (YR287), 27km Bike (YR486) & Swim (YR487) **Jan 1-Dec 31**
Sponsoring Club: AVA-142, Peninsula Pathfinders
POC: James Geith, 804-851-1829. PO Box 7100, Hampton VA 23666

Start Point: Tazewell Fitness Ctr, Williamsburg Lodge.

Event Info: Mon-Fri, 6-8; Sat, 8-7; Sun, 9-5; Swim times: Daily, 10-noon & 2-4. Swim is in an indoor pool. Walk trail is rated 2. Strollers are not recommended. Pets must be leashed. No rating was given for bike trail.

Winchester - 10km Walk (YR590) **Jan 2-Dec 31**
Sponsoring Club: AVA-151, Northern Virginia Volksmarchers
POC: Mimi Pollow, 703-780-3010. PO Box 7096, Fairfax Station VA 22039-7096

Start Point: Winchester-Frederick County Visitor Center, 703-662-4118. 1360 S. Pleasant Valley Rd. From I-81, take exit 313, follow Rt 50 W to Pleasant Valley Rd and turn right. Center is on right near corner.

Event Info: Daily-start 9-1:45. Finish by 4:45. Rated 1+. Manageable by strollers. Pets must be leashed.

Yorktown - 10km Walk (YR285), 15km Walk (YR284) & 25km Bike (YR485)
Sponsoring Club: AVA-142, Peninsula Pathfinders
POC: James Geith, 804-851-1829. PO Box 7100, Hampton, VA 23666

Start Point: Gift Shop, Visitors Center, Yorktown Battlefield, Colonial National Historical Park

Event Info: Jan 1-Mar 31, 8:30-5; Apr 1-Jun 16, 8:30-5:30; Jun 17-Aug 20, 8:30-6; Aug 21-Oct 27, 8:30-5:30; Oct 28-Dec 31, 8:30-5. Closed Christmas. Trails are rated 1+. Pets must be leashed.

WASHINGTON

Anacortes - Two 10km Walks (YR418-Downtown & YR656-Guemes Island) **Jan 1-Dec 31**
Sponsoring Club: AVA-482, Skagit Tulip Trekkers
POC: (YR656) Jean/Larry Nelson, 206-293-4217. 4006 L Ave, Anacortes, WA 98221
POC: (YR418) Jolynn Woodbury, 206-766-6664. 786 Samish Island Rd, Bow, WA 98232

Start Point: Island Hospital, 1213 24th St.

Event Info: Daily, dawn to dusk . Pets must be leashed. YRE 418 is rated 1. YR656 is rated 2+. Start is a short ferry ride away. Check ferry schedule so you don't get caught spending the night on the island. Carry your own water for this one.

Bellevue - 11km Walk (YR135) **Jan 2-Dec 31**
Sponsoring Club: AVA-638, Northwest Striders
POC: Richard Gamble, 206-255-3214. 2616 NE 20th St, Renton, WA 98056

Start Point: Quality Food Center, 549 156th Ave SE. I-90 exit 11B, north on 148th Ave, right on Lake Hills Blvd, left on 156th Ave.

Event Info: Daily, dawn to dusk. Closed Thanksgiving & Christmas. Rated 2.

Bellevue - Two 10km Walks (YR638 & YR639) **Jan 1-Dec 31**
Sponsoring Club: AVA-638, Northwest Striders
POC: Richard Gamble, 206-255-3214. 2616 NE 20th St, Renton, WA 98056

Start Point: Red Lion Hotel, 300 112th Ave SE. I-405, exit 12. West on 8th, right on 112th.

Event Info: Daily, dawn to dusk. Trails are rated 2.

Camas/Washougal - Two 10km Walks (YR680 & YR681) **Jan 1-Dec 31** Credit Only Events
Sponsoring Club: AVA-551, All Weather Walkers
POC: Judy Noall, 206-699-2467 X4017. c/o Clark County Parks, PO Box 9810, Vancouver WA 98666

Start Point: Danielson Thriftway Store, 3300 NE 3rd Ave. East on Hwy 14 past Camas. Left on 6th St to E St. Left 1 1/2 block to Lacamas Center.

Event Info: Daily, dawn to dusk. Closed Christmas. YR680 is rated 1. Suitable for strollers & wheelchairs. Pets must be leashed. YR681 is rated 3. No wheelchairs. A rough go for strollers.

Carnation - 10km Walk (YR181) **Apr 1-Oct 31**
Sponsoring Club: AVA-503, Hopkins Telephone Pioneers
POC: Ruth Kalies, 206-630-2728/Sandy Cramer, 206-565-5678. 19905 SE 300th St, Kent, WA 98042

Start Point: Remlinger Farms, 32610 NE 32nd. From I-90 take exit 22 (Fall City-Preston). Turn right on the Fall City-Preston Rd through Preston and across the bridge at Fall City. Turn left onto Fall City-Carnation Rd (SR 203). Follow SR 203 approximately six miles & turn right on NE 32nd St at Remlinger Farms sign.

Event Info: Daily, 9-6 in Apr, May, Sep & Oct. Daily, 8-6 in Jun, Jul & Aug. Trail is rated 1+.

Cathlamet - 10/21km Walk (YR803) & 25km Bike (YR804) **Jan 1-Dec 31**
Sponsoring Club: AVA-621, P.E.O. Pathfinders
POC: Liz Johnson, 206-838-3454. PO Box 6164, Federal Way, WA 98063

Start Point: Island Market, 206-849-4218. 485 State Hwy 409

Des Moines - 11km Walk (YR449) **Jan 1-Dec 31** Credit Only Event
Sponsoring Club: AVA-540, Star Walkers Volkssports Club.
POC: Sally Moore, 206-272-0846. 706 Sheridan, Tacoma WA 98406

Start Point: Masonic Home of WA, 23660 Marine View Dr S. I-5 to exit 149. West to Hwy 99. Left to S 240. Right to Marine View Dr. Right to Home.

Event Info: Daily, dawn to dusk (Home opens at 8 am). Rated 2+. Pets must be leashed.

Edmonds - 10km Walk (YR204) & 11km Walk (YR451) **Jan 2-Dec 30** YR204 is a Credit Only Event
Sponsoring Club: AVA-403, Puget Sound Sloshers
POC: Lorrie Pederson, 206-542-8694. 24132-102nd Place W, Edmonds WA 98020

Start Point: Harbor Square Athletic Club, 206-778-3546. 160 W Dayton. Exit 177-West on SR 104 to Dayton. Left for 1 block, left to Harbor Square.

Event Info: Mon-Fri, 5:30 to dusk; Sat & Sun, 7:30 to dusk. Closed major holidays. Trails are rated 2+.

Everett - 10km Walk (YR786) **Jan 1-Dec 31** Credit Only Event
Sponsoring Club: AVA-403, Puget Sound Sloshers
POC: Linda McFarland, 206-252-9865. 2232 1/2 Rainier Ave, Everett, WA 98201 or Mary Tipping, 206-776-7195. 7924 212th St SW #213, Edmonds, WA 98026

Start Point: Providence General Medical Ctr, Colby Campus, 1321 Colby Ave. Exit I-5 to Broadway. Follow Broadway to 13th St. West on 13th to parking garage on Rockefeller Ave.

Event Info: Daily, dawn to dusk. Rated 1+. Suitable for strollers but wheelchairs may have difficulty with curbs. Pets must be leashed.

Fall City - 10km Walk (YR359) & 32km Bike (YR360) **Apr 1-Oct 31** Bike is a Credit Only Event
Sponsoring Club: AVA-318, Emerald City Wanderers
POC: David W. Madsen, 206-296-5479. 1112 NW 61st, Seattle, WA 98107

Start Point: The Herbfarm, 32804 Issaquah-Fall City Rd. From I-90 exit 22 to Preston. Right on Preston-Fall City Rd. 3.3 miles. Left on 328th Way SE. Right on SE 46th (or Issaquah-Fall City Rd). Farm is on left.

Event Info: Daily, 9-6. Trails are rated 1+. Walk is not suitable for strollers or wheelchairs.

Federal Way - Two Walks 11/14km (YR205) 12km (YR802) **Jan 1-Dec 31** Credit Only Events
Sponsoring Club: AVA-133, Sea-Tac Volkssports Club
POC: Boyd Wilton, 206-839-1546. 30042 12th Lane SW, Federal Way WA 98023

Start Point: Hallmark Manor, 32300 1st Ave S; 206-874-3580. From I-5 take exit #143. Go west on S. 320th St 1 1/2 miles to the traffic light at 1st Ave. S. Turn left and go 1/2 block to the start on the left.

Event Info: Mon-Fri, 8-8; Sat, Sun, and Holidays, 10-6. Maps are available at the front entrance for those who wish to start earlier. YR205 is rated 1+. Suitable for wheelchairs & strollers. Optional 3km extension may be difficult for strollers & wheelchairs. YR802 is rated 3. Not suitable for strollers or wheelchairs.

Federal Way - 10km Walk (YR616) **Jan 1-Dec 31** Credit Only Event
Sponsoring Club: AVA-754, The Over-The-Hill Gang
POC: Alicia L. Maxcy, 206-927-4580. PO Box 23057, Federal Way WA 98093

Start Point: Jim's Market & Deli, 4612 SW 320th St. From I-5 take exit 143 (S 320th St). From Northbound, turn left on S 320th St. From southbound, turn right. Proceed down 320th heading west 4.5 miles until it intersects Hoyt Rd. Jim's is on your right at the east end of the shopping center.

Event Info: Daily, 7-7. Rated 2. Suitable for strollers & wheelchairs. Pets must be leashed.

Federal Way - Two 10km Walks (YR838-Enchanted Village) & (YR921-Street of Flags) 38km Bike (YR839-Plateau-Tideflats) **Jan 1-Dec 31**
Sponsoring Club: AVA-779, Third Planet Volkstours
POC: Dorman Batson, 206-927-2495. 35806 1st Ave S, Federal Way, WA 98003

Start Point: Private Residence, 35806 1st Ave South. From I-5 exit 143B to 1st Ave. Left to South 358th St. Park in drive of 35806 1st Ave South, on South 358th St or in designated area behind house off South 358th St.

Event Info: YR838 rated 2. Not suitable for wheelchairs & strollers will have difficulty. YR921 rated 1+. Suitable for strollers and wheelchairs. Pets must be leashed. Bike is rated 3+.

Greenwater - 10km Walk (YR711) **May 1-Sept 15**
Sponsoring Club: AVA-115, Evergreen Wanderers
POC: Chuck Repik, 206-582-7474. Box 111943, Tacoma, WA 98411-1943

Start Point: Wapiti Woolies Store, 58414- FR 14E

Issaquah - 10km Walk (YR790) **Jan 1-Dec 31**
Sponsoring Club: AVA-536, Tri-Mountain Volkssport Club
POC: Jennifer Littke, 206-222-5715. 36002 SE 46th, Fall City, WA 98024

Start Point: City Lights Video, 82 Front Street, South. From I-90 take exit #17 and go south on Fron Street to 2nd traffic light, about 7/10 of a mile. Turn left on Sunset Way. Go one block and turn right on Rainier Avenue. Park in the Issaquah City Hall parking area. City Video is on the corner of 1st Avenue SE and SE Andrews St.

Event Info: Mon-Fri, 6-dusk; Sat, 8-dusk; Sun 12-dusk. Maps will be available in a box outside of store for early walkers. Rated 2. No strollers or wheelchairs. Leashed pets.

Kelso - 10km Walk (YR423) **Jan 1-Dec 31** Credit Only Event
Sponsoring Club: AVA-530, Border Crossers
POC: James B. Gorman, 206-577-3404 days. 11 Larry Ln, Longview WA 98632

Start Point: Red Lion Inn Lobby, 206-636-4400. 510 Kelso Dr. Take I-5, exit 39. Go to frontage road, turn right.

Event Info: Daily, dawn to dusk. Rated 2. Wheelchairs & strollers with difficulty. Pets must be leashed.

Kirkland - 11/20km Walk (YR134) **Jan 1-Dec 31**
Sponsoring Club: AVA-384, Interlaken Trailblazers
POC: James L. Ridgway, 206-789-2118 (days). 821 5th St, Kirkland WA 98033

Start Point: Peter K's Deli, 206-889-0711. 215 Central Way. Exit 18 off I-405 and go west toward Lake Washington on Central Ave. Deli is on the left at 3rd and Central. Metro bus routes 230, 251, 254, 255, & 258 bring you right to the start point.

Event Info: Daily, dawn to dusk. Rated 2. Strollers & wheelchairs okay. Leashed pets.

La Conner - 10km Walk (YR657) **Jan 1-Dec 31**
Sponsoring Club: AVA-482, Skagit Tulip Trekkers
POC: Patsy Reinard, 206-856-6054. 1911 Alta Vista Dr, Sedro-Woolley, WA 98294

Start Point: Market Place, 106 South 1st. From I-5 exit on #230 west. Follow Hwy 20 west to intersection of Hwy 20 and Whitney-La Conner Rd south into La Conner. At the three way intersection with Morris & Chilberg, turn right onto Morris Rd. Go six blocks to the river. Market is on the left.

Event Info: Daily, dawn to dusk. Rated 2+.

Lacey - 10km Walk (YR819) **Jan 1-Dec 31**
Sponsoring Club: AVA-148, Capitol Volkssport Club
POC: Ron Brown, 206-456-0142. PO Box 3231, Lacey, WA 98503

Start Point: Albertsons Food Center, 206-491-8283. 6100 Pacific Avenue, SE. From I-5 northbound, take exit 109. Turn right onto Martin Way, straight to Carpenter Rd (3rd stop light). Turn right. Start is on your right just before Pacific Ave. From I-5 southbound, take exit 109. Turn left onto Martin Way then to Carpenter Rd, (4th stop light). Turn right. Start is on your right.

Event Info: Daily, 8-dusk. Closed Christmas. Rated 1+. Suitable for strollers & wheelchairs. Pets must be leashed

Lake Chelan - 10km Walk (YR785) **Apr 1-Nov 1**
Sponsoring Club: AVA-210, Bavarian Volkssport Assn
POC: Gary & Sandy Miller, 509-687-3598. 1961 Lakeshore Dr, Manson, WA 98831-9746

Start Point: Campbell's Lodge (Resort). From Wenatchee, take Hwy 97A going North to Chelan. Approaching Chelan at the first intersection take the road that continues around the lake and takes you past the Forest Service. Cross bridge, Resort is located directly on the opposite side. Please park outside resort.

Event Info: Daily, dawn to dusk. Rated 1+. Not for strollers or wheelchairs. Leashed pets.

Leavenworth - 11km Walk (YR168) **Apr 1-Dec 1**
Sponsoring Club: AVA-210, Bavarian Volkssport Assn.
POC: Russ & Bobbi Ferg, 509-548-6112. PO Box 25, Leavenworth, WA 98826

Start Point: Alpen Inn, 509-548-4326. 405 Hwy 2.

Longview - 11km Walk (YR227) **Jan 1-Dec 31** Credit Only Event
Sponsoring Club: AVA-530, Border Crossers
POC: James B. Gorman, 206-577-3404 days. 11 Larry Ln, Longview WA 98632

Start Point: St. John's Medical Ctr, 206-423-1530. 1614 E Kessler Blvd. From I-5, exit 36 northbound or exit 40 southbound. Follow hospital signs. Start at Tel-Med Desk.

Event Info: Daily, 6-6. Rated 1. Wheelchairs & strollers may have difficulty on park paths. Pets must be leashed.

Mercer Island - 10km Walk (YR712) **Jan 1-Dec 31** Credit Only Event
Sponsoring Club: AVA-447, Mercer Island Volkssport Association
POC: Jim Peterson, 206-232-8980. PO Box 1435, Mercer Island WA 98040-1435

Start Point: McDonald's, 2807 77th St SE.

Event Info: Daily, 7-dusk. Rated 2. Suitable for strollers & wheelchairs. Leashed pets.

Mt Rainier National Park - 10km Walk (YR683) **Jun 10-Sep 10**
Sponsoring Club: AVA-360, Yakima Valley Sun Striders
POC: Millie Haupt, 509-453-8710. PO Box 10523, Yakima WA 98909

Start Point: Ohanapecosh Campground. From Hwy 410 or Hwy 12 take Hwy 123 to campground.

Event Info: Daily, dawn to dusk. Rated 3. Not for strollers or wheelchairs. No pets.

Mt St Helens - 10km Walk (YR765) **May 1-Oct 31** Credit Only Event
Sponsoring Club: AVA-557, Vancouver USA Volkssporters
POC: Naomi Kihn, 206-892-5148. PO Box 2121, Vancouver, WA 98668

Registration: Rose Tree Restaurant, located at Exit 49. From I-5 take exit 49 Castle Rock.

Start Point: Coldwater Ridge Visitor Center. Mt. St. Helens National Volcanic Monument, Mile Post 43 on State Hwy 504. After registering, follow State Route 504 east for 43 miles.

Event Info: Daily, 9-6. Rated 4+. No strollers or wheelchairs. Carry your own water. Trail descends 800 ft in 1 1/4 kilometers. Climb 800 ft to the finish. Dogs are not allowed. You MUST stay on the trail.

North Bend - 10km Walk (YR179), 11km Walk (YR120) & 27km Bike (YR158) **Apr 1-Oct 31** Bike is a Credit Only Event

Sponsoring Clubs: AVA-388, Cascade Ramblers (YR120 & YR158) & AVA-779, Third Planet Volkstours (YR179)

POC: Dorman Batson, 206-927-2495. 35806 1st Ave S, Federal Way WA 98003

Start Point: Factory Stores of America Office, 461 S Fork Ave. From I-90, 30 miles East of Seattle. Take exit #32 to North Bend Blvd. Turn left into Factory Stores parking lot. Office is approximately in the center of the complex immediately to the left of the flags.

Event Info: Daily, 8-6. Walks are rated 1+, suitable for strollers. Bike is rated 2+. Bikers must sign waiver. Helmets are recommended.

North Bend - 14km Walk (YR781) **May 1-Oct 31** Credit Only Event

Sponsoring Club: AVA-534, Four Plus Foolhardy Folks

POC: Richard Gamble, 206-255-3214. 2616 NE 20th St, Renton, WA 98056

Start Point: Factory Stores of America, 461 South Fork Ave, SW. From I-90 take exit 31. Go north on North Bend Blvd. Turn left into mall. Start is in the office located near the flag poles.

Event Info: Daily, 8-6. Rated 5. Walk is on Mt. Si with an elevation gain of 3,400 ft.

Olympia - 10km Walk (YR500) **Jun 1-Sep 30**

Sponsoring Club: AVA-115, Evergreen Wanderers

POC: Gene Shaw, 206-588-8532. Box 111943, Tacoma, WA 98411-1943

Start Point: Nisqually Plaza Park, 206-491-3831. 10020 Martin Way E. (Walk will start at Nisqually Wildlife Refuge.) From North or South take Exit 114. Southbound exit goes right into Martin Waay. Northbound turns right at the end of the ramp and another right at Martin Way. Look for the Texaco Station with a combination store & ice cream parlor on the right.

Event Info: Fee of $2.00 per family daily is required. Daily, 8 to dusk. Rated 1. Pets, bicycles, jogging & speed walking is prohibited.

Olympia - Two Walks, 10km (YR260), 11km (YR820) **Jan 1-Dec 31**

Sponsoring Club: AVA-148, Capital Volkssport Club

POC: Laura Theis, 206-534-9695. 4131 41st Loop SE, Olympia, WA 98501

Start Point: Bayview Market Place Deli, 516 W 4th. I-5 North: Exit 105. Follow directions to Port of Olympia. Left on Plum St. Left on State which becomes 4th. Market is on right. I-5 South: Exit 105 then 105B. See above.

Event Info: Daily, 8-dusk. Closed Christmas. Walks are rated 1+. Strollers will have some difficulty. No wheelchairs. Pets must be leashed.

Port Angeles - 10km Walk (YR833) & 11/16km Walk (YR361) **Jan 1-Dec 31** Credit Only Event

Sponsoring Club: AVA-517, Olympic Peninsula Explorers

POC: Dick Cable, 206-681-2504. PO Box 1706, Sequim WA 98382

Start Point: Swain's General Store, 601 E 1st St. Follow Hwy 101 to Port Angeles. From the east follow Hwy 101 (Front St) to Albert St, turn left. Proceed one block to First St. Turn Left. Swain's is on your right 1/2 block down. Please park in back of lot. From the west, follow Hwy 101 (First St) to Swain's on the right.

Event Info: Daily 9-5. Closed New Year's, Christmas & Thanksgiving. YR361 is rated 2. Not recommended for strollers or wheelchairs due to stairs. YR833 is rated 2+

Port Townsend - 10km Walk (YR421) **Jan 1-Dec 31** Credit Only Event
Sponsoring Club: AVA-517, Olympic Peninsula Explorers
POC: Frances Johnson, 206-732-4623. 4081 West Valley Rd, Chimacum, WA 98325

Start Point: Port Townsend Athletic Club, 206-385-6560. 229 Monroe St. (downtown).

Event Info: Mon-Fri, 6-dusk; Sat, 9-8; Sun, 10-5. Closed major holidays and the third Saturday in May. Rated 3. Not recommended for strollers & wheelchairs.

Poulsbo - 10km Walk (YR530) **Jan 1-Dec 31**
Sponsoring Club: AVA-359, die Bremertoner Stadtmusikanten
POC: Don or Carol Young, 206-871-2502. 4576 SE Orchard Lane, Port Orchard, WA 98366

Start Point: Shoreline Deli-Mart, 206-779-6609. Anderson Pkwy

Event Info: Daily, dawn to dusk.

Preston - 10km Walk (YR180) & 30km Bike (YR705) **Apr 1-Oct 31**
Sponsoring Club: AVA-536, Tri-Mountain Volkssport Club
POC: Jennifer Littke, 206-222-5715. 36002 SE 46th, Fall City WA 98024

Start Point: Preston General Store, 30365 Preston-Fall City Rd SE. From I-90 E or W, take exit 22. Turn north and then turn right at Yield sign onto Preston-Fall City Rd. Turn immediately right into the Preston General Store parking area. Please park behind the store.

Event Info: Walk is rated 1. Not recommended for wheelchairs or strollers but an alternate route is available on request. Pets must be leashed. Bike is rated 2+.

Puyallup - 10km Walk (YR242) **Jan 1-Dec 31**
Sponsoring Club: AVA-336, Daffodil Valley Volkssport Association
POC: Gretchen Carter, 206-863-7186. 1623 Voight, Sumner, WA 98390

Start Point: Happy Donuts, 305 2nd St NE. I-5 exit 127 (SR512). East to Puyallup. Take Meridian exit turn left and drive past fairgrounds. Street name becomes 3rd then 2nd. Cross railroad tracks. Donut shop is on right.

Event Info: Daily, 5 A.M.-6 P.M. Closed Easter, Thanksgiving, Christmas & New Year's. Rated 1. Strollers & wheelchairs may have some difficulty.

Redmond - 10km Walk (YR784) **Jan 1-Dec 31** Credit Only Event
Sponsoring Club: AVA-638, Northwest Striders
POC: Richard Gamble, 206-255-3214. 2616 NE 20th St, Renton, WA 98056

Start Point: Safeway, 630 228th Ave NE. From I-90, take exit 17. Go north on E Lake Sammamish Pkwy, right on SE 43rd Way/228th Ave.

Event Info: Daily, dawn to dusk. Rated 2. Strollers okay, no wheelchairs. Leashed pets.

Renton - 11km Walk (YR659) & 25km Bike (YR660) **Jan 1-Dec 31** Credit Only Events
Sponsoring Club: AVA-561, Global Adventurers
POC: Larry Lehman, 206-271-3053. 2023 Aberdeen Ave SE, Renton WA 98055-4537

Start Point: APSI Chevron Food Mart, 206-255-1774. 301 Grady Way. From I-405 take exit 2, (SR167) Rainier Ave. to Grady Way. Turn right on Grady Way, go past Holiday Inn.

Event Info: Daily, dawn to dusk. Trails are rated 1. Suitable for strollers but not wheelchairs. Pets must be leashed.

Renton - 10km Walk (YR789) **Apr 1-Oct 31**
Sponsoring Club: AVA-384, Interlaken Trailblazers
POC: Shirley Lindberg, 206-226-3484. 3610 Park Avenue North, Renton, WA 98056

Start Point: Safeway, 206-451-2191. 6911 Coal Creek Parkway. Take exit #10 from I-405 onto Coal Creek Parkway. Drive east for 2.6 miles.

Event Info: Daily, dawn to dusk. Rated 3. No strollers or wheelchairs. Leashed pets.

Richland - 10km Walk (YR430), 11km Walk (YR604), 25km Bike (YR809), 30km Bike (YR431) & 40km Bike (YR432) **Jan 1-Dec 31** Credit Only Events
Sponsoring Club: AVA-590, Tri Cities Windwalkers
POC: Don Wicks, 509-943-5118. 1807 Hunt Ave, Richland WA 99352

Start Point: Shilo Inn-Rivershore, 509-946-4661. 50 Comstock. Take I-182 at the George Washington Exchange. Turn right at the 1st traffic light to the Shilo Inn.

Event Info: Daily, dawn to dusk. Walks are rated 1+. Bikes are rated 2. All routes are suitable for strollers & wheelchairs. Pets must be leashed. Bike rental available at Richland Schwinn bike shop, 509-943-4496. 1374 Jadwin Ave, in the Uptown Shopping Mall. "Puncture Weed" grows along the trails.

Seattle - 10km Walk (YR351) & 11km Walk (YR408) **Jan 1-Dec 31** Credit Only Event
Sponsoring Club: AVA-373, Seattle Strasse Striders
POC for YR408: Libbie Loux, 206-285-1621. 102 W Garfield, Seattle WA 98119
POC for YR351: Nancy Treibel, 206-363-9820. 357 NE 149th St, Seattle, WA 98155

Start Point: Benny Lyles Burgerworks, 1802 N 34th St. Take I-5 45th St exit. Go west one mile, turn left on Wallingford to 34th.

Event Info: Mon-Fri, 6:30-9:00; Sat & Sun, 8-3. Closed major holidays. Rated 1. Not suitable for wheelchairs. Strollers may have difficulty with stairs. Pets must be leashed.

Seattle - 10km Walk (YR655) **Jan 1-Dec 31**
Sponsoring Club: AVA-WA, Evergreen State Volkssport Association
POC: Fat Ellison, 206-863-5388. 7413D 142nd Ave East, Sumner, WA 98390

Start Point: 7-11 Store, 2429 Harbor Ave SW. From I-5 exit 163 (Spokane St). Cross the W Seattle Bridge to Harbor Ave (not Island) exit. Right on Harbor Ave. 7-11 is on left one mile down. Do not park in store lot.

Event Info: Daily, dawn to dusk. Rated 1. Strollers & wheelchairs okay. Leashed pets.

Seattle - Two 10km Walks (YR011 & YR054) **Jan 1-Dec 31**
Sponsoring Club: AVA-249, F.S. Family Wanderers
POC: Robin Bajus, 206-522-5169. 4545 Sand Point Way NE, #606, Seattle, WA 98105

Start Point: The Seattle Inn, 206-728-7666. 225 Aurora Ave N (Between John & Thomas)

Event Info: Daily, dawn to dusk.

Sedro-Woolley - 10km Walk (YR658) **Jan 1-Dec 31**
Sponsoring Club: AVA-482, Skagit Tulip Trekkers
POC: Patsy Reinard, 206-856-6054. 1911 Alta Vista Dr, Sedro-Woolley, WA 98284

Start Point: Payless Drug, 406 Crossroad Square. From I-5 exit on #232 east. Follow Cook Rd for 5 miles. Crossroad Square is on your right.

Event Info: Mon-Fri, 9-9; Sat & Sun, 9-6. Closed major holidays. Rated 1. Leashed pets.

Sequim - 10km Walk (YR834-Town), 11km Walk (YR640-Marina) & 12km Walk (YR641-Bell Hill) **Jan 1-Dec 31** Credit Only Events

Sponsoring Club: AVA-517, Olympic Peninsula Explorers

POC: Dorothy Kobernik, 206-683-8371. 101 Kaufman Dr, Sequim, WA 98382

Start Point: Econo-Lodge, 206-683-7113. 801 East Washington St (Hwy 101 & Brown Rd)

Event Info: YR833 is rated 2+, YR640 is rated 2 & YR 641 is rated 3. Country roads with no shoulders. Not suitable for wheelchairs. Pets must be leashed.

Shelton - 11km Walk (YR403) **Jan 1-Dec 31**

Sponsoring Club: AVA-148, Capital Volkssport Club

POC: Bobbi Grieb, 206-877-6740. N27060 Hwy 101, Hoodsport WA 98548

Start Point: Mason General Hospital, 206-426-1611. 2100 Sherwood Lane. I-5 North and South, exit 104, Hwy 101 to Shelton. Exit to Wallace Blvd. Right turn into North Olympic Hwy. Left turn at I Street. At dead-end, turn right, then left into Hospital parking lot. Park in gravel lot, enter at employees entrance.

Event Info: Daily, 8-6:30. Closed Christmas. Rated 1+. Suitable for strollers or wheelchairs. Pets must be leashed.

Snoqualmie - 10/12km Walk (YR182) **Apr 1-Oct 31**

Sponsoring Club: AVA-133, Sea-Tac Volkssport Club

POC: Glenda Chambers, 206-630-2728. 19905 SE 300th St, Kent, WA 98042

Start Point: Isadora's, 206-888-1345. 132 Railroad Avenue. From I-90 East take exit 27. From I-90 West take exit 31. Follow signs to Snoqualmie. Start is directly across from the train depot.

Event Info: Mon-Fri, 7-5; Sat, 10-5; Sun, 11-5. Outside box for early starters. You must finish prior to 5 P.M. Call to verify hours if in doubt.

Sumner - 10km Walk (YR159) & 28km Bike (YR407) **Jan 1-Dec 31** BIKE is a Credit Only Event

Sponsoring Club: AVA-336, Daffodil Valley Volkssport Association

POC: Pat Ellison, 206-863-5388. 7413D 142nd Ave E, Sumner WA 98390

Start Point: Spartan Drive-In, 15104 E Main St. SR 410 east to 2nd Sumner exit. turn left to Main. Turn right for one block to Spartan.

Event Info: Daily, 9-dusk. Closed Easter, Thanksgiving, Christmas & New Year's. Maps are outside for early starters. Trails are rated 1. Suitable for wheelchairs & strollers. Pets must be leashed. Bikers must sign waiver. Helmets are recommended

Tacoma - 10km Walk (YR753) **Jan 2-Dec 31**

Sponsoring Club: AVA-809, Tacma Easy Walkers Club

POC: Ethel Roy, 206-472-3236. 6210 S Sheridan Ave, Tacoma, WA 98408-4709

Start Point: Mary Bridge Children's Hospital Gift Shop. Martin King Jr Way (Formerly K St)

Event Info: Holidays vary. Please call POC if in doubt. Mon-Fri, 9-8; Sat, 10-7; Sun noon-7. For earlier start, maps are located at Gift Shop entrance. Suitable for strollers. Wheelchairs may have difficulty. Profits from hat pin sales will be donated to the hospital for purchase of Orthotic shoes for children.

Tacoma - 10km Walk (YR007) **Jan 1-Dec 31**

Sponsoring Club: AVA-115, Evergreen Wanderers
POC: Sandra Dunning, 206-752-0809. 5413 N 10th Street, Tacoma, WA 98406

Start Point: Freighthouse Square, 206-272-6178. 2501 East "D" Street. From I-5 North exit 135 or I-5 South exit 133. Follow the Tacoma City Center exits and then the Tacoma Dome exit signs. Turn right on E 26th and left on E "D".

Event Info: Daily, 7-7. Trails are rated 2. Not suitable for wheelchairs. Strollers would have to be carried down a flight of stairs. Pets must be leashed.

Tukwila - 10km Walk (YR799) **Jan 1-Dec 31** Credit Only Event

Sponsoring Club: AVA-478, Cedar River Rovers
POC: Nancy Fairman, 206-235-7012. 3500 Shattuck Avenue S, Renton, WA 98055

Start Point: Kinko's, 112 Andover Park East. DO NOT PARK IN KINKO'S LOT. **From South**: Take I-5 to Southcenter Pkwy exit. Turn right. Turn left on Strander Blvd and left again on Andover Park East. Turn right on Baker Blvd and left on Christensen Rd. **From North**: Take I-5 to Southcenter Blvd. Turn left on Southcenter and turn right at the light. Cross I-405 and turn left on Tukwila Pkwy. Turn right on Andover Park East, left on Baker Blvd and right on Christensen Rd. **From East**: Take I-90 to I-405 South to Southcenter Blvd. Follow directions above.

Event Info: Daily, dawn to dusk. Rated 1. Strollers & wheelchairs okay. Leash your pets.

Vancouver - Two 10km Walks (YR424 & YR425) & 25/41/50km Bike (YR426) **Jan 1-Dec 31** Credit Only Events

Sponsoring Club: AVA-551, All Weather Walkers
POC: Judy Noall, 206-699-2467 X4017. c/o Clark County Parks, PO Box 9810, Vancouver WA 98666

Start Point: AM/PM Store, E 39th & Main St. From I-5 take exit 2. Left on 39th St. Drive 4 blocks to Main.

Event Info: Daily, dusk to dawn. Walks are rated 2. A rough go for strollers. No wheelchairs. Bike is rated 2. Bikers must sign a waiver, Helmets are encouraged. Pets must be leashed.

Vancouver - 10km Walk (YR138) & 11/12km Walk (YR632) **Jan 1-Dec 31** & 40km Bike (YR782) **Mar 1-Dec 31**

Sponsoring Club: AVA-557, Vancouver USA Volkssporters
POC: Margie Bickford, 206-693-6430. PO Box 2121, Vancouver, WA 98668

Start Point: Red Lion Inn at the Quay. 100 Columbia. From I-5 North or South, take exit 1C, Mill Plain Blvd. Turn west on Mill Plain Blvd which becomes 15th St to Columbia St. Turn left on Columbia St to Red Lion Inn at the Quay.

Event Info: Daily, dawn to dusk. YR138 is rated 1+. YR632 is rated 1. Both are suitable for strollers. YR782 is rated 3. Bikers must sign waiver and helmets are required.

Vancouver - 10km Walk (YR116) & 40km Bike (YR251) **Mar 1-Dec 31** Credit Only Events

Sponsoring Club: AVA-557, Vancouver USA Volkssporters
POC: (Walk) Margie Bickford, 206-693-6430. (Bike) Mac McKnight, 206-896-4142. PO Box 2121, Vancouver, WA 98668

Start Point: Health Experience Athletic Club. 5411 East Mill Plain. From I-5 into Vancouver, exit 1-C to Mill Plain Blvd. Go east 3 miles to intersection of Mill Plain & MacArthur Blvd. Turn right on MacArthur for one block. Start is on the left.

Event Info: Weekdays, dawn to dusk; weekends, 8-8. Closed all major holidays. Walk is rated 1. Suitable for strollers & wheelchairs. Pets must be leashed. Bike is rated 3. Bikers must sign a waiver. Helmets are required.

Walla Walla - 10km Walk (YR654) **Jan 1-Dec 31** Credit Only Event
Sponsoring Club: AVA-572, Walla Walla Volkssporters
POC: Trudy Schrader, 509-525-0392. %1540 Ruth Ave, Walla Walla, WA 94362

Start Point: St. Mary's Medical Center, 401 W. Poplar. From Hwy 12, take the 2nd Ave exit and turn right. Go 8 blocks to Poplar St and turn right. Go another 3 blocks and St Mary's Medical Center will be on your left between 5th & 7th Sts.

Event Info: Daily, dawn to dusk. Rated 1+. Strollers & wheelchairs okay. Leash you pets.

Wenatchee - Two 10km Walks (YR298-Skyline & YR297-Riverfront) & 25km Bike (YR299) **Mar 1-Dec 1**
Bike is a Credit Only Event
Sponsoring Club: AVA-210, Bavarian Volkssport Association
POC: Gib Edwards, 509-663-3356. 2015 Overlook Dr, Wenatchee WA 98801

Start Point: Orchard Inn, 509-662-3443. 1401 N. Miller.

Event Info: Daily, dawn to dusk. Riverfront is rated 1. Suitable for strollers & wheelchairs. Skyline is rated 2+. Bike is rated 3. Pets must be leashed. Bikers must sign waiver.

Westport - Two 10km Walks (YR636 & YR637) **Jan 1-Dec 31** Credit Only Events
Sponsoring Club: AVA-775, Puyallup Elk Hoofers
POC: Glorica or Sis Siciliano, 206-589-4005. 21609 135th St. East, Sumner WA 98390

Start Point: Ted's Red Apple Store, Montesano St. From I-5 north or south exit 104. Follow signs to Aberdeen, then signs to Westport. Stay on main road (Montesano St) until you come to start on your right just before stop light.

Event Info: Daily, dawn to dusk. Both trails are rated 1. Strollers & wheelchairs may have difficulty with YR636 but should be okay on YR637. Pets must be leashed.

Winlock - 10km Walk (YR843), 28km Bike (YR844) 42km Bike (YR845) **Jan 1-Dec 31** Credit Only Events
Sponsoring Club: AVA-642, Northwest Volksbikers
POC: Jim Henkle, 206-864-2218. 114 Otter Creek Dr, Toledo, WA 98591

Start Point: Hillcrest Deli Mart (EXXON Gas Station), 206-785-3239. 476 SR 505. From I-5 take exit 63 (Winlock). Turn west for one mile to the Deli.

Event Info: Daily, dawn to dusk. Trails are rated 2+. Water and restrooms at start/finish only. Pets must be leashed. Biker must sign waiver. Helmets are recommended.

Woodland - 27/33km Bike (YR821) **Jan 1-Dec 31** Credit Only Event
Sponsoring Club: AVA-530, Border Crossers
POC: James Gorman, 206-577-3404/425-5428. 11 Larry Lane, Longview, WA 98632 or Peter Hauser, 206-577-7435. 2325 Nichols Blvd. Longview, WA 98632

Start Point: Woodland Thriftway, 206-225-9491. 1325 Lewis River Rd, SR 503. From I-5 Southbound, take exit 22 (Dike Access Rd). At the stop sign, turn left. Proceed under the interstate following North Goerig St (unmarked) around to the right to the stop sign at Scott St. Continue strait ahead to the junction with SR 503/Lewis River Rd. Bear right on SR 503 and proceed approximately 600 meters to the start on your right. From Northbound I-5, take exit 21 (SR 503). At the stop light, turn right for one block. Proceed on SR 503 for another 300 meters to start on your left.

Event Info: Please park away from the store. Daily, dawn to 5. Rated 1+. Participants must sign waiver. Please carry your own water. All bikers MUST wear a bike helmet that is SNEL or ANSI approved.

Yacolt (Moulton Falls Park) - 10km Walk (YR570) **May 1-Oct 31** Credit Only Event
Sponsoring Club: AVA-743, Pathways to Adventure
POC: Judy Noall, 206-699-2467/Judy Berry, 503-244-7073. 7065 SW Hunt Club, Portland OR 97223

Register: The Pomeroy House, Rt 1, 20902 NE Lucia Falls Rd.

Start Point: From Battleground, N on SR503; right on NE Rock Creek Rd 5.5 miles.

Event Info: Daily, 8:30-5. Rated 2+. Not suitable for strollers or wheelchairs.

Yakima - 10km Walk (YR682) **Jan 1-Dec 31** Credit Only Event
Sponsoring Club: AVA-360, Yakima Valley Sun Striders
POC: Marina Rose, 509-453-2923. PO Box 10523, Yakima WA 98909

Start Point: Rio Mirada Motor Inn, 509-457-4444. 1602 Terrace Heights Rd. From I-82 take exit 33, Yakima/Terrace Heights. If southbound, turn left on Terrace Heights. If northbound, turn right on Terrace Heights. Proceed east to the Rio Mirada Motor Inn on your left.

Event Info: Daily, 7:30 to dusk. Rated 1. Strollers & wheelchairs okay. Leash your pets.

WEST VIRGINIA

Barboursville - 10km Walk (YR877) **Jan 2-Dec 31** Credit Only Event
Sponsoring Club: AVA-664, Charleston Riverfront Ramblers
POC: Karen Maes, 304-727-4749. PO Box 28, St. Albans, WV 25177

Start Point: Beech Fork State Park Hqs. 5601 Long Branch Rd. From I-64 exit 20 and turn south to US 60. Turn right onto US 60 then left on Alt Rt 10. Take Alt Rt 10 to Rt 10 and turn north. Turn left onto Hughes Branch Rd. Follow the signs to Park.

Event Info: Mon-Fri, 8-4. Closed weekends. Memorial Day - Labor Day, Mon-Sun, 8am-10 P.M. Closed Thanksgiving & Christmas. Walk has three trails. Only one event credit allowed even if completing all trails. One trail is rated 1, suitable for strollers. Second trail is rated 3 and the third is rated 5. Not suitable for strollers or wheelchairs. Leash your pets.

Cairo - 11km Walk (YR878) & 25km Bike (YR879) **Apr 15-Oct 15** Credit Only Event
Sponsoring Club: AVA-664, Charleston Riverfront Ramblers
POC: Karen Maes, 304-727-4749. PO Box 28, St. Albans, WV 25177

Start Point: Country Trails Bikes, 304-628-3100. From I-79 take US 50 exit and turn west. From I-77 take the US 50 exit and turn east. Take US 50 to WV 31 to Cairo.

Event Info: Mon-Fri, 9-5; closed Wednesday; Sat & Sun, 9-7. Closed major holidays. Walk is rated 1. Suitable for strollers but not recommended for wheelchairs. Pets must be leashed. Bike is rated 1+. Bikers must sign waiver. Helmets are recommended

Charleston - 10km Walk (YR880) **Apr 15-Oct 15** Credit Only Event
Sponsoring Club: AVA-664, Charleston Riverfront Ramblers
POC: Karen Maes, 304-727-4749. PO Box 28, St. Albans, WV 25177

Start Point: D & M Stables, Kanawha State Forest. From I-64/I-79 through Charleston, heading east or west, take exit 58A/US119/Oakwood Rd. At the T intersection turn right onto Oakwood Rd/US 119 South. In one mile, at the 2nd set of stop lights, turn left onto Oakwood Rd (watch for brown & white Kanawha State Forest sign). Stay on Oakwood Rd when it turns left after 1/2 mile. In another 2/5 of a mile, turn right onto Bridge Rd. At the first stop sign, Bridge Rd becomes Loudon Heights Rd. Stay on Loudon Heights. In another 3/5 miles, turn right onto Connell Rd. After 2 1/5 miles, turn left at T intersection onto Loudendale Rd. After 2 2/5 miles you will enter the State Forest. The stables is 2 miles from the entrance.

Event Info: Mon-Fri, 10-5; Sat & Sun, 9-5. Closed major holidays. Call POC if in doubt. Only one event credit even if completing both trails. One trail is rated 1. It is suitable for strollers but wheelchairs may have problems. The other trail is rated 3. Not suitable for strollers or wheelchairs and should not be walked when wet. Pets must be leashed.

Richwood - 10/20km Ski (YR047) **Jan 7-Apr 2** 10/20km Walk (YR113) & 30/55km Bike (YR114) **Apr 1-Nov 26**
Sponsoring Club: AVA-545, Hillbilly Hikers
POC: Kitra A. Burnham, 304-846-2201. 6 Front Street, Richwood, WV 26261

Start Point: Cranberry Mountain Visitor Center, 304-653-4826. Monongaheala National Forest, 23 miles east of Richwood.

Event Info Ski: Weekends (Sat & Sun) Only: 9-4. You may only walk on the last weekend **if** there has been **no** opportunity to ski the event. Skiers must sign waiver.

Event Info Walk/Bike: Weekends (Sat & Sun) only in April; (Fri, Sat & Sun) in May, Sept, & Oct; & (Sat & Sun) in Nov. Daily from Memorial Day to Labor Day. 9-5. Not suitable for strollers or wheelchairs. Pets must be leashed. Bikers must sign waiver.

St Albans - 10km Walk (YR881) **Jan 2-Dec 31** Credit Only Event
Sponsoring Club: AVA-664, Charleston Riverfront Ramblers
POC: Karen Maes, 304-727-4749. PO Box 28, St. Albans, WV 25177

Start Point: Universal Health Club, 304-727-4749. 808 B Street. From St. Albans exit off I-64. Turn right on Hwy 35. Cross Hwy 60 and immediately turn left onto Main St West. After crossing Coal River, turn right onto Kanawha Terrace and pull into first parking lot on your left.

Event Info: Mon-Fri, 8-7; Sat, 10-3; Sun, 10-2. Closed major holidays. Rated 3. Not suitable for wheelchairs. Pets must be leashed.

WISCONSIN

Cedarburg - 10km Walk (YR136) **Apr 1-Oct 31**
Sponsoring Club: AVA 490, Deutschstadt Volkssporters
POC: W. R. Breen, 414-375-0383. W51 N176 Fillmore Ave, Cedarburg, WI 53012

Start Point: Washington House Inn. W62 N573 Washington Ave.

Event Info: Daily, 9-2. Off trail by 5. Rated 1. Not for strollers & wheelchairs. No pets.

Madison - 10km Walk (YR763) **Jan 1-Dec 31**
Sponsoring Club: AVA-490, Deutschstadt Volkssporters
POC: Susan Sanders, 608-238-6047. 3723 Ross St, Madison, WI 53705

Start Point: Inn on the Park, 608-257-8811. 22 S Carroll St. From the Beltline Hwy south of the city (Hwy 12-14-18-151) Exit on John Nolen Dr. Follow John Nolen to Blair and Wilson St. Turn left on Wilson go 5 blocks and turn right on ML King Blvd. Go 1 block and turn right on Doty St. Go 1 block turn right on Pickney and turn left immediately into Doty St parking ramp. From the ramp, walk 1 block north (towards capital) to Main St. Turn left, walk 2 blocks to start.

Event Info: Daily, dawn to dusk. Rated 2. Not for strollers or wheelchairs. No pets.

St Croix Falls - 10km Walk (YR720) **Apr 15-Oct 31**
Sponsoring Club: AVA-796, St. Croix Valley Volkssporters
POC: Dianne Hoffman, 715/483-0234/483-3918. 684 Moody Rd, St. Croix Falls, WI 54024

Start Point: Polk County Information Ctr, 715-483-1410. Intersection of Hwy 35 & Hwy 8. 55 miles from Minneapolis and St. Paul.

Event Info: Daily, 9-2. Finish by 5. Rated 3. Portions difficult for strollers. Closed Easter.

WYOMING

Buffalo - 10km Walk (YR835) **May 1-Sept 30**
Sponsoring Club: AVA-806, Clear Creek Volkssport Assn.
POC: Frank Schleicher, 307-684-2739. 213 High St, Buffalo, WY 82834

Start Point: Super 8 Motel, 655 East Hart (junction of Hwy 16 & I-25). From I-90 exit #56b to I-25 southbound. Then exit at #299. Turn right at stop sign at bottom of off ramp. From I-25 northbound, exit at #299. Turn left at stop sign at bottom of off ramp. Turn left immediately after Col Bozeman's Restaurant. From Hwy 16 west, turn left at Main St (2nd stoplight). Go to Hart St (next light) and turn right. Turn right before Cole Bozeman's.

Event Info: Daily, dawn to dusk. Rated 2. Not for strollers or wheelchairs. No pets.

Casper - 10km Walk (YR040) **May 27-Sep 30**
Sponsoring Club: AVA-501, Wyoming State Parks & Historic Sites
POC: Ron Green, 307-635-2313. 611 Rodeo Ave, Cheyenne WY 82009

Start Point: Entrance Fee Booth, Edness K. Wilkins State Park, 307-577-5150. Off I-25, just east of Casper near Evansville.

Event Info: If fee booth is closed, drive in and look for park employee. Daily 9-5. Suitable for wheelchairs & strollers. Rated 1. Please carry water. 5200 ft elevation.

Cheyenne - 25km Bike (YR024) **Jan 2-Dec 31** Credit Only Event
Sponsoring Club: AVA-093, Cheyenne High Plains Wanderers
POC: Gaylord C. Fosdick, 307-638-8538. 1415 Madison Ave, Cheyenne WY 82001

Start Point: Bicycle Station, 3515 E Lincoln Way. From I-80 take exit 364 (College Dr) and go north to 12th St. Turn left on 12 and go west to Kingham Dr. Turn right on Kingham and go north into the Cheyenne Plaza. From I-25 take the Eastbound I-80 exit #8 and follow directions above.

Event Info: One sanction but two trails available. Only one event stamp allowed. Call 307-634-4268 for bike rental availability. Mon-Fri, 9:30-6:30; Sat, 9-5; Sun, 11:30-4:30. Rated 2. Participants must sign waiver form. Helmets are recommended. Altitude is 6020 ft.

Cheyenne - 10km Walk (YR002) **Jan 2-Dec 31**
Sponsoring Club: AVA-093, Cheyenne High Plains Wanderers
POC: Mike & Carol Jennings, 307-632-9072. 1600 Kopsa Ct, Cheyenne, WY 82007

Start Point: Wrangler Western Wear Store, 307-632-9072. 1518 Capitol Ave.

Start Point (During Frontier Days-July 21-30): Brown's Shoe Fit Company, 1701 Carey Ave.

Event Info: Rated 1. Strollers & wheelchairs will find some high curbs. Altitude is 6020 ft.

Cheyenne - 11km Walk (YR015) **Jan 2-Dec 31**
Sponsoring Club: AVA-093, Cheyenne High Plains Wanderers
POC: Mike & Carol Jennings, 307-632-9072. 1600 Kopsa Ct, Cheyenne, WY 82007

Start Point: Brown's Shoe Fit Company, 307-632-6293. 1701 Carey Ave.

Event Info: Mon-Sat, 9-5:30. Closed Sunday. Rated 1. Strollers & wheelchairs will find some high curbs. Altitude is 6020 ft.

☆ Devils Tower - 10km Walk (YR522) **May 1-Sept 30**
Sponsoring Club: AVA-177, Northern Hills Walking Club
POC: Cindy Waller, 307-283-2310. PO Box 912, Sundance WY 82729

Start Point: Devils Tower KOA Campground Office. Located at entrance to Devils Tower Nat'l Monument

Event Info: May 30-Sept 5, 8-8. May 1-May 30 & Sept 6-Sept 30, hours limited. Rated 3.

Ft Bridger - 10km Walk (YR507) **May 27-Sep 30**
Sponsoring Club: AVA-501, Wyoming State Parks & Historic Sites
POC: Ron Green, 307-635-2313. 611 Rodeo Ave, Cheyenne WY 82009

Start Point: Ft. Bridger State Historic Site. 307-782-3842. 3 miles S of I-80 at Mountain View exit.

Event Info: Jun-Aug, 8-5:30; Sept, 8:30-5. Rated 1. 6,700 ft. elevation. Closed September 1-4 due to Mountain Man Rendezvous. A fun time to visit. Walk the day before or after. Some parts not suitable for strollers or wheelchairs but close by areas will allow passage.

Guernsey - 10km Walk (YR041) **May 27-Sep 30**
Sponsoring Club: AVA-501, Wyoming State Parks & Historic Sites
POC: Ron Green, 307-635-2313. 611 Rodeo Ave, Cheyenne WY 82009

Start Point: Museum, Guernsey State Park, 307-836-2334. 15 miles E of I-25, 4 miles N of Guernsey.

Event Info: Daily, 10-6. Early start available. Rated 3+. Not suitable for strollers or wheelchairs. Please carry water. Good shoes recommended.

☆ Guernsey - 10km Walk (YR388) **Jan 1-Dec 31**
Sponsoring Club: AVA-501, Wyoming State Parks & Historic Sites
POC: Ron Green 307-635-2313. 611 Rodeo Ave, Cheyenne WY 82009

Start Point: Bunkhouse Motel, 307-836-2356. Hwy 26. Downtown Guernsey.

Event Info: Daily, 9-6. Rated 2. Not suitable for strollers or wheelchairs. Please carry water.

Lander - 10km Walk (YR039) **May 27-Sept 5**
Sponsoring Club: AVA-501, Wyoming State Parks & Historic Sites
POC: Ron Green, 307-635-2313. 611 Rodeo Ave, Cheyenne WY 82009

Start Point: Visitor's Center, Sinks Canyon State Park, 307-332-6333. 3079 Sinks Canyon Rd. 7 miles S of Lander on County Rd 131.

Event Info: Daily, 9-7. Rated 3. Not for strollers or wheelchairs. Carry water. Good shoes recommended.

Laramie - 10km Walk (YR816) **Jan 2-Dec 31**
Sponsoring Club: AVA-093, Cheyenne High Plains Wanderers
POC: Mike & Carol Jennings, 307-632-9072. 1600 Kopsa Ct, Cheyenne, WY 82007

Start Point: Dodds' Bootery, 307-632-9072. 401 S Second.

Event Info: Mon-Sat, 9:30-5:30. Sun, 12-4; winter months only. Rated 1. Suitable for strollers & wheelchairs.

Moorcroft - 10km Walk (YR140) **May 27-Sep 30**
Sponsoring Club: AVA-501, Wyoming State Parks & Historic Sites
POC: Ron Green, 307-635-2313. 611 Rodeo Ave, Cheyenne WY 82009

Start Point: Marina at Keyhole State Park. 307-756-3596. 353 McKean Rd. 8 miles N of I-90 between Moorcroft & Sundance on Pineridge Rd.

Event Info: Daily, 8-6. Rated 2+. Please carry water. Not suitable for strollers or wheelchairs. Good shoes recommended. 4,200 foot elevation.

Newcastle - 10km Walk (YR028-Historical) **Apr 29-Sep 30**
Sponsoring Club: AVA-763, NACC Volkssports
POC: Allan Ward, Chamber Office 307-746-2739. PO Box 331, Newcastle WY 82701

Start Point: Sundowner Inn, 451 W Main.

Event Info: Daily, 8 to dusk. Rated 2. Strollers & wheelchairs with difficulty. Pets on leash.

Pine Bluffs - 10km Walk (YR318) **May 1-Oct 31**
Sponsoring Club: AVA-093, Cheyenne High Plains Wanderers
POC: Emma Fosdick, 307-638-8538. 1415 Madison Ave, Cheyenne, WY 82001

Start Point: Gator's Travelyn Motel, 307-245-3226. 7th & Parsons (515 West 7th)

Event Info: Daily, dawn to dusk. Rated 3+. No wheelchairs or strollers.

Pine Bluffs - 300m Swim (YR319) **May 27-Aug 27**
Sponsoring Club: AVA-093, Cheyenne High Plains Wanderers
POC: Sonja Carlson, 307-245-9230. 403 Pine, Pine Bluffs, WY 82082

Start Point: Pine Bluffs Swimming Pool, 307-245-3783. 200 East 8th

Event Info: Outdoor Pool. May be closed due to bad weather.

South Pass City - 10km Walk (YR042) **May 27-Sep 30**
Sponsoring Club: AVA-501, Wyoming State Parks & Historic Sites
POC: Ron Green, 307-635-2313. 611 Rodeo Ave, Cheyenne WY 82009

Start Point: Smith-Sherlock Store, South Pass City State Historic Site, 307-332-3684. 131 South Pass Main. 35 miles S of Lander off Wyoming Hwy 28.

Event Info: Daily, 9-6. Trails is rated 4. Not suitable for strollers or wheelchairs. Please carry water. Good shoes recommended. 8,300 ft. elevation.

Sundance - 10km Walk (YR497) **May 1-Sept 30**
Sponsoring Club: AVA-177, Northern Hills Walking Club
POC: Susan Worthington, 307-283-1182(wk) 283-1677(hm). Box 189, Sundance WY 82729

Start Point: Country Cottage/Bear Lodge Motel, 5th & Cleveland St.

Alternate Start Point: Bear Lodge Motel, 3rd & Cleveland.

Event Info: May 30-Sep 5, 9 A.M.-9 P.M.; May 1-May 30 & Sep 6-Sep 30, hours limited. Rated 2.

Thermopolis - 10km Walk (YR038) **Jan 1-Dec 31**
Sponsoring Club: AVA-501, Wyoming State Parks & Historic Sites
POC: Ron Green, 307-635-2313. 611 Rodeo Ave, Cheyenne WY 82009

Start Point: Hot Springs State Park Bath House. 307-864-2176. 220 Park St.

Event Info: Mon-Sat, 8-6; Sun & holidays, noon-6. Closed Christmas. Rated 1+. Elevation 4,326 ft. Suitable for strollers & wheelchairs. Pets must be leashed.

VOLKSSPORTS ASSOCIATE

❑ Yes, I want to support volkssporting across the United States. Please sign me up as follows:

❑ Individual-$20 per year ❑ Family-$25 per year (List names below) ❑ Corporate-$200 per year

Enclosed is my check for $_____ made payable to Volkssports Associate. I understand a portion of this fee is designated for my subscription to THE AMERICAN WANDERER.

Please charge my ❑ VISA ❑ MASTERCARD ❑ DISCOVER ❑ AMERICAN EXPRESS

Card No.: _____ Exp date: _____

Signature:_____

I belong to the following AVA Club: _____

A portion of your membership fee will be distributed to the club you designate.

Please rush my membership packet to:

Name: _____ Phone: _____

Address: _____

City/State/Zip: _____

FAMILY MEMBERS: _____

STARTING POINT

Please send copies of the AVA Year Round Event Book, **STARTING POINT** to:

Name: _____ Phone: _____

Address: _____

City/State/Zip: _____

$5.00 each + shipping
$4.00 for Volkssports Associate Members + shipping

Volkssports Associate Membership No. _____

SHIPPING: $1.50 for each book sent BOOK RATE or $3.00 for each book sent FIRST CLASS.

❏ Enclosed is my check/money order for $ _____ made payable to AVA.

Please charge my ❏ VISA ❏ MASTERCARD ❏ DISCOVER ❏ AMERICAN EXPRESS

Card No.: _____ Exp date: _____

Signature: _____

Send completed form to: AVA National Headquarters
1001 Pat Booker Road, Suite 101
Universal City, TX 78148-4147.

Phone orders accepted for purchase with your credit card. Call (210) 659-2112 or fax (210) 659-1212.